Mastering Bootstrap 4

Learn how to build beautiful and highly customizable web interfaces by leveraging the power of Bootstrap 4

Benjamin Jakobus
Jason Marah

BIRMINGHAM - MUMBAI

Mastering Bootstrap 4

First published: September 2016

Production reference: 2171016

Published by Packt Publishing Ltd.
Livery Place
35 Livery Street
Birmingham
B3 2PB, UK.

ISBN 978-1-78398-112-0

www.packtpub.com

Credits

Authors

Benjamin Jakobus
Jason Marah

Reviewer

Marija Zaric

Acquisition Editor

Rahul Nair

Content Development Editor

Samantha Gonsalves

Technical Editor

Huzefa Unwala

Production Coordinator

Shraddha Falebhai

Copy Editor

Safis Editing

Project Coordinator

Kinjal Bari

Proofreader

Safis Editing

Indexer

Rekha Nair

Graphics

Jason Monteiro

About the Authors

Benjamin Jakobus graduated with a BSc in Computer Science from University College Cork and obtained an MSc in Advanced Computing from Imperial College London. As a software engineer, he has worked on various web-development projects across Europe and Brazil.

To Marina Barrenne De Artagão Quental, for all your kindness and support. To Eduardo Quental, for giving me so much of your time.

Jason Marah is a software engineer who is currently developing `AerLingus.com` in Dublin, Ireland, as a lead UI developer. Jason is a University College Cork alumnus, graduating with a BSc in Computer Science. Jason has worked as a full-stack engineer specializing in JavaScript around Europe on various projects.

To Heather, for so much love, support and understanding. To my family and friends for the never-ending encouragement.

About the Reviewer

Marija Zaric is a web designer who loves coding and works with clients from USA and all over the world. She is a relentless learner. Marija creates various Bootstrap themes for the global market.

She was a technical reviewer for the books *Responsive Media in HTML5, Mastering Responsive Web Design*, and *Responsive Web Design Patterns* for Packt.

Her projects can be found at `http://www.marijazaric.com/`.

www.PacktPub.com

For support files and downloads related to your book, please visit `www.PacktPub.com`.

Did you know that Packt offers eBook versions of every book published, with PDF and ePub files available? You can upgrade to the eBook version at `www.PacktPub.com` and as a print book customer, you are entitled to a discount on the eBook copy. Get in touch with us at `service@packtpub.com` for more details.

At `www.PacktPub.com`, you can also read a collection of free technical articles, sign up for a range of free newsletters and receive exclusive discounts and offers on Packt books and eBooks.

`https://www.packtpub.com/mapt`

Get the most in-demand software skills with Mapt. Mapt gives you full access to all Packt books and video courses, as well as industry-leading tools to help you plan your personal development and advance your career.

Why subscribe?

- Fully searchable across every book published by Packt
- Copy and paste, print, and bookmark content
- On demand and accessible via a web browser

Table of Contents

Preface

Bootstrap is a free CSS and JavaScript framework that allows developers to rapidly build responsive web interfaces. The framework was first conceived by Mark Otto and Jacob Thornton while working at Twitter in 2010. Since its release as an open source project in August of 2011, Bootstrap has become a household name among frontend web developers. The framework's ease-of-use along with its cross-browser compatibility, support for mobile user interfaces, and responsive web design capabilities, make it an essential building block for any modern web application. Totaling over 600 contributors, and more than 34,000 GitHub forks, Bootstrap has become the world's most popular responsive web development framework. However, despite its popularity, there are relatively few advanced resources on the fourth, and latest, version of Bootstrap. As such, the motivation behind this book is to provide a comprehensive, step-by-step guide for developers that wish to build a complete, production-ready, website using Bootstrap 4. Once you turn the final pages of this book, you should be mastering the framework's ins and outs, and building highly customizable and optimized web interfaces. You will know how to both extend the framework, integrate it with third-party components and frameworks, as well as optimize and automate your Bootstrapped builds.

What this book covers

Chapter 1, *Revving Up Bootstrap*, places the Bootstrap framework into context by highlighting the relevant features that come bundled with it. It briefly deals with various ways to include the framework and concludes by setting up the required files for the book's demo project.

Chapter 2, *Making a Style Statement*, introduces the Bootstrap markup and style rules for the mobile-first grid system and HTML image elements. It also goes into the handy helper classes and responsive utilities that Bootstrap makes available to boost development speed.

Chapter 3, *Building the Layout*, focuses on starting to flesh out the demo project set up in Chapter 1, *Revving Up Bootstrap*, by adding a style guide for commonly used HTML elements and structuring the page layout.

Chapter 4, *On Navigation, Footers, Alerts, and Content*, shows you how to take advantage of Bootstrap to build footers and alerts, and how you can add and style various types of content using Bootstrap's built-in classes.

Chapter 5, *Speeding Up Development Using jQuery Plugins*, focuses on how to use the handy third-party jQuery plugins to add interactivity and fun to a web page.

Chapter 6, *Customizing Your Plugins*, delves into the Bootstrap jQuery plugins' code and customizes it to jazz up this book's demo page. Plugins will be examined and extended throughout this chapter in an effort to not only make our page better, but to also improve our knowledge of how jQuery plugins are built and how they behave within Bootstrap's ecosystem.

Chapter 7, *Integrating Bootstrap with Third-Party Plugins*, will identify new features or improvements that we want to make to our demo website. Consequently, the chapter will introduce libraries to help us achieve those goals, and figure out how these can be gracefully integrated with our existing architecture.

Chapter 8, *Optimizing Your Website*, shows how your website can be optimized for maximum performance and fast loading time on any device.

Chapter 9, *Integrating with AngularJS and React*, teaches the essentials of using Bootstrap within AngularJS and React. AngularJS is a Model-View-* JavaScript framework, while React is a JavaScript library that concentrates solely on the View part of the Model-View-Controller type stack. A vast amount of web pages are built with the frameworks or libraries such as AngularJS and React as they provide very useful abstractions on top of JavaScript and the DOM.

What you need for this book

This book targets intermediate-level frontend web developers. The book is not intended to be an introduction to web development. As such, we assume that readers have a firm grasp of the basic concepts behind web development, essential HTML, JavaScript, and CSS skills, as well as practical experience of applying this knowledge. Furthermore, the reader should have an understanding of jQuery. Elementary knowledge about AngularJS, build tools, and React are desirable for the book's final two chapters. However, unfamiliarity with the two frameworks will not stop readers from completing and understanding the examples.

Who this book is for

This book targets intermediate-level frontend web developers. The book is not intended to be an introduction to web development. As such, the book assumes that readers have a firm grasp on the basic concepts behind web development, as well as essential HTML, JavaScript, and CSS skills.

Conventions

In this book, you will find a number of text styles that distinguish between different kinds of information. Here are some examples of these styles and an explanation of their meaning.

Code words in text, database table names, folder names, filenames, file extensions, pathnames, dummy URLs, user input, and Twitter handles are shown as follows: "Create a blank index.html file and insert the following HTML code:"

A block of code is set as follows:

```
<meta charset="utf-8">
<meta name="viewport" content="width=device-width,
initial-scale=1, shrink-to-fit=no">
<meta http-equiv="x-ua-compatible" content="ie=edge">
<title>MyPhoto</title>
```

Any command-line input or output is written as follows:

```
npm install -g bower
```

New terms and **important words** are shown in bold. Words that you see on the screen, for example, in menus or dialog boxes, appear in the text like this: "Clicking the **Next** button moves you to the next screen."

 Warnings or important notes appear in a box like this.

 Tips and tricks appear like this.

Reader feedback

Feedback from our readers is always welcome. Let us know what you think about this book—what you liked or disliked. Reader feedback is important for us as it helps us develop titles that you will really get the most out of. To send us general feedback, simply e-mail feedback@packtpub.com, and mention the book's title in the subject of your message. If there is a topic that you have expertise in and you are interested in either writing or contributing to a book, see our author guide at www.packtpub.com/authors.

Customer support

Now that you are the proud owner of a Packt book, we have a number of things to help you to get the most from your purchase.

Downloading the example code

You can download the example code files for this book from your account at `http://www.packtpub.com`. If you purchased this book elsewhere, you can visit `http://www.packtpub.com/support` and register to have the files e-mailed directly to you.

You can download the code files by following these steps:

1. Log in or register to our website using your e-mail address and password.
2. Hover the mouse pointer on the **SUPPORT** tab at the top.
3. Click on **Code Downloads & Errata**.
4. Enter the name of the book in the **Search** box.
5. Select the book for which you're looking to download the code files.
6. Choose from the drop-down menu where you purchased this book from.
7. Click on **Code Download**.

Once the file is downloaded, please make sure that you unzip or extract the folder using the latest version of:

- WinRAR / 7-Zip for Windows
- Zipeg / iZip / UnRarX for Mac
- 7-Zip / PeaZip for Linux

The code bundle for the book is also hosted on GitHub at `https://github.com/PacktPublishing/Mastering-Bootstrap-4`. We also have other code bundles from our rich catalog of books and videos available at `https://github.com/PacktPublishing/`. Check them out!

Downloading the color images of this book

We also provide you with a PDF file that has color images of the screenshots/diagrams used in this book. The color images will help you better understand the changes in the output. You can download this file from `http://www.packtpub.com/sites/default/files/downloads/MasteringBootstrap4_ColorImages.pdf`.

Errata

Although we have taken every care to ensure the accuracy of our content, mistakes do happen. If you find a mistake in one of our books-maybe a mistake in the text or the code-we would be grateful if you could report this to us. By doing so, you can save other readers from frustration and help us improve subsequent versions of this book. If you find any errata, please report them by visiting http://www.packtpub.com/submit-errata, selecting your book, clicking on the **Errata Submission Form** link, and entering the details of your errata. Once your errata are verified, your submission will be accepted and the errata will be uploaded to our website or added to any list of existing errata under the Errata section of that title.

To view the previously submitted errata, go to https://www.packtpub.com/books/content/support and enter the name of the book in the search field. The required information will appear under the **Errata** section.

Piracy

Piracy of copyrighted material on the Internet is an ongoing problem across all media. At Packt, we take the protection of our copyright and licenses very seriously. If you come across any illegal copies of our works in any form on the Internet, please provide us with the location address or website name immediately so that we can pursue a remedy.

Please contact us at copyright@packtpub.com with a link to the suspected pirated material.

We appreciate your help in protecting our authors and our ability to bring you valuable content.

Questions

If you have a problem with any aspect of this book, you can contact us at questions@packtpub.com, and we will do our best to address the problem.

1
Revving Up Bootstrap

Bootstrap is a web development framework that helps developers build web interfaces. Originally conceived at Twitter in 2011 by Mark Otto and Jacob Thornton, the framework is now open source and has grown to be one of the most popular web development frameworks to date. Being freely available for private, educational, and commercial use meant that Bootstrap quickly grew in popularity. Today, thousands of organizations rely on Bootstrap, including NASA, Walmart, and Bloomberg. According to `BuiltWith.com`, over 10% of the world's top 1 million websites are built using Bootstrap (`http://trends.builtwith.com/docinfo/Twitter-Bootstrap`). As such, knowing how to use Bootstrap will be an important skill and will serve as a powerful addition to any web developer's tool belt.

The framework itself consists of a mixture of JavaScript and CSS, and provides developers with all the essential components required to develop a fully functioning web user interface. Over the course of this book, we will be introducing you to all of the most essential features that Bootstrap has to offer by teaching you how to use the framework to build a complete website from scratch. As CSS and HTML alone are already the subject of entire books in themselves, we assume that you, the reader, has at least a basic knowledge of HTML, CSS, and JavaScript.

We begin this chapter by introducing you to our demo website, `MyPhoto`. This website will accompany us throughout this book, and serve as a practical point of reference. Therefore, all lessons learned will be taught within the context of `MyPhoto`.

We will then discuss the Bootstrap framework, listing its features and contrasting the current release to the last major release (Bootstrap 3).

Last but not least, this chapter will help you set up your development environment. To ensure equal footing, we will guide you towards installing the right build tools, and precisely detail the various ways in which you can integrate Bootstrap into a project. More advanced readers may safely skip this last part and continue to Chapter 2, *Making a Style Statement*.

To summarize, this chapter will do the following:

- Introduce you to what exactly we will be doing
- Explain what is new in the latest version of Bootstrap, and how the latest version differs to the previous major release
- Show you how to include Bootstrap in our web project

Introducing our demo project

This book will teach you how to build a complete Bootstrap website from scratch. Starting with a simple layout in Chapter 2, *Making a Style Statement* and Chapter 3, *Building the Layout*, we will build and improve the website's various sections as we progress through each chapter. The concept behind our website is simple: to develop a landing page for photographers. Using this landing page, (hypothetical) users will be able to exhibit their wares and services. While building our website, we will be making use of the same third-party tools and libraries that you would if you were working as a professional software developer. We chose these tools and plugins specifically because of their widespread use. Learning how to use and integrate them will save you a lot of work when developing websites in the future. Specifically, the tools that we will use to assist us throughout the development of MyPhoto are **Bower**, **node package manager (npm)**, and **Grunt**.

From a development perspective, the construction of MyPhoto will teach you how to use and apply all of the essential user interface concepts and components required to build a fully functioning website. Among other things, you will learn how to do the following:

- Use the Bootstrap grid system to structure the information presented on your website
- Create a fixed, branded, navigation bar with animated scroll effects

- Use an image carousel for displaying different photographs, implemented using Bootstrap's `carousel.js` and jumbotron (jumbotron is a design principle for displaying important content). It should be noted that carousels are becoming an increasingly unpopular design choice; however, they are still heavily used and are an important feature of Bootstrap. As such, we do not argue for or against the use of carousels as their effectiveness depends very much on how they are used, rather than on whether they are used.
- Build custom tabs that allow users to navigate across different contents
- Use and apply Bootstrap's modal dialogs
- Apply a fixed page footer
- Create forms for data entry using Bootstrap's input controls (text fields, text areas, and buttons) and apply Bootstrap's input validation styles
- Make best use of Bootstrap's context classes
- Create alert messages and learn how to customize them
- Rapidly develop interactive data tables for displaying product information
- Use drop-down menus, custom fonts, and icons

In addition to learning how to use Bootstrap 4, the development of `MyPhoto` will introduce you to a range of third-party libraries such as Scrollspy (for scroll animations), SalvattoreJS (a library for complementing our Bootstrap grid), Animate.css (for beautiful CSS animations, such as fade-in effects at `https://daneden.github.io/animate.css/`), and Bootstrap DataTables (for rapidly displaying data in tabular form).

The website itself will consist of different sections:

- A **Welcome** section
- An **About** section
- A **Services** section
- A **Gallery** section
- A **Contact Us** section

The development of each section is intended to teach you how to use a distinct set of features found in third-party libraries. For example, by developing the **Welcome** section, you will learn how to use Bootstrap's jumbotron and alert dialogs along with different font and text styles, while the **About** section will show you how to use cards. The **Services** section of our project introduces you to Bootstrap's custom tabs. That is, you will learn how to use Bootstrap's tabs to display a range of different services offered by our website.

Following on from the **Services** section, you will need to use rich imagery to really show off the website's sample services. You will achieve this by really mastering Bootstrap's responsive core along with Bootstrap's carousel and third-party jQuery plugins. Last but not least, the **Contact Us** section will demonstrate how to use Bootstrap's form elements and helper functions. That is, you will learn how to use Bootstrap to create stylish HTML forms, how to use form fields and input groups, and how to perform data validation.

Finally, toward the end of the book, you will learn how to optimize your website, and integrate it with the popular JavaScript frameworks AngularJS (`https://angularjs.org/`) and React (`http://facebook.github.io/react/`). As entire books have been written on AngularJS alone, we will only cover the essentials required for the integration itself.

Now that you have glimpsed a brief overview of `MyPhoto`, let's examine Bootstrap 4 in more detail, and discuss what makes it so different to its predecessor. Take a look at the following screenshot:

Figure 1.1: A taste of what is to come: the MyPhoto landing page

What Bootstrap 4 Alpha 4 has to offer

Much has changed since Twitter's Bootstrap was first released on August 19th, 2011. In essence, Bootstrap 1 was a collection of CSS rules offering developers the ability to lay out their website, create forms, buttons, and help with general appearance and site navigation. With respect to these core features, Bootstrap 4 Alpha 4 is still much the same as its predecessors. In other words, the framework's focus is still on allowing developers to create layouts, and helping to develop a consistent appearance by providing stylings for buttons, forms, and other user interface elements. How it helps developers achieve and use these features, however, has changed entirely. Bootstrap 4 is a complete rewrite of the entire project, and, as such, ships with many fundamental differences to its predecessors. Along with Bootstrap's major features, we will be discussing the most striking differences between Bootstrap 3 and Bootstrap 4 in the sub-sections that follow.

Layout

Possibly the most important and widely used feature is Bootstrap's ability to lay out and organize your page. Specifically, Bootstrap offers the following:

- Responsive containers
- Responsive breakpoints for adjusting page layout in response to differing screen sizes
- A 12 column grid layout for flexibly arranging various elements on your page
- Media objects that act as building blocks and allow you to build your own structural components
- Utility classes that allow you to manipulate elements in a responsive manner. For example, you can use the layout utility classes to hide elements, depending on screen size

We will be discussing each of these features in detail in Chapter 2, *Making a Style Statement* and Chapter 3, *Building the Layout*.

Content styling

Just like its predecessor, Bootstrap 4 overrides the default browser styles. This means that many elements, such as lists or headings, are padded and spaced differently. The majority of overridden styles only affect spacing and positioning; however, some elements may also have their border removed. The reason behind this is simple: to provide users with a clean slate upon which they can build their site.

Building on this clean slate, Bootstrap 4 provides styles for almost every aspect of your web page such as buttons (*Figure 1.2*), input fields, headings, paragraphs, special inline texts, such as keyboard input (*Figure 1.3*), figures, tables, and navigation controls. Aside from this, Bootstrap offers state styles for all input controls, for example, styles for disabled buttons or toggled buttons. Take a look at the following screenshot:

Figure 1.2: The six button styles that come with Bootstrap 4 are btn-primary, btn-secondary, btn-success, btn-danger, btn-link, btn-info, and btn-warning

Take a look at the following screenshot:

Figure 1.3: Bootstrap's content styles. In the preceding example, we see inline styling for denoting keyboard input

Components

Aside from layout and content styling, Bootstrap offers a large variety of reusable components that allow you to quickly construct your website's most fundamental features. Bootstrap's UI components encompass all of the fundamental building blocks that you would expect a web development toolkit to offer: modal dialogs, progress bars, navigation bars, tooltips, popovers, a carousel, alerts, drop-down menus, input groups, tabs, pagination, and components for emphasizing certain contents.

Let's have a look at the following modal dialog screenshot:

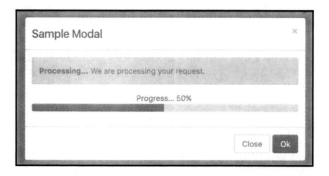

Figure 1.4: Various Bootstrap 4 components in action. In the preceding screenshot we see a sample modal dialog, containing an info alert, some sample text, and an animated progress bar.

Mobile support

Similar to its predecessor, Bootstrap 4 allows you to create mobile-friendly websites without too much additional development work. By default, Bootstrap is designed to work across all resolutions and screen sizes, from mobile, to tablet, to desktop. In fact, Bootstrap's *mobile-first* design philosophy implies that its components must display and function correctly at the smallest screen size possible. The reasoning behind this is simple. Think about developing a website without consideration for small mobile screens. In this case, you are likely to pack your website full of buttons, labels, and tables. You will probably only discover any usability issues when a user attempts to visit your website using a mobile device only to find a small web page that is crowded with buttons and forms. At this stage, you will be required to rework the entire user interface to allow it to render on smaller screens. For precisely this reason, Bootstrap promotes a bottom-up approach, forcing developers to get the user interface to render correctly on the smallest possible screen size, before expanding upwards.

Utility classes

Aside from ready-to-go components, Bootstrap offers a large selection of utility classes that encapsulate the most commonly needed style rules. For example, rules for aligning text, hiding an element, or providing contextual colors for warning text.

Cross-browser compatibility

Bootstrap 4 supports the vast majority of modern browsers, including Chrome, Firefox, Opera, Safari, Internet Explorer (version 9 and onwards; Internet Explorer 8 and below are not supported), and Microsoft Edge.

Sass instead of Less

Both **Less** and **Sass (Syntactically Awesome Stylesheets)** are CSS extension languages. That is, they are languages that extend the CSS vocabulary with the objective of making the development of many, large, and complex style sheets easier. Although Less and Sass are fundamentally different languages, the general manner in which they extend CSS is the same, both rely on a preprocessor. As you produce your build, the preprocessor is run, parsing the Less/Sass script and turning your Less or Sass instructions into plain CSS.

Less is the official Bootstrap 3 build, while Bootstrap 4 has been developed from scratch, and is written entirely in Sass. Both Less and Sass are compiled into CSS to produce a single file, `bootstrap.css`. It is this CSS file that we will be primarily referencing throughout this book (with the exception of `Chapter 3`, *Building the Layout*). Consequently, you will not be required to know Sass in order to follow this book. However, we do recommend that you take a 20 minute introductory course on Sass if you are completely new to the language. Rest assured, if you already know CSS, you will not need more time than this. The language's syntax is very close to normal CSS, and its elementary concepts are similar to those contained within any other programming language.

From pixel to root em

Unlike its predecessor, Bootstrap 4 no longer uses **pixel (px)** as its unit of typographic measurement. Instead, it primarily uses **root em (rem)**. The reasoning behind choosing rem is based on a well known problem with px; websites using px may render incorrectly, or not as originally intended, as users change the size of the browser's base font. Using a unit of measurement that is relative to the page's root element helps address this problem, as the root element will be scaled relative to the browser's base font. In turn, a page will be scaled relative to this root element.

Typographic units of measurement

Simply put, typographic units of measurement determine the size of your font and elements. The most commonly used units of measurement are px and em. The former is an abbreviation for pixel, and uses a reference pixel to determine a font's exact size. This means that, for displays of 96 **dots per inch (dpi)**, 1 px will equal an actual pixel on the screen. For higher resolution displays, the reference pixel will result in the px being scaled to match the display's resolution. For example, specifying a font size of 100 px will mean that the font is exactly 100 pixels in size (on a display with 96 dpi), irrespective of any other element on the page.

Em is a unit of measurement that is relative to the parent of the element to which it is applied. So, for example, if we were to have two nested div elements, the outer element with a font size of 100 px and the inner element with a font size of 2 em, then the inner element's font size would translate to 200 px (as in this case 1 em = 100 px). The problem with using a unit of measurement that is relative to parent elements is that it increases your code's complexity, as the nesting of elements makes size calculations more difficult.

The recently introduced rem measurement aims to address both em's and px's shortcomings by combining their two strengths; instead of being relative to a parent element, rem is relative to the page's root element.

No more support for Internet Explorer 8

As was already implicit in the preceding feature summary, the latest version of Bootstrap no longer supports Internet Explorer 8. As such, the decision to only support newer versions of Internet Explorer was a reasonable one, as not even Microsoft itself provides technical support and updates for Internet Explorer 8 anymore (as of January 2016). Furthermore, Internet Explorer 8 does not support rem, meaning that Bootstrap 4 would have been required to provide a workaround. This in turn would most likely have implied a large amount of additional development work, with the potential for inconsistencies. Lastly, responsive website development for Internet Explorer 8 is difficult, as the browser does not support CSS media queries. Given these three factors, dropping support for this version of Internet Explorer was the most sensible path of action.

A new grid tier

Bootstrap's grid system consists of a series of CSS classes and media queries that help you lay out your page. Specifically, the grid system helps alleviate the pain points associated with horizontal and vertical positioning of a page's contents and the structure of the page across multiple displays. With Bootstrap 4, the grid system has been completely overhauled, and a new grid tier has been added with a breakpoint of 480 px and below. We will be talking about tiers, breakpoints, and Bootstrap's grid system extensively in `Chapter 2`, *Making a Style Statement*.

Bye-bye GLYPHICONS

Bootstrap 3 shipped with a nice collection of over 250 font icons, free of use. In an effort to make the framework more lightweight (and because font icons are considered bad practice), the GLYPHICON set is no longer available in Bootstrap 4.

Bigger text: no more panels, wells, and thumbnails

The default font size in Bootstrap 4 is 2 px bigger than in its predecessor, increasing from 14 px to 16 px. Furthermore, Bootstrap 4 replaced panels, wells, and thumbnails with a new concept: **cards**. To readers unfamiliar with the concept of wells, a well is a UI component that allows developers to highlight text content by applying an inset shadow effect to the element to which it is applied. A panel also serves to highlight information, but by applying padding and rounded borders. Cards serve the same purpose as their predecessors, but are less restrictive as they are flexible enough to support different types of content, such as images, lists, or text. They can also be customized to use footers and headers. Take a look at the following screenshot:

Figure 1.5: The Bootstrap 4 card component replaces existing wells, thumbnails, and panels

New and improved form input controls

Bootstrap 4 now allows for input control sizing, as well as classes for denoting block and inline level input controls. However, one of the most anticipated new additions is Bootstrap's input validation styles, which used to require third-party libraries or a manual implementation, but are now shipped with Bootstrap 4 (see *Figure 1.6*). Take a look at the following screenshot:

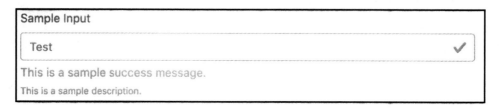

Figure 1.6: The new Bootstrap 4 input validation styles, indicating the successful processing of input

Last but not least, Bootstrap 4 also offers custom forms in order to provide even more cross-browser UI consistency across input elements (*Figure 1.7*). As noted in the Bootstrap 4 Alpha 4 documentation, the input controls are *"built on top of semantic and accessible markup, so they're solid replacements for any default form control"* (source: http://v4-alpha.getbootst rap.com/components/forms/). Take a look at the following screenshot:

Figure 1.7: Custom Bootstrap input controls that replace the browser defaults in order to ensure cross-browser UI consistency

Customization

The developers behind Bootstrap 4 have put specific emphasis on customization throughout the development of Bootstrap 4. As such, many new variables have been introduced that allow for the easy customization of Bootstrap. Using the $enabled-*- Sass variables, one can now enable or disable specific global CSS preferences.

Setting up our project

Now that we know what Bootstrap has to offer, let us set up our project:

1. Create a new project directory named MyPhoto. This will become our project root directory.
2. Create a blank index.html file and insert the following HTML code:

```
<!DOCTYPE html>
<html lang="en">
<head>
    <meta charset="utf-8">
    <meta name="viewport" content="width=device-width,
    initial-scale=1, shrink-to-fit=no">
    <meta http-equiv="x-ua-compatible" content="ie=edge">
    <title>MyPhoto</title>
</head>
<body>
    <div class="alert alert-success">
        Hello World!
    </div>
</body>
</html>
```

Note the three `meta` tags. The first tag tells the browser that the document in question is `utf-8` encoded. Since Bootstrap optimizes its content for mobile devices, the subsequent `meta` tag is required to help with viewport scaling. The last `meta` tag forces the document to be rendered using the latest document rendering mode available if viewed in Internet Explorer.

3. Open the `index.html` in your browser. You should see just a blank page with the words **Hello World**.

Now it is time to include Bootstrap. At its core, Bootstrap is a glorified CSS style sheet. Within that style sheet, Bootstrap exposes very powerful features of CSS with an easy-to-use syntax. It being a style sheet, you include it in your project as you would with any other style sheet that you might develop yourself. That is, open the `index.html` and directly link it to the style sheet.

Viewport scaling

The term "viewport" refers to the available display size to render the contents of a page. The `viewport meta` tag allows you to define this available size. Viewport scaling using `meta` tags was first introduced by Apple and, at the time of writing, is supported by all major browsers.

Using the `width` parameter, we can define the exact width of the user's viewport. For example, `<meta name="viewport" content="width=320px">` will instruct the browser to set the viewport's `width` to 320px. The ability to control the viewport's width is useful when developing mobile-friendly websites; by default, mobile browsers will attempt to fit the entire page onto their viewports by zooming out as far as possible. This allows users to view and interact with websites that have not been designed to be viewed on mobile devices. However, as Bootstrap embraces a mobile-first design philosophy, a zoom out will, in fact, result in undesired side-effects. For example, breakpoints (which we will discuss in `Chapter 2`, *Making a Style Statement*) will no longer work as intended, as they now deal with the zoomed-out equivalent of the page in question. This is why explicitly setting the viewport width is so important. By writing `content="width=device-width, initial-scale=1, shrink-to-fit=no"`, we are telling the browser the following:

- We want to set the viewport's width equal to the actual device's screen width.
- We do not want any zoom, initially.

- We do not wish to shrink the content to fit the viewport.

For now, we will use the Bootstrap builds hosted on Bootstrap's official **Content Delivery Network (CDN)**. This is done by including the following HTML tag into the head of your HTML document (the head of your HTML document refers to the contents between the `<head>` opening tag and the `</head>` closing tag):

```
<link rel="stylesheet" href="https://maxcdn.bootstrapcdn.com/
bootstrap/4.0.0-alpha.4/css/bootstrap.min.css">
```

Bootstrap relies on jQuery, a JavaScript framework that provides a layer of abstraction in an effort to simplify the most common JavaScript operations (such as element selection and event handling). Therefore, before we include the Bootstrap JavaScript file, we must first include jQuery. Both inclusions should occur just before the `</body>` closing tag:

```
<script src="https://ajax.googleapis.com/ajax/libs/jquery/2.1.4
/jquery.min.js">
</script>
<script src="https://maxcdn.bootstrapcdn.com/bootstrap/4.0.0-alpha.4
/js/bootstrap.min.js"></script>
```

Note that, while these scripts could, of course, be loaded at the top of the page, loading scripts at the end of the document is considered best practice to speed up page loading times and to avoid JavaScript issues preventing the page from being rendered. The reason behind this is that browsers do not download all dependencies in parallel (although a certain number of requests are made asynchronously, depending on the browser and the domain). Consequently, forcing the browser to download dependencies early on will block page rendering until these assets have been downloaded. Furthermore, ensuring that your scripts are loaded last will ensure that once you invoke **Document Object Model (DOM)** operations in your scripts, you can be sure that your page's elements have already been rendered. As a result, you can avoid checks that ensure the existence of given elements.

What is a Content Delivery Network?

The objective behind any Content Delivery Network (CDN) is to provide users with content that is highly available. This means that a CDN aims to provide you with content, without this content ever (or rarely) becoming unavailable. To this end, the content is often hosted using a large, distributed set of servers. The BootstrapCDN basically allows you to link to the Bootstrap style sheet so that you do not have to host it yourself.

Save your changes and reload the `index.html` in your browser. The **Hello World** string should now contain a green background:

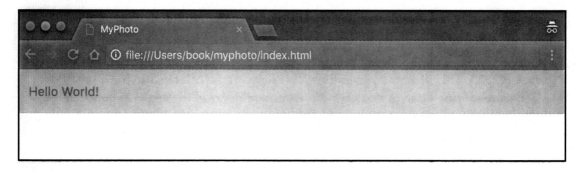

Figure 1.8: Our "Hello World" styled using Bootstrap 4

Now that the Bootstrap framework has been included in our project, open your browser's developer console (if using Chrome on Microsoft Windows, press *Ctrl + Shift + I; o*n Mac OS X you can press *cmd + alt + I*). As Bootstrap requires another third-party library Tether, for displaying popovers and tooltips, the developer console will display an error (*Figure 1.6*). Take a look at the following screenshot:

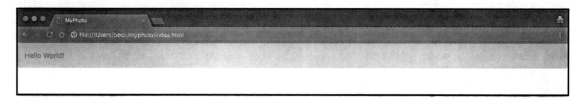

Figure 1.9: Chrome's Developer Tools can be opened by going to View, selecting Developer, and then clicking on Developer Tools. At the bottom of the page, a new view will appear. Under the Console tab, an error will indicate an unmet dependency.

Tether is available via the CloudFare CDN, and consists of both a CSS file and a JavaScript file. As before, we should include the JavaScript file at the bottom of our document while we reference Tether's style sheet from inside our document head:

```
<!DOCTYPE html>
<html lang="en">
<head>
    <meta charset="utf-8">
    <meta name="viewport" content="width=device-width, initial-
    scale=1, shrink-to-fit=no">
    <meta http-equiv="x-ua-compatible" content="ie=edge">
    <title>MyPhoto</title>
    <link rel="stylesheet" href="https://maxcdn.bootstrapcdn.com/
    bootstrap/4.0.0-alpha.4/css/bootstrap.min.css">
    <link rel="stylesheet" href="https://cdnjs.cloudflare.com/ajax/
    libs/tether/1.3.1/css/tether.min.css">
</head>
<body>
```

```
<div class="alert alert-success">
    Hello World!
</div>
<script src="https://ajax.googleapis.com/ajax/libs/jquery/
2.1.4/jquery.min.js"></script>
<script src="https://cdnjs.cloudflare.com/ajax/libs/tether/
1.3.1/js/tether.min.js"></script>
<script src="https://maxcdn.bootstrapcdn.com/bootstrap/4.0.0-
alpha.4/js/bootstrap.min.js"></script>
</body>
</html>
```

While CDNs are an important resource, there are several reasons why, at times, using a third-party CDN may not be desirable:

- CDNs introduce an additional point of failure, as you now rely on third-party servers.
- The privacy and security of users may be compromised, as there is no guarantee that the CDN provider does not inject malicious code into the libraries that are being hosted. Nor can one be certain that the CDN does not attempt to track its users.
- Certain CDNs may be blocked by the Internet Service Providers of users in different geographical locations.
- Offline development will not be possible when relying on a remote CDN.
- You will not be able to optimize the files hosted by your CDN. This loss of control may affect your website's performance (although typically you are more often than not offered an optimized version of the library through the CDN).

Instead of relying on a CDN, we could manually download the jQuery, Tether, and Bootstrap project files. We could then copy these builds into our project root and link them to the distribution files. The disadvantage of this approach is the fact that maintaining a manual collection of dependencies can quickly become very cumbersome, and next to impossible as your website grows in size and complexity. As such, we will not manually download the Bootstrap build. Instead, we will let Bower do it for us. Bower is a package management system, that is, a tool that you can use to manage your website's dependencies. It automatically downloads, organizes, and (upon command) updates your website's dependencies. To install Bower, head over to `http://bower.io/`.

How do I install Bower?

Before you can install Bower, you will need two other tools: Node.js and Git. The latter is a version control tool, in essence; it allows you to manage different versions of your software. To install Git, head over to `http://gi`

t-scm.com/ and select the installer appropriate for your operating system. NodeJS is a JavaScript runtime environment needed for Bower to run. To install it, simply download the installer from the official NodeJS website: h ttps://nodejs.org/Once you have successfully installed Git and NodeJS, you are ready to install Bower. Simply type the following command into your terminal:

```
npm install -g bower
```

This will install Bower for you, using the JavaScript package manager npm, which happens to be used by, and is installed with, NodeJS.

Once Bower has been installed, open up your terminal, navigate to the project root folder you created earlier, and fetch the bootstrap build:

bower install bootstrap#v4.0.0-alpha.4

This will create a new folder structure in our project root:

```
|__bower_components
  |__bootstrap
    |__Gruntfile.js
    |__LICENSE
    |__README.md
    |__bower.json
    |__dist
    |__fonts
    |__grunt
    |__js
    |__less
    |__package.js
    |__package.json
```

We will explain all of these various files and directories later on in this book. For now, you can safely ignore everything except for the `dist` directory inside `bower_components/bootstrap/`. Go ahead and open the `dist` directory. You should see three sub directories:

- `css`
- `fonts`
- `js`

The name `dist` stands for distribution. Typically, the distribution directory contains the production-ready code that users can deploy. As its name implies, the `css` directory inside `dist` includes the ready-for-use style sheets. Likewise, the `js` directory contains the JavaScript files that compose Bootstrap. Lastly, the `fonts` directory holds the font assets that come with Bootstrap.

To reference the local Bootstrap CSS file in our `index.html`, modify the `href` attribute of the link tag that points to the `bootstrap.min.css`:

```
<link rel="stylesheet" href="bower_components/bootstrap/dist/css
/bootstrap.min.css">
```

Let's do the same for the Bootstrap JavaScript file:

```
<script src="bower_components/bootstrap/dist/js/bootstrap.min.js"></script>
```

Repeat this process for both jQuery and Tether. To install jQuery using Bower, use the following command:

```
bower install jquery
```

Just as before, a new directory will be created inside the `bower_components` directory:

```
|__bower_components
  |__jquery
    |__AUTHORS.txt
    |__LICENSE.txt
    |__bower.json
    |__dist
    |__sizzle
    |__src
```

Again, we are only interested in the contents of the `dist` directory, which, among other files, will contain the compressed jQuery build `jquery.min.js`.

Reference this file by modifying the `src` attribute of the script tag that currently points to Google's `jquery.min.js` by replacing the URL with the path to our local copy of jQuery:

```
<script src="bower_components/jquery/dist/jquery.min.js"></script>
```

Last but not least, repeat the steps already outlined for Tether:

```
bower install tether
```

Once the installation completes, a similar folder structure than the ones for Bootstrap and jQuery will have been created. Verify the contents of `bower_components/tether/dist` and replace the CDN Tether references in our document with their local equivalent.

The final `index.html` should now look as follows:

```html
<!DOCTYPE html>
<html lang="en">
<head>
    <meta charset="utf-8">
    <meta name="viewport" content="width=device-width, initial-scale=1,
    shrink-to-fit=no">
    <meta http-equiv="x-ua-compatible" content="ie=edge">
    <title>MyPhoto</title>
    <link rel="stylesheet" href="bower_components/bootstrap/dist/css
    /bootstrap.min.css">
    <link rel="stylesheet" href="bower_components/tether/dist/css
    /tether.min.css">
</head>
<body>
    <div class="alert alert-success">
        Hello World!
    </div>
    <script src="bower_components/jquery/dist/jquery.min.js"></script>
    <script src="bower_components/tether/dist/js/tether.min.js">
    </script>
    <script src="bower_components/bootstrap/dist/js/bootstrap.min.js">
    </script>
</body>
</html>
```

Refresh the `index.html` in your browser to make sure that everything works.

What IDE and browser should I be using when following the examples in this book?

While we recommend a JetBrains IDE or Sublime Text along with Google Chrome, you are free to use whatever tools and browser you like. Our taste in IDE and browser is subjective on this matter. However, keep in mind that Bootstrap 4 does not support Internet Explorer 8 or below. As such, if you do happen to use Internet Explorer 8, you should upgrade it to the latest version.

Summary

Aside from introducing you to our sample project MyPhoto, this chapter was concerned with outlining Bootstrap 4, highlighting its features, and discussing how this new version of Bootstrap differs to the last major release (Bootstrap 3). The chapter provided an overview of how Bootstrap can assist developers in the layout, structuring, and styling of pages. Furthermore, we noted how Bootstrap provides access to the most important and widely used user interface controls through the form of components that can be integrated into a page with minimal effort. By providing an outline of Bootstrap, we hope that the framework's intrinsic value in assisting in the development of modern websites has become apparent to the reader. Furthermore, during the course of the wider discussion, we highlighted and explained some important concepts in web development, such as typographic units of measurement or the definition, purpose, and justification of the use of Content Delivery Networks. Last but not least, we detailed how to include Bootstrap and its dependencies inside an HTML document. This sets the scene for Chapter 2, *Making a Style Statement* in which we will introduce you to the Bootstrap grid system by building a general layout for the first page of our sample project.

2
Making a Style Statement

In the previous chapter, we showed you a first glimpse of `MyPhoto`, the Bootstrap website that we are going to build up throughout the following chapters. Now it is time to get our hands dirty, and actually start building the first section of this website. A first pass at an element of the **Services** section that presents the list of print sizes available to order. We will achieve this by building a grid using Bootstrap's grid system, creating image elements within the grid system, applying image modifiers, and leveraging Bootstrap's utility classes to create visual indicators and optimized layouts specific to different display resolutions.

By the end of this chapter, through code examples and studying the Bootstrap source code, you will have gained a deep understanding of the following:

- Bootstrap's grid system
- Responsive images within Bootstrap
- Bootstrap's helper classes
- Bootstrap's responsive utilities

The grid system

Bootstrap's grid system is arguably its most impressive and most commonly used feature. Therefore, mastering it is essential for any Bootstrap developer as the grid system removes many of the pain-points associated with page layouts, especially responsive page layouts. The grid system solves issues such as the horizontal and vertical positioning of a page's contents and the structure of the page across multiple display widths.

As already noted in Chapter 1, *Revving up Bootstrap*, Bootstrap 4 is mobile-first. As such, it should come as no surprise that the grid system is optimized for smaller viewports and scales up to suit larger viewports, as opposed to scaling down to smaller viewports.

What is a viewport?

A viewport is the available display size to render the contents of a page. For example, the size of your browser window, minus the toolbars, scrollbars, and so on, on your display is your viewport. As already noted in Chapter 1, *Revving Up Bootstrap*, mobile devices may indicate their viewport to be larger than it actually is, in order to allow for the display of websites that have not been optimized for display on mobile devices. As a consequence, websites that take mobile viewports into consideration, may often not render as intended. As a remedy, the viewport meta tag was introduced by Apple on iOS, and has since been uniformly adopted by all other major browsers. The viewport meta tag allows you to define the viewport's display size.

The grid is a structure that consists of three distinct, but fundamentally linked, parts: an all encapsulating **container**, split into horizontal **rows** which are themselves split into 12 equal **columns**. We will take an in depth look into the three building blocks of Bootstrap's grid system:

container												
row 1	col 1	col 2	col 3	col 4	col 5	col 6	col 7	col 8	col 9	col 10	col 11	col 12
row 2												
row 3												
row 4												

Figure 2.1: The Bootstrap grid structure: a container (outermost box) containing a table-like structure consisting of rows and 12 columns. It is important to note that rows must be contained inside the container. Likewise, columns can only exist within the context of rows. While grids can be used to construct tables, they are not tables in themselves. Unlike tables, independent rows may consist of a different number of columns. So, for example, row 1 may consist of 12 columns, while row 2 may contain only three columns.

Flexbox support

Flexbox is a CSS box model which allows for simple implementation of complex layouts, as opposed to the CSS2 layout modules such as block, inline, table, and positioned. Flexbox is designed to allow a layout to make the most use out of the available space, through a set of simple rules. Bootstrap 4 allows the developer to configure the framework to use flexbox for certain components, by changing one variable in `_variables.scss-$enable-flex`. Set `$enable-flex` to `true`, recompile Bootstrap and a number of Bootstrap components will have their display property set to `flex`. This includes the grid system itself, input groups, and the media component. You can find out more about flexbox at `https://www.w3.org/TR/css-flexbox-1/`.

Containers

Containers are at the core of Bootstrap's grid system, and practically the parent of all Bootstrap pages. A container is exactly what it sounds like. It encapsulates all other content within a section of a page, providing the base for how the section is rendered. You can think of a container as representing a canvas in a browser window for your content to be displayed on a canvas that can transform based on its environment. Unless explicitly specified, your content will never creep outside of this canvas, regardless of the viewport. A container can apply to the entire contents of a page, where you would have one root container element, or to different sections of a page, where you would have numerous container elements on the page.

There are two types of container classes provided by Bootstrap: `container` and `container-fluid`.

container

The `container` class renders the contents of the page to a fixed width. This width is typically based upon the width of the viewport, leveraging CSS media queries to determine which width is most suitable.

What are media queries?

Media queries are expressions, which resolve to a Boolean value. They are used to trigger `@media` rules that define styles for different media types. See `https://developer.mozilla.org/en-US/docs/Web/Guide/CSS/Media_queries`for further information.

The grid system has five core **breakpoints** it references, which are defined in `_variables.scss`. These are, extra-small (`xs`), small (`sm`), medium (`md`), large (`lg`) and extra-large (`xl`).

What are Breakpoints?

Breakpoints in relation to web development layouts are predefined vertical and horizontal dimensions at which the style rules change. As these rules break, they trigger another set of rules optimized for those dimensions. These rules are triggered by media queries, querying the dimensions of the viewport. For example, `@media (min-width: 768px)` will trigger a set of rules when the viewport is more than `768px` wide.

Let's take a look at `_variables.scss`:

```scss
$grid-breakpoints: (
    // Extra small screen / phone
    xs: 0,
    // Small screen / phone
    sm: 544px,
    // Medium screen / tablet
    md: 768px,
    // Large screen / desktop
    lg: 992px,
    // Extra large screen / wide desktop
    xl: 1200px
) !default;
```

Here, Bootstrap is defining the five breakpoints' minimum and maximum width variables, and the associated display types. Bootstrap will reference these variables throughout all its Sass code as the breakpoints can now be accessed as properties of `$grid-breakpoints`. We can also see the variables for the various container sizes, associated with the appropriate breakpoints. Look at the following code:

```scss
// Grid containers
//
// Define the maximum width of `.container` for different screen sizes.
```

```
$container-max-widths: (
    sm: 576px,
    md: 720px,
    lg: 940px,
    xl: 1140px
) !default;
// Grid columns
//
// Set the number of columns and specify the width of the gutters.
$grid-columns: 12 !default;
$grid-gutter-width:    1.875rem !default; // 30px
```

For example, container-tablet is set to 750 px: 720px plus the value of grid-gutter-width, which is 30px. As you can see from the comments in the code, container-** is associated directly with screen-**. Then, these sizes are leveraged via media queries in _grid.scss to set the desired width of the container. Let's take a look inside _grid.scss at the .container class:

```
.container {
    @include make-container();
    @include make-container-max-widths();
}
```

Let's break this down.

The make-container() and make-container-max-widths() are mixins with rules to center the container within the viewport and set max-width rules, respectively.

What is a mixin?

A mixin in this context is a set of predefined style rules encapsulated in a variable, which can be used within another rules definition. This is great for code maintenance and **don't repeat yourself (DRY)** principles.

You will also find make-container and make-container-max-widths within _grid.scss. The make-container mixin centralizes the alignment of the container using margin and padding rules. Have a look at the following code:

```
@mixin make-container($gutter: $grid-gutter-width) {
    margin-left: auto;
    margin-right: auto;
    padding-left: ($gutter / 2);
    padding-right: ($gutter / 2);
    @if not $enable-flex {
    @include clearfix();
```

```
        }
    }
```

The `make-container-max-widths` mixin is more complex. The mixin loops through the global `$breakpoint` variable, synonymous with `$grid-breakpoints`, and sets a `max-width` rule for each breakpoint, using media queries. Take a look at the following code:

```
// For each breakpoint, define the maximum width of the
container in a media query
@mixin make-container-max-widths($max-widths: $container-max-widths) {
    @each $breakpoint, $container-max-width in $max-widths {
        @include media-breakpoint-up($breakpoint) {
            max-width: $container-max-width;
        }
    }
}
```

The completed code then looks like the following:

```
@media (min-width: 544px) {
    .container {
        max-width: 576px;
                }
}
@media (min-width: 768px) {
    .container {
        max-width: 720px;
                }
}
@media (min-width: 992px) {
    .container {
        max-width: 940px;
                }
}
@media (min-width: 1200px) {
    .container {
        max-width: 1140px;
                }
}
```

There are four media queries, defining the horizontal breakpoint to trigger a `width` style rule. For example, `@media (min-width: 768px)` instructs the browser to only set the `width` property to the `max-width` of the container to `720px` for viewports wider than or equal to `768px`. This property is then superseded by the `@media (min-width: 992px)` rule when the viewport is wider than or equal to `992px`.

In the vast majority of cases, the width of the contents of the page is fixed to the width of the container. There are cases where the width of the container is ignored. One such case is Bootstrap's `navbar` class, in which the `navbar` element is allowed to fill the entire horizontal width of the viewport. We will come across this scenario in a later chapter.

Now that we have seen how the container is constructed and the theory behind the container, let us see it in practice. A container is generally a `div` with a container class in the body of the markup, wrapping around the page's main content. For example:

```
<body>
    <div class="container">
        <h1>Help, I'm trapped in a container!</h1>
    </div>
    <div>
        <h1>I'm free!</h1>
    </div>
</body>
```

Take a look at the following screenshot:

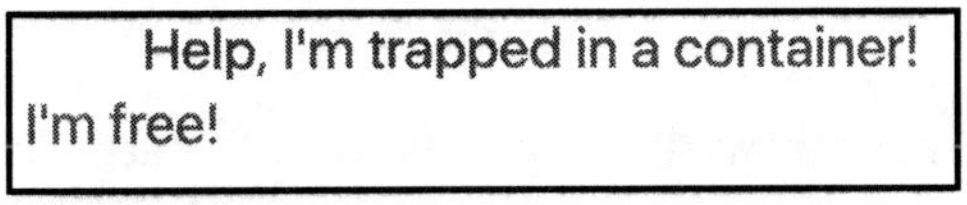

Figure 2.2: Using the container class

container-fluid

The other type of container, `container-fluid`, differs from `container` in two distinct ways:

- It takes up the full-width of the viewport, except for 15 pixels padding left and right
- It doesn't concern itself with breakpoints

The `container-fluid` allows the page to be fully responsive to all widths, providing smoother transitions. When responding to breakpoints, `container` snaps the layout to the appropriate width, while `container-fluid` progressively alters the layout.

The only difference in the markup is that instead of the `container` class being applied to the container `div`, the `container-fluid` class is applied. Look at the following code snippet:

```
<body>
    <div class="container-fluid">
        <h1>Help, I'm trapped in a container!</h1>
    </div>
    <div>
        <h1>I'm free!</h1>
    </div>
</body>
```

Take a look at the following screenshot:

Help, I'm trapped in a container!
I'm free!

Figure 2.3: Using the container-fluid class

Note that the container element now sits 15 pixels from the edge of the browser. When we use `container`, the container already has a hard-coded width defined. This width is based on the viewport. For example, at a resolution of 1200 px wide, the container would be 1140 px wide. At a resolution of 1280 pixels, the container would remain at 1170 px wide, because the container only responds to certain breakpoints. When we use `container-fluid`, the container width is dynamic, because `container-fluid` responds to every horizontal change and bases the width solely on the padding values from the make-container mixin. `container`, on the other hand, responds only at specific widths. `container-fluid` is the approach to take when building a page which needs to work across all display sizes and forms, especially when building mobile-first applications.

The `container` ensures that our contents will always display within a defined area on the page. But what about positioning content within the container? This is where rows come into play.

Box sizing

In CSS, every element is represented as a rectangle, or box. Each box has a number of properties associated with it to define how the element is rendered. This is the CSS Box Model. The box-sizing property of an element defines how the Box Model should calculate the width and height of elements.

 The default value for box-sizing in the CSS box model is content-box. The content-box property only includes the content of an element when calculating the size of that element.

Bootstrap 4 defaults the value of box-sizing to border-box. The border-box property includes the padding and border, as well as the content of the element in the calculation of the height and width of the element. Note that the margin is not included in the calculation. The third possible value for box-sizing is padding-box. The padding-box property, as the name suggests, only uses the content and the padding in calculating the size of an element.

Rows

A row is used to define a selection of elements that should be dealt with as a horizontal group. As such, rows reside within a container element. The power of the row lies in being able to stack content vertically. Almost like containers within a container, or defining a section of the page. Creating a row is as simple as applying the row class to the desired element:

```
<body>
    <div class="container">
        <h1>Help, I'm trapped in a container!</h1>
        <div class="row">
            <div>Section 1</div>
        </div>
        <div class="row">
            <div>Section 2</div>
        </div>
        <div class="row">
            <div>Section 3</div>
        </div>
    </div>
    <div>
```

```
        <h1>I'm free!</h1>
    </div>
</body>
```

Take a look at the following screenshot:

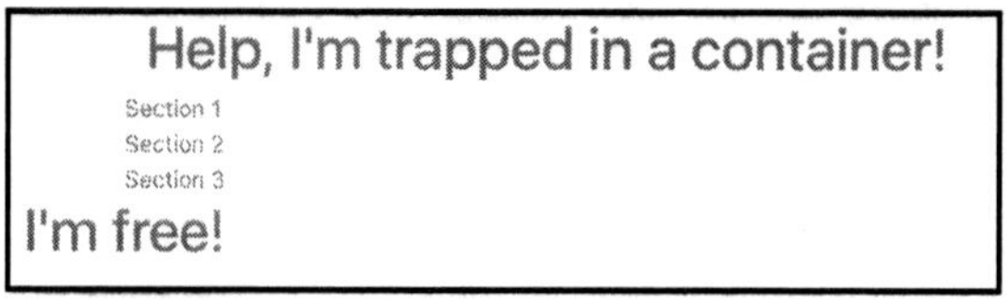

Figure 2.4: Using rows

The true power of rows only becomes apparent when they are used with columns.

Columns

Arguably, columns are the most important piece of the grid system. Rows exist within containers, and those rows are split up into 12 equal columns. Before we get into the nitty-gritty details, let's take a look at an example, by taking the first step into creating the print sizes section of MyPhoto. There will be 12 print sizes offered. Let's list those sizes horizontally:

```
<div class="container">
    <h1>Our Print Sizes</h1>
    <div class="row">
        <div class="col-sm-1">6x5</div>
        <div class="col-sm-1">8x10</div>
        <div class="col-sm-1">11x17</div>
        <div class="col-sm-1">12x18</div>
        <div class="col-sm-1">16x20</div>
        <div class="col-sm-1">18x24</div>
        <div class="col-sm-1">19x27</div>
        <div class="col-sm-1">20x30</div>
        <div class="col-sm-1">22x28</div>
        <div class="col-sm-1">24x36</div>
        <div class="col-sm-1">27x39</div>
        <div class="col-sm-1">27x40</div>
    </div>
</div>
```

As usual, we have our `container`. Within that `container`, we have a `row`, and within that `row` we have twelve individual elements with the `col-sm-1`. This produces a very neat list of evenly spaced elements in a single row on the page. Observe the following screenshot:

Figure 2.5: Using columns to display print sizes

Let's break down `col-xs-1` and explain each part individually:

- `col`: This means that we want this element to act as a column.
- `sm`: This is a reference to all viewports above or equal to `544px`. This class means we apply this rule for all viewports equal to or larger than `544px`.
- `1`: This means that the element takes up one column width of the row (1/12 of the row width).

Because `col-sm-1` references viewports larger than `544px`, smaller viewports (such as phones) revert to a stacked view. Take a look at the following screenshot:

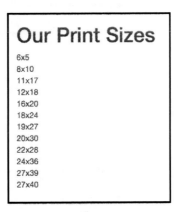

Figure 2.6: Viewports smaller than 544px revert to a stacked view when using col-sm-1

Columns are split up into five distinct breakpoints:

- `col-xs-`: This is for viewports below `544px` (extra-small)
- `col-sm-`: This is for viewports of `544px` or greater (small)
- `col-md-`: This is for viewports of `768px` or greater (medium)
- `col-lg-`: This is for viewports of `992px` or greater (large)

- `col-xl-`: This is for viewports of `1200px` or greater (extra-large)

The Bootstrap 3 column breakpoints

Bootstrap 3 did not have `col-xl`. Furthermore, its four distinct breakpoints were:

- `col-xs-`: This was for viewports below `768px` (extra-small)
- `col-sm-`: This was for viewports of `768px` or greater (small)
- `col-md-`: This was for viewports of `992px` or greater (medium)
- `col-lg-`: This was for viewports of `1200px` or greater (large)

These classes are then appended with the number of columns an element should cover. Let's split the print sizes into five separate categories, namely: **Small**, **Medium**, **Large**, and **Extra Large**. As we know, a row is split into 12 columns. We have four print size categories, so we divide the number of columns by the number of elements, and that is the number of columns we want the element to cover. So, we append the number 3 to the `col-sm-` classname:

```
<div class="container">
    <h1>Our Print Sizes</h1>
    <div class="row">
        <div class="col-sm-3">Small</div>
        <div class="col-sm-3">Medium</div>
        <div class="col-sm-3">Large</div>
        <div class="col-sm-3">Extra Large</div>
    </div>
</div>
```

Check out the following screenshot:

Figure 2.7: Print Categories split it into even columns across the grid system

But again, on an extra small viewport we are going to see the elements stacked. That is, the elements will appear one on top of the other. But what if we do not want this to happen? What if we would like the elements to take up a different number of columns as the viewport size changes? Well luckily Bootstrap allows you to define the column widths for all breakpoints, and it will decide which rule to apply. Let's try the following:

```html
<div class="container">
    <h1>Our Print Sizes</h1>
    <div class="row">
        <div class="col-xs-6 col-sm-3">Small</div>
        <div class="col-xs-6 col-sm-3">Medium</div>
        <div class="col-xs-6 col-sm-3">Large</div>
        <div class="col-xs-6 col-sm-3">Extra Large</div>
    </div>
</div>
```

We have retained `col-sm-3`, but now we have included `col-xs-6`. This means that for viewports below `544px` wide, we want each element to take up 6 columns. This will result in the first two elements displaying on one line, and the last two below that.

On a viewport of `544px` or wider, the categories appear in one horizontal row (as previously suggested, this is a drastic change from Bootstrap 3; with the previous version of Bootstrap, using the code, categories would appear in a horizontal row for viewports of `768px` or wider). Look at the following screenshot:

Figure 2.8: The print sizes at a resolution above 544px

On a viewport of less than `544px` wide, the categories are split across two rows. Observe the following screenshot:

Figure 2.9: The print sizes at a resolution below 544px

Nesting

Not only does the grid system split rows horizontally into columns, it also allows you to split the columns vertically, by supporting nested rows. These nested rows themselves are split into 12 columns within the space provided by the parent column. There is nothing special needed in terms of mark up to achieve row inception. All that is needed to achieve this is to nest the elements appropriately and apply the row and column classes.

Let's organize our print sizes into the relevant categories. We want 12 size options, split equally into the four size categories. Each category will contain one row element with each print size taking up one column in the grid. Let's try the following:

```html
<div class="container">
    <h1>Our Print Sizes</h1>
    <div class="row">
        <div class="col-xs-6 col-sm-3">
            <h5>Small</h5>
            <div class="row">
                <div class="col-sm-4">6x5</div>
                <div class="col-sm-4">8x10</div>
                <div class="col-sm-4">11x17</div>
            </div>
        </div>
        <div class="col-xs-6 col-sm-3">
            <h5>Medium</h5>
            <div class="row">
                <div class="col-sm-4">12x18</div>
                <div class="col-sm-4">16x20</div>
                <div class="col-sm-4">18x24</div>
            </div>
        </div>
        <div class="col-xs-6 col-sm-3">
            <h5>Large</h5>
            <div class="row">
                <div class="col-sm-4">19x27</div>
                <div class="col-sm-4">20x30</div>
                <div class="col-sm-4">22x28</div>
            </div>
        </div>
        <div class="col-xs-6 col-sm-3">
            <h5>Extra Large</h5>
            <div class="row">
                <div class="col-sm-4">24x36</div>
                <div class="col-sm-4">27x39</div>
                <div class="col-sm-4">27x40</div>
            </div>
        </div>
    </div>
```

```
        </div>
    </div>
```

Check out the following screenshot:

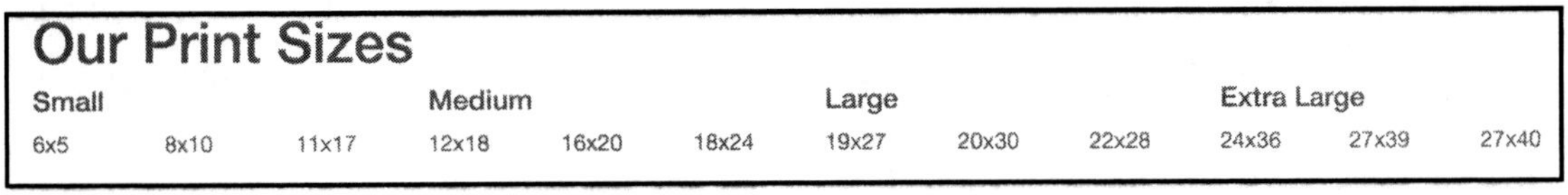

Our Print Sizes

Small			Medium			Large			Extra Large		
6x5	8x10	11x17	12x18	16x20	18x24	19x27	20x30	22x28	24x36	27x39	27x40

Figure 2.10: The print sizes using nesting

Within our category columns, we have nested a row. We split each row into three equal columns for viewports larger than or equal to 544px wide, using col-sm-4, to display the print sizes. Simple as that. Typically, it is good practice to ensure that the sum total of columns defined within the nested rows doesn't exceed the 12 columns allocated, as Bootstrap applies widths based on the assumption of 12 columns. Exceeding the 12 columns may result in unequal or unexpected column widths. However, on some occasions you may want to force a column onto another line at certain resolutions. For example, text content of columns may slightly overlap at certain resolutions.

In that case, we would like to force certain columns onto another line at a small resolution. To do this, we add col-md-* classes, and give the columns requiring a new line at 544px the class col-sm-12. Let's force the third size in the **Large** category onto its own line and force all **Extra Large** sizes onto separate lines. Let's try the following:

```
<div class="col-xs-6 col-sm-3">
    <h5>Large</h5>
    <div class="row">
        <div class="col-sm-4">19x27</div>
        <div class="col-sm-4">20x30</div>
        <div class="col-sm-12 col-md-4">22x28</div>
    </div>
</div>
<div class="col-xs-6 col-sm-3">
    <h5>Extra Large</h5>
    <div class="row">
        <div class="col-sm-12 col-md-4">24x36</div>
        <div class="col-sm-12 col-md-4">27x39</div>
        <div class="col-sm-12 col-md-4">27x40</div>
    </div>
</div>
```

Observe the following screenshot:

Our Print Sizes

Small			Medium			Large		Extra Large
6x5	8x10	11x17	12x18	16x20	18x24	19x27	20x30	24x36
						22x28		27x39
								27x40

Figure 2.11: The print sizes with the "Extra Large" category forced onto a separate line for viewports below 544px

Nice and neat. If you have been paying attention, then you will have noticed that we do not actually need to define the resolutions below **Medium** if we want the elements to have separate lines, as this is the default behavior. We would only need to define it if we wanted a resolution below that (such as xs) to have a different behavior. So, this does the trick:

```
<div class="col-xs-6 col-sm-3">
    <h5>Large</h5>
    <div class="row">
        <div class="col-sm-4">19x27</div>
        <div class="col-sm-4">20x30</div>
        <div class="col-md-4">22x28</div>
    </div>
</div>
<div class="col-xs-6 col-sm-3">
    <h5>Extra Large</h5>
    <div class="row">
        <div class="col-md-4">24x36</div>
        <div class="col-md-4">27x39</div>
        <div class="col-md-4">27x40</div>
    </div>
</div>
```

Columns and flexbox

If the grid system has flexbox enabled, by setting $enable-flex to true as described previously, it is possible to have Bootstrap automatically set the column sizes to equal width. To do this simply use col-*, where * is the breakpoint. An example would be col-xs. Given two sibling elements in a row, both with the class col-xs, then both of those columns will automatically be given the same width.

The grid system also lets you order your columns independently of how they are ordered in the markup. Bootstrap 4 achieves this through the `pull-*-*` and `push-*-*` classes. These classes took the form of `col-*-pull-*` and `col-*-push-*` in Bootstrap 3.

Pulling and pushing

The `pull-*-*` and `push-*-*` classes allow for columns to be moved horizontally along their parent row. For instance, perhaps you wanted the **Extra Large** category to appear as the first category in certain resolutions. You would simply dynamically apply the appropriate `push` and `pull` classes to the appropriate columns. In this case, apply `push-sm-9` to the **Extra Large** column, as you are pushing the column 9 columns left, and `pull-sm-3` to the rest, as you are pulling those three columns to the right. Take a look at the following code snippet:

```
<div class="container">
    <h1>Our Print Sizes</h1>
    <div class="row">
        <div class="col-xs-6 col-sm-3 push-sm-3">
            <h5>Small</h5>
            <div class="row">
                <div class="col-sm-4">6x5</div>
                <div class="col-sm-4">8x10</div>
                <div class="col-sm-4">11x17</div>
            </div>
        </div>
        <div class="col-xs-6 col-sm-3 push-sm-3">
            <h5>Medium</h5>
            <div class="row">
                <div class="col-sm-4">12x18</div>
                <div class="col-sm-4">16x20</div>
                <div class="col-sm-4">18x24</div>
            </div>
        </div>
        <div class="col-xs-6 col-sm-3 push-sm-3">
            <h5>Large</h5>
            <div class="row">
                <div class="col-sm-4">19x27</div>
                <div class="col-sm-4">20x30</div>
                <div class="col-md-4">22x28</div>
            </div>
        </div>
        <div class="col-xs-6 col-sm-3 pull-sm-9">
            <h5>Extra Large</h5>
            <div class="row">
                <div class="col-md-4">24x36</div>
```

```
                <div class="col-md-4">27x39</div>
                <div class="col-md-4">27x40</div>
            </div>
        </div>
    </div>
</div>
```

Observe the following screenshot:

Our Print Sizes

Extra Large			Small			Medium			Large		
24x36	27x39	27x40	6x5	8x10	11x17	12x18	16x20	18x24	19x27	20x30	22x28

Figure 2.12: Using Bootstrap's pull-*-* to re-arrange the Extra Large category column

You may have noticed that in the markup, we have only applied `sm` pull and push classes, even though we have `xs` classes applied. The reason for that is simple. The push and pull classes only work on groups of columns that exist on a single horizontal plane. Pushing **Extra Large** 9 columns to the left will just force them out of the viewport completely. Pushing **Extra Large** 6 columns will only push the columns to the position of **Large,** an unfortunate shortcoming of this feature.

Offsetting

One neat feature of the grid system is how it allows you to create empty space within your row by using columns. If you wanted to list the categories and sizes, but for some reason you wanted to leave the space for **Medium** empty, in other grid systems you might need to add the empty elements to the markup to get the desired effect. For example:

```
<div class="container">
    <h1>Our Print Sizes</h1>
    <div class="row">
        <div class="col-xs-6 col-sm-3 push-sm-3">
            <h5>Small</h5>
            <div class="row">
                <div class="col-sm-4">6x5</div>
                <div class="col-sm-4">8x10</div>
                <div class="col-sm-4">11x17</div>
            </div>
        </div>
        <div class="col-xs-6 col-sm-3 push-sm-3">
        </div>
        <div class="col-xs-6 col-sm-3 push-sm-3">
            <h5>Large</h5>
```

```
            <div class="row">
                <div class="col-sm-4">19x27</div>
                <div class="col-sm-4">20x30</div>
                <div class="col-md-4">22x28</div>
            </div>
        </div>
        <div class="col-xs-6 col-sm-3 pull-sm-9">
            <h5>Extra Large</h5>
            <div class="row">
                <div class="col-md-4">24x36</div>
                <div class="col-md-4">27x39</div>
                <div class="col-md-4">27x40</div>
            </div>
        </div>
    </div>
  </div>
</div>
```

Observe the following screenshot:

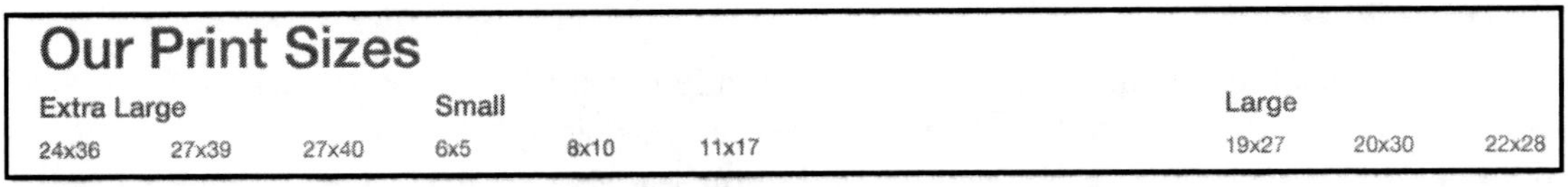

Our Print Sizes

Extra Large			Small			Large		
24x36	27x39	27x40	6x5	8x10	11x17	19x27	20x30	22x28

Figure 2.13: Adding spacing between columns

While it has the desired effect, it is adding markup simply for the sake of layout, which isn't really what we want to do if we can avoid it. Bootstrap allows us to avoid it via the `offset` classes. The `offset` classes follow the same convention as the rest of the `column` classes, `offset-*-*`. Now, we can remove the empty layout elements and simply add the `offset` classes to the **Large** columns. Take a look at the following code:

```
<div class="col-xs-6 col-sm-3 push-sm-3">
    <h5>Small</h5>
    <div class="row">
        <div class="col-sm-4">6x5</div>
        <div class="col-sm-4">8x10</div>
        <div class="col-sm-4">11x17</div>
    </div>
</div>
<div class="col-xs-6 col-xs-offset-6 col-sm-3 offset-sm-3 push-sm-3">
    <h5>Large</h5>
    <div class="row">
        <div class="col-sm-4">19x27</div>
        <div class="col-sm-4">20x30</div>
        <div class="col-md-4">22x28</div>
    </div>
```

```
        </div>
        <div class="col-xs-6 col-sm-3 pull-sm-9">
            <h5>Extra Large</h5>
            <div class="row">
                <div class="col-md-4">24x36</div>
                <div class="col-md-4">27x39</div>
                <div class="col-md-4">27x40</div>
            </div>
        </div>
    </div>
```

Voila. The same result with less code. The goal we all aim to achieve.

With containers, rows, and columns, we can now reason about our layout more easily. By splitting a viewport into understandable chunks and concepts, the grid system gives us a structure to apply our content.

Image elements

As a next step, let us add an image to each column in our grid. Each image will act as a category heading, as well as allow us to display our photographic wares. The images used in the following part, and throughout the rest of the book, are provided with this book. Take a look at the following code:

```
<div class="col-xs-6 col-sm-3 push-sm-3">
    <img src="images/small.jpg">
    <h5>Small</h5>
    <div class="row">
        <div class="col-sm-4">6x5</div>
        <div class="col-sm-4">8x10</div>
        <div class="col-sm-4">11x17</div>
    </div>
</div>
<div class="col-xs-6 col-sm-3 push-sm-3">
    <img src="images/medium.jpg">
    <h5>Medium</h5>
    <div class="row">
        <div class="col-sm-4">12x18</div>
        <div class="col-sm-4">16x20</div>
        <div class="col-sm-4">18x24</div>
    </div>
</div>
<div class="col-xs-6 col-sm-3 push-sm-3">
    <img src="images/large.jpg">
    <h5>Large</h5>
    <div class="row">
```

```
            <div class="col-sm-4">19x27</div>
            <div class="col-sm-4">20x30</div>
            <div class="col-md-4">22x28</div>
        </div>
    </div>
    <div class="col-xs-6 col-sm-3 pull-sm-9">
        <img src="images/extra-large.jpg">
        <h5>Extra Large</h5>
        <div class="row">
            <div class="col-md-4">24x36</div>
            <div class="col-md-4">27x39</div>
            <div class="col-md-4">27x40</div>
        </div>
    </div>
```

And that results in the following screenshot as seen in *Figure 2.14*:

Figure 2.14: An unexpected outcome: Adding an image to the column in each grid results in the images failing to respect the boundaries of parent columns

That isn't what we expected. As you can see, images do not respect the boundaries of the parent column. Obviously, we can fix this with some styling, but we don't need to do that from scratch. Bootstrap comes with a class to handle this case, called `img-fluid`.

Responsive images

It is as straightforward as you would hope, just apply the `img-fluid` class to the element:

```
<div class="col-xs-6 col-sm-3 push-sm-3">
    <img src="images/small.jpg" class="img-fluid">
    <h5>Small</h5>
    <div class="row">
        <div class="col-sm-4">6x5</div>
        <div class="col-sm-4">8x10</div>
        <div class="col-sm-4">11x17</div>
    </div>
</div>
<div class="col-xs-6 col-sm-3 push-sm-3">
    <img src="images/medium.jpg" class="img-fluid">
    <h5>Medium</h5>
    <div class="row">
        <div class="col-sm-4">12x18</div>
        <div class="col-sm-4">16x20</div>
        <div class="col-sm-4">18x24</div>
    </div>
</div>
<div class="col-xs-6 col-sm-3 push-sm-3">
    <img src="images/large.jpg" class="img-fluid">
    <h5>Large</h5>
    <div class="row">
        <div class="col-sm-4">19x27</div>
        <div class="col-sm-4">20x30</div>
        <div class="col-md-4">22x28</div>
    </div>
</div>
<div class="col-xs-6 col-sm-3 pull-sm-9">
    <img src="images/extra-large.jpg" class="img-fluid">
    <h5>Extra Large</h5>
    <div class="row">
        <div class="col-md-4">24x36</div>
        <div class="col-md-4">27x39</div>
        <div class="col-md-4">27x40</div>
    </div>
</div>
```

Take a look at the following screenshot:

Figure 2.15: Making images responsive using Bootstrap's img-fluid class results in images that respect the boundaries of parent elements

That is more like it. `img-fluid` is exceedingly simple in itself, essentially just adding a `max-width: 100%` rule to the image element. Now, the `img` element will respect the boundaries of its parent.

Responsive images in Bootstrap 3

Images in Bootstrap 3 were made responsive using the `img-responsive` class. The `img-fluid` class in Bootstrap 4 is, in essence, the equivalent of `img-responsive`, just with a different name.

However, this simple approach also means that the feature is very basic. The browser still downloads the full resolution image, even though it may only be rendered at a fraction of the size. There are other libraries and services which help resolve the responsive images problem.

Bootstrap does, however, provide a neat mixin to help mitigate issues with retina displays. The `img-retina` mixin basically extends `background-image` and `background-size` rules, by allowing for two images and two sizes to be defined one for standard displays, and one for retina. `img-retina` takes the form:

```
.img-retina(std-res-img, hi-res-img, standard-width, standard-height)
```

For standard displays, `img-retina` will set the `background-image` to `std-res-img`, with the defined width and height. For retina display, `img-retina` will set `background-image` to `hi-res-img`, with the defined width and height values doubled.

For example, if we wanted to make sure that the **Extra Large** image loaded at high resolution on retina displays, we could give it a class `extra-large-image`, and apply that to a `div`:

```
<div class="extra-large-image"></div>
```

We would define `extra-large-image` as:

```
.extra-large-image {
    .img-retina('/images/extra-large_std-res.png',
    '/images/extra-large_hi-res.png', 700px, 400px)
}
```

This will result in `/images/extra-large_std-res.png` being loaded with the dimensions 700 x 400 at standard resolution, and `/images/extra-large_hi-res.png` being loaded at 1400 x 800 on retina displays.

Image modifiers

Bootstrap also comes with some useful built-in image modifiers namely `img-rounded`, `img-thumbnail`, and `img-circle`. Let's apply these to the images in our example:

```
<div class="container">
    <h1>Our Print Sizes</h1>
    <div class="row">
        <div class="col-xs-6 col-sm-3 push-sm-3">
            <img src="images/small.jpg" class="img-fluid
            img-circle">
            <h5>Small</h5>
            . . .
        </div>
        <div class="col-xs-6 col-sm-3 push-sm-3">
            <img src="images/medium.jpg" class="img-fluid
            img-rounded">
            <h5>Medium</h5>
            . . .
        </div>
        <div class="col-xs-6 col-sm-3 push-sm-3">
            <img src="images/large.jpg" class="img-thumbnail">
            <h5>Large</h5>
            . . .
```

```
        </div>
        <div class="col-xs-6 col-sm-3 pull-sm-9">
            <img src="images/extra-large.jpg" class="img-fluid">
            <h5>Extra Large</h5>
            ...
        </div>
    </div>
</div>
```

Take a look at the following screenshot:

Figure 2.16: Applying Bootstrap's image modifiers: img-rounded, img-circle and img-thumbnail

You may notice that in the previously mentioned code, for the **Small** and **Medium** images, we have kept `img-fluid`, but removed `img-fluid` from **Large**. This is because `img-thumbnail` actually uses `img-fluid` as a mixin, while `img-circle` and `img-rounded` pay zero respect to the parent column width, so the `img-fluid` class is necessary. These images scale nicely down to `xs` displays, but it does look a little cluttered on a small viewport.

Take a look at the following screenshot:

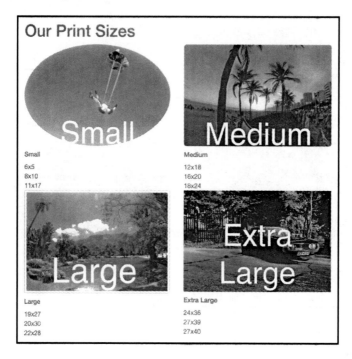

Figure 2.17: Dealing with smaller viewports by utilizing Bootstrap's responsive utilities

Bootstrap provides some really useful responsive utilities to tackle the issue of cluttered viewports.

Responsive utilities

Responsive utilities are a group of media query-based classes that control when an element should be hidden or shown depending on the viewport. One popular use case for this is controlling display specific navigations. For example, a page may have a navigation bar on large displays and have a hidden navigation on small displays which is only displayed when a user chooses to open the navigation.

Let's look at a quick example with our **Print Size** page. Add the `hidden-xs-down` class to the `img` elements:

```
<div class="container">
    <h1>Our Print Sizes</h1>
    <div class="row">
```

```
<div class="col-xs-6 col-sm-3 push-sm-3">
    <img src="images/small.jpg" class="img-fluid img-circle
    hidden-xs-down">
    <h5>Small</h5>
    ...
</div>
<div class="col-xs-6 col-sm-3 push-sm-3">
    <img src="images/medium.jpg" class="img-fluid img-rounded
    hidden-xs-down">
    <h5>Medium</h5>
    ...
</div>
<div class="col-xs-6 col-sm-3 push-sm-3">
    <img src="images/large.jpg" class="img-thumbnail
    hidden-xs-down">
    <h5>Large</h5>
    ...
</div>
<div class="col-xs-6 col-sm-3 pull-sm-9">
    <img src="images/extra-large.jpg" class="img-fluid
    hidden-xs-down">
    <h5>Extra Large</h5>
    ...
</div>
</div>
</div>
```

Take a look at the following screenshot:

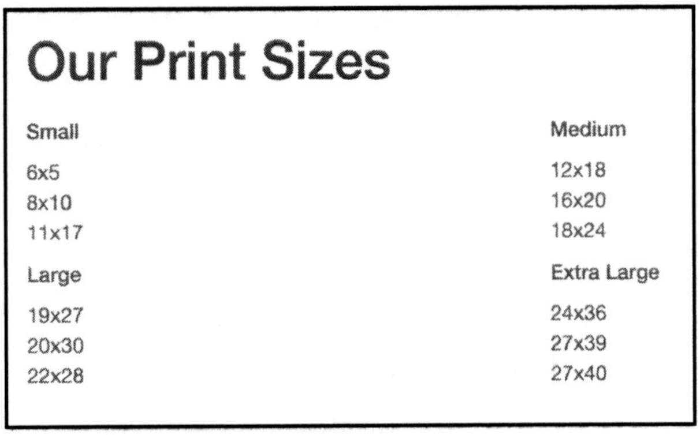

Our Print Sizes

Small	Medium
6x5	12x18
8x10	16x20
11x17	18x24
Large	Extra Large
19x27	24x36
20x30	27x39
22x28	27x40

Figure 2.18: Hiding elements based on the viewport size using the hidden-xs-down class

The `hidden-xs-down` property hides the element only when the display is extra-small, according to Bootstrap's grid system.

Hiding in Bootstrap 3

Bootstrap 3 only offers hidden-* (where * refers to the viewport size. For example, hidden-xs). As such, to hide an element only when the display is extra-small, we would add the class hidden-xs to our element.

The hidden classes stick to the conventions found in the grid system, along with hidden-xs-*, there are hidden-sm-*, -md-*, and -lg-* classes. In the grid system, col-md targets all **Medium** displays and below. Likewise, hidden-md-down will target only **Medium** displays or displays smaller than **Medium** (that is, small and extra small).

Aside from hidden-xs-down, Bootstrap also offers the hidden-*-up class, which hides an element if the viewport is at or above the threshold. For example, hidden-lg-up would hide the element when the display is **Large** or **Extra Large** (that is, unless the viewport is extra small, small or medium)

Let's apply the hidden classes so that:

- Images are hidden on xs, sm, and md displays.
- The page title is hidden on md or smaller displays
- Category titles are hidden on lg and bigger displays.

Observe the following code:

```
<div class="container">
    <h1 class="hidden-lg-down">Our Print Sizes</h1>
    <div class="row">
        <div class="col-xs-6 col-sm-3 push-sm-3">
            <img src="images/small.jpg"
            class="img-fluid img-circle hidden-md-down">
            <h5 class="hidden-lg-up">Small</h5>
            ...
        </div>
        <div class="col-xs-6 col-sm-3 push-sm-3">
            <img src="images/medium.jpg" class="img-fluid img-rounded
            hidden-md-down">
            <h5 class="hidden-lg-up">Medium</h5>
            ...
        </div>
        <div class="col-xs-6 col-sm-3 push-sm-3">
            <img src="images/large.jpg" class="img-thumbnail
            hidden-md-down">
            <h5 class="hidden-lg-up">Large</h5>
            ...
```

```
        </div>
        <div class="col-xs-6 col-sm-3 pull-sm-9">
            <img src="images/extra-large.jpg" class="img-fluid
            hidden-md-down">
            <h5 class="hidden-lg-up">Extra Large</h5>
            ...
        </div>
    </div>
</div>
```

Viewing the page on a viewport smaller than 544px, the categories will be displayed over two rows, with the category title text instead of images. Have a look at the following screenshot:

Small		Medium
6x5		12x18
8x10		16x20
11x17		18x24
Large		**Extra Large**
19x27		24x36
20x30		27x39
22x28		27x40

Figure 2.19: Screenshot depicting our page with the title and image elements hidden at displays smaller than sm

Viewing the page on a viewport larger than 768px (md) and smaller than 992px (lg), the categories will be displayed over one row with both the category title text and images, as in *Figure 2.20*. Viewing the page on a viewport larger than 992px will remove the category title text. Take a look at the following screenshot:

Figure 2.20: Screenshot depicting our page with the title element hidden for lg displays

Helper classes

Bootstrap also provides some utility classes, which Bootstrap refers to as helper classes. The helper classes provide some basic styles to accentuate information on a page. Their purpose is to give the user some context to the information they are receiving and to provide the developer with styling techniques, outside of the grid system.

Context

Bootstrap defines six context types to give a visual indicator to the user of what type of information is being conveyed: `muted`, `primary`, `success`, `info`, `warning`, and `danger`, as well as providing the developer with simple classes to assign context to elements via text color, `text-<context>` or background color, `bg-<context>`.

Let's apply some context to our example. We will add two prices to each size: a regular price and a special offer price. We will apply a `success` context to the special offer price and a `muted` context to the regular price. Print sizes with prices reduced by €10 or more will be given an `info` context background. The code should look similar to the following code snippet:

```
<div class="container">
    <h1 class="hidden-lg-down">Our Print Sizes</h1>
    <div class="row">
        <div class="col-xs-6 col-sm-3 push-sm-3">
            <img src="images/small.jpg" class="img-fluid img-circle
            hidden-md-down">
            <h5 class="hidden-lg-down">Small</h5>
            <div class="row">
                <div class="col-sm-4 bg-info">6x5
                    <div class="row">
                        <div class="col-sm-3 text-muted">€15</div>
                        <div class="col-sm-3 text-success">€8</div>
                    </div>
                </div>
                <div class="col-sm-4">8x10
                    <div class="row">
                        <div class="col-sm-3 text-muted">€18</div>
                        <div class="col-sm-3 text-success">€11</div>
                    </div>
                </div>
                <div class="col-sm-4">11x17
                    <div class="row">
                        <div class="col-sm-3 text-muted">€25</div>
                        <div class="col-sm-3 text-success">€20</div>
```

```
            </div>
         </div>
      </div>
   </div>
   <div class="col-xs-6 col-sm-3 push-sm-3">
   <img src="images/medium.jpg" class="img-fluid img-rounded
   hidden-md-down">
      ...
   </div>
```

Take a look at the following screenshot:

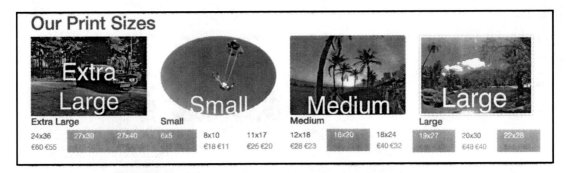

Figure 2.20: Bootstrap's context classes in action: note the changes in color for the various dimension and price blocks

As you can see, regular prices are gray, the special offer prices are green, and sizes with large discounts have a blue background.

Centering and floating

Bootstrap also provides handy classes for centering and floating elements.

Bootstrap 3 had a center-block class, which used margins to align an element centrally and sets the display property to block. This comes in very useful outside of the grid system. This has been removed from Bootstrap 4, in favor of two other classes, d-block and m-x-auto. The d-block class is responsible for setting the element's display property to block, while the m-x-auto class sets the margin properties to auto. As you may imagine, Bootstrap 4 also comes with the d-inline and d-inline-block classes, as well as an array of m-*-* classes for various margin options. More than that, there are also various padding options, with the p-*-* convention. Let us update our example with a new heading, **Special Offers**, inside a div we want to take up 50% of the viewport and we'll give it a primary background using the contextual classes.

Let's see it without the use of `m-x-auto` first. Observe the following code:

```
<div style="width:50%">
    <h1 class="bg-primary">Special Offers</h1>
</div>
<div class="container">
    <h1 class="hidden-lg-down">Our Print Sizes</h1>
    <div class="row">
```

Take a look at the following screenshot:

Figure 2.21: Applying Bootstrap's bg-primary class

Pretty ugly. Let's make it a little less ugly by centering the heading using `center-block` and `text-xs-center`. In Bootstrap 3, we would have used `center-block`, but as the element already has the `display: block` property, we can just use `m-x-auto` instead to control the margins. This can be done in the following manner:

```
<div class="m-x-auto" style="width:50%">
    <h1 class="bg-primary text-xs-center">Special Offers</h1>
</div>
```

For the time being, we have also used inline styles here to set the `width` of **Special Offers** to 50%. Inline styles should in general be avoided as they decrease maintainability of the code base. Ideally, we should use a class here to apply this style rule. We will address this in a later chapter. Let's check out the result in the following screenshot:

Figure 2.22: Applying Bootstrap's m-x-auto, text-xs-center and bg-primary classes

Nice, a little less ugly.

Along with this, Bootstrap gives us useful classes for floating elements left and right: `pull-*-right` and `pull-*-left`. These classes follow the same semantics as the previously discussed `hidden` classes and simply result in the appropriate `float` property being applied to the element together with an `!important` rule. The rules only get applied when the display is at or above the given breakpoint (the supported breakpoints are: `xs`, `sm`, `md`, `lg`, and `xl`).

Let's add a caveat to the page, indicating that **Terms and Conditions Apply**. We will use the `pull-xs-right` class to float it to the far right, the contextual `danger` class to indicate that it is worth noting to the user, and Bootstrap's `label` class to make the text look a little prettier. Since `pull-xs-right` floats elements to the right when the display is extra small or larger, the **Terms and Conditions** element will be floating to the right for all display sizes. Take a look at the following code:

```
<div class="bg-danger pull-xs-right">
    <p class="label">Temperatures may not be accurate</p>
</div>
```

Take a look at the following screenshot:

Figure 2.23: Using pull-xs-right to align an element to the right, for all display sizes

Nice and neatly docked to the right-hand side.

Aligning elements in Bootstrap 3

Bootstrap 3 only offers pull-left and pull-right, independent of display size. To align elements conditionally one would need to write custom CSS rules.

Toggling visibility

None of these utility classes are very complex. Nor would a developer not be able to implement the required logic themselves. However, they greatly help speed up development. The classes Bootstrap provides to toggle content visibility are a clear example of this. The `invisible` class simply sets the elements `visbility` property to `hidden`, with an `!important` rule. However, there are a few very useful display utility classes that are slightly more complex such as `text-hide`, `sr-only`, and `sr-only-focusable`.

The `sr-only` class hides an element except from screen-readers. `sr-only-focusable` extends this functionality to become visible when the element becomes focused, for instance in the case of keyboard access.

The `text-hide` class allows the developer to couple an image with a text element. The text will be read by a screen-reader, but by using `text-hidden`, it is not visible. Let's see this in action with the images in our example. Replace the `hidden-**` classes we added to our category text elements with `text-hide`. Have a look here:

```
<h5 class="text-hide">Small</h5>
```

Give it a try with a screen-reader to see (actually, hear!) the results.

Text alignment and transformation

Using the grid system, we learned how to lay out a website's basic building blocks. However, generally we need an additional level of control that allows us to more finely align the content contained within these building blocks. This level of control is provided Bootstrap's text alignment classes:

- `text-justify`: This justifies the text, so that it fills an entire area evenly (see *Figure 2.24*)
- `text-*-left`: This aligns the text in the element to which this class is applied to the left on viewports of size * or wider, where * can be one of the following: xs, sm, md, lg, and xl
- `text-*-right`: This aligns the text in the element to which this class is applied to the right on viewports of size * or wider, where * can be one of the following: xs, sm, md, lg, and xl
- `text-*-center`: This aligns the text in the element to which this class is applied to the center on viewports of size * or wider, where * can be one of the following: xs, sm, md, lg, xl

This can be observed in the following screenshot:

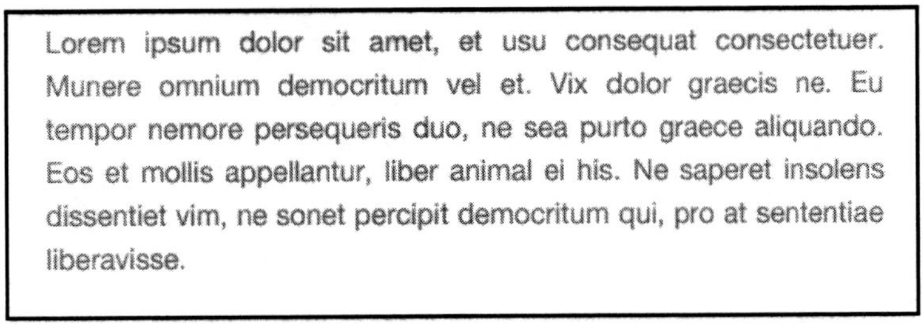

> Lorem ipsum dolor sit amet, et usu consequat consectetuer. Munere omnium democritum vel et. Vix dolor graecis ne. Eu tempor nemore persequeris duo, ne sea purto graece aliquando. Eos et mollis appellantur, liber animal ei his. Ne saperet insolens dissentiet vim, ne sonet percipit democritum qui, pro at sententiae liberavisse.

Figure 2.24: An example of using the text-justify class to justify text

Aside from text alignment classes, Bootstrap also provides classes for transforming text contained within elements to which the classes are applied. Specifically:

- Text can be converted to all lower case by applying the `text-lowercase` class
- Text can be converted to all upper case by applying the `text-uppercase` class
- The first letter in each word can be capitalized by applying the `text-capitalize` class

The appearance (that is, its font weight) of text can be modified by applying `font-weight-normal`, `font-weight-bold`, and `font-italic`.

Summary

In this chapter, we covered the most important aspect of Bootstrap. We learned how Bootstrap's grid system operates, gaining an understanding of its many features. We have seen how we can leverage Bootstrap to manage responsive images, as well as how to target specific content to specific displays. On top of that, we have learned how to use the extremely useful Bootstrap helper classes. We also discovered a very nice feature of all the layout specific utility classes: the fact that they can also be used as mixins, and are indeed used as mixins within other Bootstrap classes. Leveraging these classes when we start writing custom style rules for MyPhoto will surely come in useful. As such, our understanding of Bootstrap is now quite deep, so let us go forward to the next chapter and build the layout for our MyPhoto page.

3
Building the Layout

In Chapter 2, *Making a Style Statement*, we learned about some of Bootstrap's core features, such as the grid system, and built out the print sizes component of MyPhoto. In this chapter, we are going to put this knowledge to further use by building out the layout of MyPhoto.

First, we will split the page into five sections, as we discussed in the previous chapters. These would be **Welcome**, **Services**, **Gallery**, **About**, and **Contact Us**, along with a footer placeholder. Here, we will use the grid system to create distinct sections on the page. We will add content to these sections using the Bootstrap components jumbotron, tabs, carousel, and wells.

Furthermore, we will discover how to integrate Bootstrap's **navbar** component into our page to provide single-page, app-like navigation, while also using it to surface Bootstrap **modal windows**.

As we learn about and implement these different components, we will also introduce how to customize the components to integrate with the styling conventions of MyPhoto.

In this chapter, we shall cover the following topics:

- Learning how to lay out a page using Bootstrap's grid system
- Learning how to integrate Bootstrap jumbotron, wells, tabs, and carousel
- Learning how to integrate Bootstrap's navbar
- Learning how to create and surface Bootstrap's modal windows
- Learning how to extend Bootstrap's component styles

Splitting it up

The MyPhoto webpage consists of five sections: **Welcome**, **Services**, **Gallery**, **About**, and **Contact Us**. The first thing we want to do is split our page into these distinct sections.

Each section will be a distinct container, so we can practically treat each section as a standalone component on the page. We want the container to take up 100% of the available horizontal space. Therefore, we will apply the container-fluid class. As we learned earlier, container-fluid allows its contents to be responsive across all resolutions, relying on the percentage width of the page, unlike the standard container class, which uses predefined horizontal breakpoints. To provide a visual cue that these are separate parts of the page, we will apply Bootstrap's **contextual background classes** to each section. We will also include a footer element in the page. The footer will contain miscellaneous bits of information, like legal information, but for now we will just include a placeholder:

```
<body>
    <div class="container-fluid bg-primary">
        <div class="row">
            <h3>Welcome</h3>
        </div>
    </div>
    <div class="container-fluid bg-info">
        <div class="row">
            <h3>Services</h3>
        </div>
    </div>
    <div class="container-fluid bg-success">
        <div class="row">
            <h3>Gallery</h3>
        </div>
    </div>
    <div class="container-fluid bg-warning">
        <div class="row">
            <h3>About</h3>
        </div>
    </div>
    <div class="container-fluid bg-danger">
        <div class="row">
            <h3>Contact Us</h3>
        </div>
    </div>
    <footer>Footer placeholder</footer>
</body>
```

So, we have five distinct containers, each with a distinct contextual background class and an inner row element, with an appropriate heading, along with a footer, producing the following screenshot:

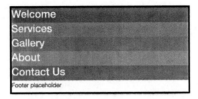

Figure 3.1: Five distinct containers, each with a different contextual background

Okay, great. All sections of our site are in place. Let's add some custom CSS to give each section some space to breathe. Create a file, `styles/myphoto.css`, and add the following rules to set the minimum height of the section:

```
.myphoto-section {
    min-height: 500px;
}
```

The `myphoto-section` class will set the height of the section to a minimum height of `500px`. Add this class to each section, except for the `footer`:

```
<div class="container-fluid myphoto-section bg-primary">
    <div class="row">
        <h3>Welcome</h3>
    </div>
</div>
```

The addition of the `myphoto-section` class results in the following screenshot:

Figure 3.2: Five distinct containers with a minimum height of 500 pixels each

Now each section is easily distinguishable. The page bears a striking resemblance to a rainbow, though. Let's apply a color scheme here. We will apply a classic dark/light style, alternating between dark and light with each section. Update `myphoto.css` with the following classes:

```
.bg-myphoto-dark {
    background-color: #504747;
    color: white;
}
.bg-myphoto-light {
    background-color: white;
    color: #504747;
}
```

These new classes adhere to the Bootstrap `.bg` naming convention and offer contrasting styles, a dark background with light text, and vice versa. Apply these to the container elements, in an even-odd manner:

```
<div class="container-fluid myphoto-section bg-myphoto-light">
    <div class="row">
        <h3>Welcome</h3>
    </div>
</div>
<div class="container-fluid myphoto-section bg-myphoto-dark">
    <div class="row">
        <h3>Services</h3>
    </div>
</div>
...
```

The **Welcome** section should now appear with a light background, the **Services** section with a dark background, and so on. Take a look at the following screenshot:

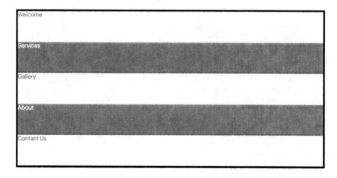

Figure 3.3: Five sections with alternating background colors

Pretty classy, right? Now, we have a responsive page, split into individual sections, powered by the grid system, with our own styling. Nothing wild here, but a nice start. Let's go ahead and add some content.

Adding Bootstrap components

MyPhoto is looking pretty bare right now, so let's take a look at integrating some Bootstrap components into our sections. First, let us add Bootstrap's JavaScript library. Bootstrap's JS relies upon jQuery UI, so let us add that too. Note that Bootstrap JS is not required for all the components we are going to use here, but it is best to get the setup out of the way. Install jQuery using Bower:

```
bower install jquery
```

Add the following code to the head of your page:

```
<script src="bower_components/jquery/dist/jquery.min.js"></script>
<script src="bower_components/bootstrap/dist/js/bootstrap.min.js">
</script>
```

With that, we're ready to use any Bootstrap component in our page.

Jumbotron

The first component we are going to integrate is Bootstrap's jumbotron.

The jumbotron component is essentially a very simple visual cue to draw attention to certain content. It is generally used as a splash to offer immediate information to the user. That is exactly what we will be doing with it.

In the **Welcome** section of our page, nest a jumbotron element into the container element:

```
<div class="container-fluid myphoto-section bg-myphoto-light">
    <div class="container">
        <div class="jumbotron">
            <h1>Welcome to MyPhoto</h1>
            <p>Photographs you can cherish!</p>
        </div>
    </div>
</div>
```

We have nested a container element in the container-fluid **Welcome** element. We do this so that our content is centered within the section, allowing for gutter space on the left and right. Within that container, we add a jumbotron element. The jumbotron class simply gives its element a hero-banner type style to attract the eye. The jumbotron itself acts in a similar way to a container, encompassing its own content. Here, we add a header and a paragraph to provide some context to the user. Take a look at the following screenshot:

Figure 3.4: The Bootstrap jumbotron class to create a banner welcoming the user to MyPhoto

Oh, not great. The jumbotron has worked as expected, but it is not grabbing our attention as we would hope against a light background. Being a photographer's page, maybe we should add some pictorial content here? We can use jumbotron to display as a hero-image. Add a new class to myphoto.css:

```
.jumbotron-welcome {
    background-image: url('/images/skyline.png');
    background-size: cover;
    color: white;
}
```

This class will simply apply a background image and a light font color to an element. Apply the class to our jumbotron element:

```
<div class="jumbotron jumbotron-welcome">
```

Take a look at the following screenshot:

Figure 3.5: Using Sao Paulo's skyline as a background image for MyPhoto's welcome banner

Pretty nice. Let's flip that, and apply the background image to the **Welcome** section `container` element, removing the `bg-myphoto-light` class. Add the following class to `myphoto.css`:

```
.bg-myphoto-welcome {
    background-image: url('/images/skyline.png');
    background-size: cover;
    color: #504747;
}
```

Then, update the **Welcome** section to the following:

```
<div class="container-fluid myphoto-section bg-myphoto-welcome">
    <div class="container">
        <div class="jumbotron">
            <h1>Welcome to MyPhoto</h1>
            <p>Photographs you can cherish!</p>
        </div>
    </div>
</div>
```

Our new class again applies the background image. It also applies a dark font color, which will be inherited by the jumbotron. We have removed the `jumbotron-welcome` class from the `jumbotron` element.

Excellent! We have added some photographic content and our jumbotron attracts attention.

Tabs

`MyPhoto` offers a trio of services. We built the UI for one of these, the **Print** service, in `Chapter 2`, *Making a Style Statement*. The UI displayed the prices for various print sizes. Obviously, we will want to integrate the **Print** service into the **Services** section of the `MyPhoto` page. We also need to include the other two services, namely, **Events**, where a photographer may take photographs of a customer's event such as a wedding or a conference, and **Personal**, where a photographer may take family photos and so on.

Rather than build the services into three separate interfaces, we are going to develop them using Bootstrap's `tabs` component.

Tabs are a part of Bootstrap's `nav` family of components. Tabs provide an elegant way of displaying and grouping related content. Under the surface, `tabs` are simply list elements linked to `div` elements, representing the tab contents, with some nice styling applied. Tabs are one of the Bootstrap components that require jQuery and `bootstrap.js` to function correctly.

First, we will add the tab list to the **Services** section:

```
<ul class="nav nav-tabs nav-justified">
    <li class="nav-item">
        <a href="#services-events" data-toggle="tab" class="nav-link
        active">Events
        </a>
    </li>
    <li class="nav-item">
        <a href="#services-personal" data-toggle="tab" class="nav-
        link">Personal</a>
    </li>
    <li class="nav-item">
        <a href="#services-prints" data-toggle="tab" class="nav-
        link">
        Prints</a>
    </li>
</ul>
```

We're wrapping the **Services** header in a `container` element, so we follow the same convention as the **Welcome** section and leave gutter space around the content. Within that container, we also include the `tabs`. We create an unordered list element (`ul`) with the `nav` base class, and the `nav-tabs` class to apply the tab styling. The list elements are then created, with the tab heading text and a `href` to the relevant tab content. The `nav-item` class is applied to each list item to denote that the item is indeed a navigation item (the `nav-item` class adjusts the margin and float of the list item, and ensures that the list items are not stacked on top of each other, but instead appear next to one another). The anchor element that is used to reference the tab's corresponding section is given a `nav-link` class. This `nav-link` class adjusts the following:

- The anchor's padding, so that it displays nicely as a tab link.
- It removes the default anchor focus and hover text decoration.
- It changes the anchor's display to `inline-block`. This has two important effects on the element:
    - The browser renders any white space contained within the element.
    - The element is placed inline, but maintains the properties of a block-level element.

The `active` class is applied to the default selected list item's anchor element. Last but not least, the anchor's `data-toggle` attribute is set to `tab`. Our **Services** section now looks like this:

Figure 3.6: Using tabs components to build out the MyPhoto's Services section

Navigation tabs in Bootstrap 3

Nav tabs in Bootstrap 3 require slightly more work than when using Bootstrap 4. For one, Bootstrap 3 does not have the `nav-item` and `nav-link` classes. Instead, we create an unordered-list element (`ul`) with the `nav` base class, namely, `nav-tabs` class, to apply the tab styling, and `nav-justified` to center the text within the tab headings. The list elements are then created, with the tab heading text and a `href` to the relevant tab content.

The `active` class is applied to the default selected list item:

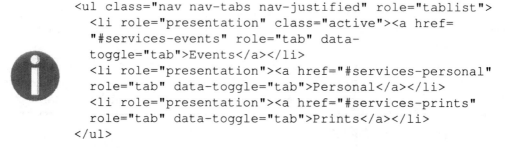

```html
<ul class="nav nav-tabs nav-justified" role="tablist">
  <li role="presentation" class="active"><a href=
  "#services-events" role="tab" data-
  toggle="tab">Events</a></li>
  <li role="presentation"><a href="#services-personal"
  role="tab" data-toggle="tab">Personal</a></li>
  <li role="presentation"><a href="#services-prints"
  role="tab" data-toggle="tab">Prints</a></li>
</ul>
```

Note that the `nav-justified` class has been removed from Bootstrap 4.

We now have some selectable tabs, with inappropriate styling and no content. Let's resolve the content issue first. We will add `Lorem Ipsum` text to the **Events** and **Personal** tab content, and we will use an `Our Print Sizes` table for the **Prints** tab content:

```html
<div class="tab-content bg-myphoto-light">
  <div role="tabpanel" class="tab-pane active" id="services-events">
    <div class="container">
      <div class="row">
        <p>Lorem Ipsum</p>
      </div>
    </div>
  </div>
  <div role="tabpanel" class="tab-pane" id="services-personal">
    <div class="container">
      <div class="row">
        <p>Lorem Ipsum</p>
      </div>
    </div>
  </div>
  <div role="tabpanel" class="tab-pane" id="services-prints">
    <div class="m-x-auto" style="width:50%">
      <h1 class="bg-primary text-xs-center">Special Offers</h1>
    </div>
    <div class="container">
      <h1 class="hidden-lg-down">Our Print Sizes</h1>
        <div class="row">
          <div class="col-xs-6 col-sm-3 push-sm-3">
            <h5 class="text-hide">Small</h5>
              <div class="row">
                <div class="col-sm-4 bg-info">6x5
                  <div class="row">
                    <div class="col-sm-3 text-muted">€15</div>
```

```
                <div class="col-sm-3 text-success">€8</div>
            </div>
        </div>
        <div class="col-sm-4">8x10
            <div class="row">
                <div class="col-sm-3 text-muted">€18</div>
                <div class="col-sm-3 text-success">€11</div>
            </div>
        </div>
        <div class="col-sm-4">11x17
            <div class="row">
                <div class="col-sm-3 text-muted">€25</div>
                <div class="col-sm-3 text-success">€20</div>
            </div>
        </div>
    </div>
</div>
<div class="col-xs-6 col-sm-3 push-sm-3">
    <h5 class="text-hide">Medium</h5>
    <div class="row">
        <div class="col-sm-4">12x18
            <div class="row">
                <div class="col-sm-3 text-muted">€28</div>
                <div class="col-sm-3 text-success">€23</div>
            </div>
        </div>
        <div class="col-sm-4 bg-info">16x20
            <div class="row">
                <div class="col-sm-3 text-muted">€35</div>
                <div class="col-sm-3 text-success">€25</div>
            </div>
        </div>
        <div class="col-sm-4">18x24
            <div class="row">
                <div class="col-sm-3 text-muted">€40</div>
                <div class="col-sm-3 text-success">€32</div>
            </div>
        </div>
    </div>
</div>
<div class="col-xs-6 col-sm-3 push-sm-3">
    <h5 class="text-hide">Large</h5>
    <div class="row">
        <div class="col-sm-4 bg-info">19x27
            <div class="row">
                <div class="col-sm-3 text-muted">€45</div>
                <div class="col-sm-3 text-success">€30</div>
            </div>
```

```
                </div>
                <div class="col-sm-4">20x30
                    <div class="row">
                        <div class="col-sm-3 text-muted">€48</div>
                        <div class="col-sm-3 text-success">€40</div>
                    </div>
                </div>
                <div class="col-md-4 bg-info">22x28
                    <div class="row">
                        <div class="col-sm-3 text-muted">€55</div>
                        <div class="col-sm-3 text-success">€40</div>
                    </div>
                </div>
            </div>
        </div>
        <div class="col-xs-6 col-sm-3 pull-sm-9">
            <h5 class="text-hide">Extra Large</h5>
            <div class="row">
                <div class="col-md-4">24x36
                    <div class="row">
                        <div class="col-sm-3 text-muted">€60</div>
                        <div class="col-sm-3 text-success">€55</div>
                    </div>
                </div>
                <div class="col-md-4 bg-info">27x39
                    <div class="row">
                        <div class="col-sm-3 text-muted">€75</div>
                        <div class="col-sm-3 text-success">€60</div>
                    </div>
                </div>
                <div class="col-md-4 bg-info">27x40
                    <div class="row">
                        <div class="col-sm-3 text-muted">€75</div>
                        <div class="col-sm-3 text-success">€60</div>
                    </div>
                </div>
            </div>
        </div>
    </div>
</div>
<div class="bg-danger pull-xs-right">
  <p class="label">Terms and Conditions Apply</p>
 </div>
    </div>
  </div>
</div>
```

We add a `tab-content` element to wrap the three services, which are declared with a `tab-pane` class. The `tab-pane` classes have an `id` attribute matching the `href` attribute of the corresponding tab heading, and each of the `tab-pane` elements has a `container` element for the contents of the pane. Now, clicking on the the **Prints** tab will surface **Our Print Sizes** chart. We have modified the print sizes chart for its new context within the `tabs` component. Take a look at the following screenshot:

Figure 3.7: Adding tab content using the tab-pane class

Let's quickly add some styling to the tab headings and panels to make them slightly more readable. Add the following classes to `myphoto.css`:

```
.bg-myphoto-dark .nav-tabs a {
    color: white;
}
```

Save and refresh. Our **Services** section now looks like the following:

Figure 3.8: Improving the look and feel of our tabs by setting the tab title color to white

With those changes, our **Services** tabs are a little more pleasing to the eye. The contents of the tabs can now be fleshed out within their own specific container elements.

Carousel

To exhibit the photographic wares, we need a gallery. To implement the `gallery` feature, we are going to integrate Bootstrap's `carousel` component. The carousel acts as a slideshow, with a list of nested elements as the slides.

Let's add a `carousel`, with three slides, to the **Gallery** section:

```
<div class="container-fluid myphoto-section bg-myphoto-light">
  <div class="container">
    <div class="row">
      <h3>Gallery</h3>
      <div id="gallery-carousel" class="carousel slide"
      data-ride="carousel" data-interval="3000">
        <div class="carousel-inner" role="listbox">
          <div style="height: 400px" class="carousel-item active">
            <img src="images/brazil.png">
            <div class="carousel-caption">
              Brazil
            </div>
          </div>
          <div style="height: 400px" class="carousel-item">
            <img src="images/datsun.png">
            <div class="carousel-caption">
              Datsun 260Z
            </div>
          </div>
          <div style="height: 400px" class="carousel-item">
            <img src="images/skydive.png">
            <div class="carousel-caption">
              Skydive
            </div>
          </div>
        </div>
        <a class="left carousel-control" href="#gallery-carousel"
        role="button" data-slide="prev">
          <span class="icon-prev" aria-hidden="true"></span>
        </a>
        <a class="right carousel-control" href="#gallery-carousel"
        role="button" data-slide="next">
          <span class="icon-next" aria-hidden="true"></span>
        </a>
        <ol class="carousel-indicators">
          <li data-target="#gallery-carousel" data-slide-
          to="0" class="active"></li>
          <li data-target="#gallery-carousel" data-slide-
          to="1"></li>
```

```
        <li data-target="#gallery-carousel" data-slide-
        to="2"></li>
      </ol>
    </div>
  </div>
  </div>
</div>
```

Take a look at the following screenshot:

Figure 3.9: Using the Bootstrap carousel to display a gallery of images. Note the arrows at both sides of the images. These are the carousel controls that allow users to navigate the image gallery.

Now, we have a fully functioning, three-slide gallery. Let's breakdown what is happening here.

The carousel in Bootstrap 3

When using the carousel feature after switching to Bootstrap 4, having used Bootstrap 3, there are two changes to be wary of. The first is that the `carousel-item` class was just called `item` class in Bootstrap 3. The second is that Bootstrap 4 comes with the `icon-next` and `icon-prev` classes that should be used with the carousel controls. A typical Bootstrap 3 carousel control may look as follows:

```
<a class="left carousel-control" href="#gallery-
carousel" role="button" data-slide="prev">
  <span class="glyphicon glyphicon-chevron-left" aria-
  hidden="true"></span>
</a>
<a class="right carousel-control" href="#gallery-
carousel" role="button" data-slide="next">
```

```
<span class="glyphicon glyphicon-chevron-right" aria-
hidden="true"></span>
</a>
```

First, we declare the `carousel` parent tag:

```
<div id="gallery-carousel" class="carousel slide" data-ride=
"carousel" data-interval="4000"></div>
```

We give the `div` an `id` that can be referenced by its nested elements, such as the carousel indicators. We use Bootstrap's `carousel` and `slide` classes. The `data-ride="carousel"` attribute indicates that the `carousel` is to automatically initialize on page load. The `data-interval` attribute indicates that the slides should change every `4000` ms. There are other options such as `data-pause`, which will indicate whether or not the carousel should pause on hover. The default value is `hover`; to prevent pausing, set this option to `false`. The `data-wrap` is a Boolean attribute, to indicate whether the carousel should be a continuous loop, or end once the last slide has been reached. The default value for `data-wrap` is `true`. The `data-keyboard` is also a Boolean attribute, to indicate whether or not the carousel is keyboard-controllable. The default value for `data-keyboard` is `true`.

Then, we add the actual slides. The slides are nested within a `carousel-inner` element, to contain the slides. The slides are also `div` elements, with the `carousel-item` class, and the active class to indicate which slide to show on initialization:

```
<div style="height: 400px" class="carousel-item active">
    <img src="images/image1.png">
    <div class="carousel-caption">
      Skydiving
    </div>
</div>
```

Within the `div`, we have an image element to act as the main content for the slide, and it has a sibling `carousel-caption` element, which is exactly what it sounds like, a caption for the slide. The `carousel-caption` element can contain nested elements.

Next, we add the right and left arrows for navigating through the slides:

```
<a class="left carousel-control" href="#gallery-carousel"
role="button" data-slide="prev">
  <span class="icon-prev" aria-hidden="true"></span>
</a>
```

These are simple anchor tags, leveraging Bootstrap's directional and `carousel-control` classes. The `data-slide` attribute indicates whether we want to cycle backward or forward through the list of slides. The `data-slide` can take the value `prev` for previous, or next. Nested within the anchor tag is a span simply applying the `icon-prev` and `icon-next` class as a directional indicator.

Finally, we declare the `carousel-indicators`:

```
<ol class="carousel-indicators">
  <li data-target="#gallery-carousel" data-slide-to="0"
  class="active"></li>
  <li data-target="#gallery-carousel" data-slide-to="1"></li>
  <li data-target="#gallery-carousel" data-slide-to="2"></li>
</ol>
```

The indicators are circles layered on the slideshow, indicating which slide is currently active. For example, if the second slide is active, then the second circle will be filled. It is mandatory to indicate which slide is active on initialization by setting `class="active"` on that element. The `data-slide-to` attribute indicates which slide the circle relates to, so if a user clicks a circle with `data-slide-to="2"`, the third slide becomes active, as the count for the slides begins at 0. Some Bootstrap framework ports, for example Angular Bootstrap, will automatically generate the carousel indicators based on the number of slides the carousel contains, but using Vanilla Bootstrap, the list has to be created and maintained manually.

With that, we now have a fully functioning carousel as our **Gallery**, with very little markup, thanks to the power of Bootstrap.

Cards

The final section we are going to look at in this chapter is the **About** section. Here, we are going to use Bootstrap's `card` component to highlight our `MyPhoto` marketing blurb. Take a look at the following code:

```
<div class="container-fluid myphoto-section bg-myphoto-dark">
<div class="container">
<div class="row">
  <h3>About</h3>
  <div class="card bg-myphoto-light">
    <div class="card-block">
      <p>The style of photography will be customised to your
      personal preference, as if being shot from your own eyes.
      You will be part of every step of the photography process,
```

```
         to ensure these photos feel like your own.</p>
         <p>Our excellent photographers have many years of experience,
         capturing moments from weddings to sporting events of absolute
         quality.</p>
         <p>MyPhoto also provides superb printing options of all shapes
         and sizes, on any canvas, in any form. From large canvas prints
         to personalised photo albums, MyPhoto provides it all.</p>
         <p>MyPhoto provides a full, holistic solution for all your
         photography needs.</p>
       </div>
     </div>
   </div>
 </div>
</div>
```

Take a look at the following screenshot:

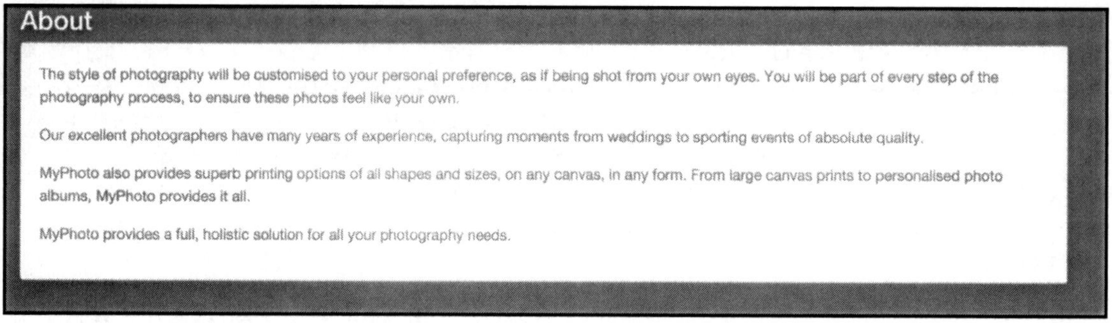

Figure 3.10: Using Bootstrap cards to display About information

There isn't much to say about cards. The `card` class gives an impression of an element being inset, to draw the eye of the user and to provide a visual cue of relatively important content. It achieves this effect by:

- Giving the element a 1 px border, along with a 0.25 rem border radius to which it is applied
- Adjusting the element's bottom margin, forcing some space between the `card` element and any subsequent elements
- Ensuring that the element's position is relative and making the element behave as a block-level element (that is, forcing the element onto a row of its own)

Along with a card, we use `card-block` to provide larger padding around the content area. The card is as effective as it is simple, and complements the content nicely.

Now that our sections have some content, we need to add some navigation and branding. To do this, we are going to leverage Bootstrap's `navbar` component.

Cards in Bootstrap 3

Cards are a new concept, introduced with Bootstrap 4. Prior to Bootstrap 4, cards did not exist. The feature replaced Bootstrap 3's wells, thumbnails, and panels. To achieve a similar effect to the one demonstrated in *Figure 3.10*, we would use the `well` and `well-lg` classes:

```
<div class="container-fluid myphoto-section bg-
myphoto-dark">
  <div class="container">
    <div class="row">
      <h3>About</h3>
      <div class="well well-lg bg-myphoto-light">
        <p>....</p>
        <p>...</p>
      </div>
    </div>
  </div>
</div>
```

Navbar

Bootstrap's navbar is a powerful, responsive component to provide sensible navigation around a website. Before getting into the details, let's add it to our page and see what happens:

```
<nav class="navbar navbar-light">
  <a class="navbar-brand" href="#">MyPhoto</a>
  <ul class="nav navbar-nav">
    <li class="nav-item"><a class="nav-link" href="#welcome">
    Welcome</a></li>
    <li class="nav-item"><a class="nav-link" href="#services">
    Services</a></li>
    <li class="nav-item"><a class="nav-link" href="#gallery">
    Gallery</a></li>
    <li class="nav-item"><a class="nav-link" href="#about">
    About</a></li>
    <li class="nav-item"><a class="nav-link" href="#contact">
    Contact Us</a></li>
  </ul>
```

```
</nav>
```

Take a look at the following screenshot:

Figure 3.11: Using Bootstrap's navbar to provide navigational links to MyPhoto's Welcome, Services, Gallery, About, and Contact Us sections

With that, we have a navigation for our single page site. Let's break it down.

For accessibility and semantic purposes, we use the `nav` tag as the parent element. We could use the `role="navigation"` attribute on a `div` element, but using `nav` is semantically clearer. We apply the `navbar` class, which is where Bootstrap starts its magic. The `navbar` class sets the dimensions and positioning of the navigation bar. The `navbar-light` property applies some styling to keep in line with Bootstrap's default style guide.

The first element in the `nav` family is a `navbar-brand` element. This element is used to apply styling to differentiate the brand of the page, such as a specific logo or font style, to the other elements within the `nav`.

We then have a `ul` element as a sibling to `navbar-brand`. Within this `ul`, we nest a list of list item elements that contain the anchors to various sections on our page. Each list item element has a `nav-item` class applied to it; each anchor has a `nav-link` class. The former adjusts the element's margin and ensures the element's positioning within the container by setting its `float` property. The latter adjusts the anchor element's styling, removing its text decoration and default colors.

If you click on **Services**, nothing happens. This is because we also need to update the sections with the corresponding `id` for each section. Let's do that now. For example, add `id="services"` to the **Welcome** section:

```
<div class="container-fluid myphoto-section bg-myphoto-
welcome" id="services">
```

Now, if we click on **Services** in the `nav`, the browser scrolls us down to the **Services** section.

Navigation in Bootstrap 3

 The entire `navbar` component has been rewritten in Bootstrap 4 in an effort to make the navbar simpler and easier to use. Bootstrap 4 introduced the `nav-item` class for use on the list items, and added the `nav-link` class for use with the anchor element. Neither of these two aforementioned classes exist in Bootstrap 3.

Take a look at the following screenshot:

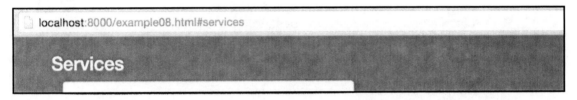

Figure 3.12: Clicking on Services in the nav, the browser scrolls us down to the Services section. Observe how the string "#services" is appended to the URL in the address bar.

In its current state, the navigation list wraps onto a new line, which wraps when the list is too long for the given resolution. Take a look at the following screenshot:

MyPhoto Welcome   Services   Gallery   About

Contact Us

Figure 3.13: The navbar items wrapping onto a new line on smaller resolutions

Not very Bootstrap-like. Of course, Bootstrap provides a straightforward solution for this. Bootstrap's solution is to use the *hamburger* interface at lower resolutions. First, let's add the hamburger. Within the `nav` element, we add the following code:

```
<button class="navbar-toggler hidden-sm-up pull-xs-right"
type="button" data-toggle="collapse" data-target="#navigation">
≡
</button>
```

Take a look at the following screenshot:

Figure 3.14: Adding a hamburger button to our navigation bar

What is a hamburger?

 A hamburger, in web development, refers to a specific style of button or icon, representing a list item. Represented as three horizontal and parallel lines (resembling a hamburger), a hamburger button generally surfaces navigation options when selected. The hamburger has become popular and useful for condensing navigations on small displays.

At lower resolutions, the hamburger now appears on the right-hand side. However, our list of sections still wraps onto a new line and the hamburger button has no effect. In order to hook the hamburger and the links together, first we add an `id` attribute to the parent `div` of the links, and then reference that `id` in a `data-target` attribute in the hamburger `button` element. We also apply the `collapse` and `navbar-collapse` classes to the link's parent element. These classes effectively make the navigation links disappear at smaller resolutions:

```
<div class="collapse navbar-collapse" id="navigation">
  <button type="button" class="navbar-toggle collapsed"
  data-toggle="collapse" data-target="#navigation"
  aria-expanded="false">
```

Take a look at the following screenshot:

Figure 3.15: Making the navigation links disappear on smaller resolutions

When a user clicks on the hamburger, the navigation menu will be surfaced. Take a look at the following screenshot:

Figure 3.16: Making the navigation links visible on smaller resolutions by clicking the hamburger menu

Now, on smaller viewports, the list of links is no longer visible, the hamburger icon appears, and the list of links appears once the button has been activated. This provides a much better experience on smaller resolutions.

Now that we have our sections and navigation working, let's add a drop-down menu to our navigation to provide the user with the secondary features **Profile, Settings**, and **Log Out**.

To do this, we are going to use Bootstrap's `dropdown` class. As a child of the list of section links, create a new list item element with Bootstrap's `nav-item` class. As previously noted, this defines the element as a Bootstrap navigation item and renders it alongside the other items within our navbar. To the same list item, we also apply the `dropdown` class and `pull-xs-right` class (recall that the latter aligns the list item element to the right of the container). Within the list element, we include an anchor tag, responsible for surfacing the drop-down navigation:

```
<li class="nav-item dropdown pull-xs-right">
  <a href="#" class="nav-link dropdown-toggle" data-toggle=
  "dropdown" role="button"
    aria-haspopup="true" aria-expanded="false">
    Profile <span class="caret"></span>
  </a>
  <div class="dropdown-menu dropdown-menu-right">
    <a class="dropdown-item" href="#" data-toggle="modal"
    data-target="#profile-modal">
      Profile
    </a>
  </div>
</li>
```

Take a look at the following screenshot:

Figure 3.17: A drop-down menu item

Great, it looks nice and neat on the right-hand side of our page. Of course, it doesn't do anything yet. We need to create the menu we want it to surface. As a child of the **Profile** anchor tag, add a `div` element, this time with Bootstrap's `dropdown-menu` class, to denote this is the element we want the `dropdown` to surface, with four list elements:

```
<li class="nav-item dropdown pull-xs-right">
  <a href="#" class="nav-link dropdown-toggle" data-toggle=
  "dropdown" role="button
    aria-haspopup="true" aria-expanded="false">
    Profile <span class="caret"></span>
  </a>
  <div class="dropdown-menu dropdown-menu-right">
    <a class="dropdown-item" href="#" data-toggle="modal"
    data-target="#profile-modal">
      Profile
    </a>
    <a class="dropdown-item" href="#" data-toggle="modal" data-target=
    "#settings-modal">
      Settings
    </a>
    <div class="dropdown-divider"></div>
    <a class="dropdown-item" href="#">
      Logout
    </a>
  </div>
</li>
```

Take a look at the following screenshot:

Figure 3.18: The expanded drop-down menu item, listing three sub-items

We also add a `dropdown-menu-right` class to align the drop-down menu to the right. Now, we have a list of links in a drop-down menu, and as you can see, we've leveraged Bootstrap's `dropdown-divider` class to provide a visual cue to the separation between **Profile** functionality, and logging out of the site.

The `dropdown` class itself simply sets the CSS position property to `relative`. There are several other classes specifying how the drop-down menu, and other items within the drop-down, such as the divider, look and behave. All these style definitions can be found in `bootstrap/scss/_dropdown.scss`. The interactions and behaviors of the `dropdown` component are actually handled and triggered by an out-of-the-box Bootstrap library, `dropdown.js`. The `dropdown.js` uses CSS selectors to hook into dropdown-specific elements, and toggles CSS classes to execute certain behaviors. You can find the `dropdown` library at `bower_components/bootstrap/js/dist/dropdown.js`.

Drop-down menus in Bootstrap 3

Notice the difference in how drop-down menus are created in Bootstrap 4. To implement the same drop-down menu functionality using Bootstrap 3, we would need another unordered-list element as a child of the **Profile** anchor tag. We would then only apply the `dropdown-menu` class. The individual menu items would be represented as list items. Furthermore, Bootstrap 4 introduced the `dropdown-divider` class, replacing the Bootstrap 3 `divider` class. The appearance of the two is the same, however, and both serve as a visual cue to the separation between **Profile** functionality, and logging out of the site.

As nice as the dropdown is, it doesn't actually do anything. Rather than have the user leave the page to use secondary functionality, let's render the functionality in modal windows instead.

What is a modal window?

A modal window in web development is an element that is layered on top of the main webpage content to give the impression of a separate window, which requires user interaction and prevents the user from using the main content.

Bootstrap makes surfacing modal windows extraordinarily simple. It is simply a case of creating the modal markup, using Bootstrap's modal classes, and using HTML attributes, `data-toggle`, `data-target`, and `data-dismiss` to surface and remove the modal.

First, let's update the `Profile` and `Settings` element with the `data-toggle` and `data-target` attributes:

```
<a class="dropdown-item" href="#" data-toggle="modal" data-target=
"#profile-modal">
  Profile
</a>
<a class="dropdown-item" href="#" data-toggle="modal" data-target=
"#settings-modal">
  Settings
</a>
```

We set `data-toggle="modal"` to tell Bootstrap we want to open a `modal`, and `data-target` is a reference to the `id` of the `modal` we want to surface. Let's go ahead and create these modals.

As a sibling to the `nav` element, we add the following `modal` markup:

```
<div class="modal" id="profile-modal" role="dialog">
  <div class="modal-dialog" role="document">
    <div class="modal-content">
      <div class="modal-header">
        <button type="button" class="close" data-dismiss="modal"
        aria-label="Close"><span aria-hidden="true">&times;</span>
        </button>
        <h4 class="modal-title" id="profile-modal-label">Profile</h4>
      </div>
      <div class="modal-body">
        Profile
      </div>
    </div>
  </div>
</div>
<div class="modal" id="settings-modal" role="dialog">
  <div class="modal-dialog" role="document">
    <div class="modal-content">
      <div class="modal-header">
        <button type="button" class="close" data-dismiss="modal"
        aria-label="Close"><span aria-hidden="true">&times;</span>
        </button>
        <h4 class="modal-title" id="settings-modal-label">Settings</h4>
      </div>
      <div class="modal-body">
        Settings
      </div>
    </div>
  </div>
```

```
</div>
```

Let's explain what is happening in this piece of code. We apply the `modal` class to the parent element. The `id` of the element corresponds to the value of the `data-target` attribute of the element we want to use to surface the modal. Within that `div`, we use Bootstrap's modal classes to define nested elements to represent the modal itself (`modal-dialog`), the content of the modal (`modal-content`), the header of the modal (`modal-header`) and the body of the modal (`modal-body`). We also define the title of the modal using `modal-title`, and a **Close** button. The **Close** button includes a `data-dismiss="modal"` attribute, which allows the user to close the modal just by clicking anywhere off the modal. Let's take a look at how the `Profile` modal renders. Take a look at the following screenshot:

Figure 3.19: Using Bootstrap's modal to display an empty dialog

Pretty nice, considering it required very little markup.

We have a pretty nice navigation in place now. Well, a functional navigation. It does not really fit in well with the rest of our site, though. Let's create our own custom navigation style for `MyPhoto`.

Styling

Bootstrap's navbar comes with two built-in styles: `navbar-light`, which we currently use, and `navbar-dark`. To add a new style, we could add a new class to `_navbar.scss`, add new color variables to `_variables.scss`, recompile Bootstrap, and then apply the class to our `navbar` element. However, applying changes directly to Bootstrap source files is bad practice. For instance, we use Bower to add Bootstrap, along with other third-party components, to our project. If we were to add new styles to Bootstrap source files, we would need to add Bootstrap to our repository and use that version, instead of Bower, or else other developers on your team would not get the changes. Also, if we wanted to use a new version of Bootstrap, even a minor or patch release, it would force us to reapply all our custom changes to that new version of Bootstrap.

Instead, we are going to apply the changes to the `MyPhoto` stylesheet. Add the following rules to `myphoto.css`:

```css
.navbar-myphoto {
  background-color: #2A2A2C;
  border-color: black;
  border-radius: 0;
  margin-bottom: 0px;
}
.navbar-myphoto.navbar-brand {
  color: white;
  font-weight: bold;
}
.navbar-myphoto.navbar-nav > li > a {
  color: white;
}
.navbar-myphoto.navbar-nav > li > a:hover {
  background-color: #2A2A2C;
  color: gray;
}
.navbar-myphoto.navbar-nav > li > a:focus {
  background-color: #504747;
  color: gray;
}
.navbar-myphoto.navbar-nav > li.active > a {
  background-color: #504747;
  color: gray;
}
.navbar-myphoto.dropdown-menu {
  background-color: #504747;
  border-color: black;
}
.navbar-myphoto.dropdown-menu > a {
  color: white;
  background-color: #504747;
}
.navbar-myphoto.dropdown-menu > a:hover {
  color: gray;
  background-color: #504747;
}
.navbar-myphoto.dropdown-menu > a:focus {
  color: gray;
  background-color: #504747;
}
.navbar-myphoto.dropdown-menu > .active > a:focus {
  color: gray;
  background-color: #504747;
}
```

```
.navbar-myphoto > .navbar-toggler {
  color: white;
}
.nav-pills > .active > a, .nav-pills > .active > a:hover {
  background-color: grey;
}
.nav-pills.nav-link.active, .nav-pills.nav-link.active:focus,
.nav-pills.nav-link.active:hover,
.nav-pills.nav-item.open.nav-link,
.nav-pills.nav-item.open.nav-link:focus,
.nav-pills.nav-item.open.nav-link:hover {
  background-color: grey;
}
```

We have added a new class, `navbar-myphoto`. The `navbar-myphoto` uses the same dark background as `bg-myphoto-dark` and removes the `margin-bottom` navbar applied by default. We then have to apply rules for the classes that are usually nested within a `navbar` element. We apply font and background rules across these classes, in their various states, to keep inline with the general style of `MyPhoto`. These rules could be made more succinct using a preprocessor, but we are not going to add that complexity to this project.

In the markup, replace `navbar-light` with `navbar-myphoto`. Take a look at the following screenshot:

Figure 3.20: The custom-styled navigation bar with drop-down

With these new styles, we now have a style-appropriate `navbar` for `MyPhoto`. Pretty neat.

Last but not least, let's try and improve the overall look and feel of our website by adding some nice fonts. We will use two freely available Google Fonts. Specifically, we will use **Poiret One** (`https://www.google.com/fonts/specimen/Poiret+One`) for our navbar and headers, and **Lato** (`https://www.google.com/fonts/specimen/Lato`) for everything else. To be able to use these fonts, we must first include them. Insert the following two lines into the head of our `index.html`:

```
<link href="https://fonts.googleapis.com/css?family=Poiret+One"
rel="stylesheet" type="text/css">
<link href="http://fonts.googleapis.com/css?family=Lato&
subset=latin,latin-ext" rel="stylesheet" type="text/css">
```

Then, insert the following lines of code into `myphoto.css`:

```
h1, h2, h3, h4, h5, h6, .nav, .navbar {
  font-family: 'Poiret One', cursive;
}
body {
  font-family: 'Lato', cursive;
}
```

Take a look at the following screenshot:

Figure 3.21: MyPhoto styled using Google Fonts: Poiret One and Lato

Summary

In this chapter, we defined the skeleton of our MyPhoto webpage using the knowledge of Bootstrap's grid system we gained from Chapter 2, *Making a Style Statement*, while also integrating some of Bootstrap's core components. We lightly customized those components with our own bespoke CSS to fit in with the design of the page, while also exploring how to link the functionality of these components together. With a functioning MyPhoto page, we can now move on to Chapter 4, *On Navigation, Footers, Alerts, and Content*, and learn how to customize these components even further.

4
On Navigation, Footers, Alerts, and Content

In the previous chapter, we built our website's basic skeleton. Using Bootstrap's grid system, we structured our website into five distinct sections. We then styled these sections and learned how to use Bootstrap's navbar and tab system to make these sections navigable. In this chapter, we will continue adding to the knowledge obtained in `Chapter 3`, *Building the Layout* by leveraging even more Bootstrap components, adding more content and streamlining our website's design. We will begin by improving our navbar. We will first learn how to fix our navbar's position. We will then use a Bootstrap plugin (Scrollspy) to automatically update the navbar tab item appearance based on the user's navigation. Next, we will customize the website's scrolling behavior, making the transition between sections smoother.

Once we have improved our website's navigation, we will focus on improving and customizing our website's overall look and feel. That is, we will learn how to apply and customize alerts, and how to use buttons and brand images. We will also discover how to style different text elements, use media objects, and apply citations and figures.

As we progress through this chapter, we will be examining each of the aforementioned components individually. This way, we will have the chance to see how they are actually composed under the hood.

To summarize, in this chapter we shall do the following:

- Learn how to fixate our navbar
- Use the Bootstrap plugin Scrollspy to improve our website's navigation
- Use icons to customize and improve the overall design of our website
- Introduce Bootstrap alerts and customize them

- Style our website's footer
- Apply buttons to improve our website's overall usability

Fixating the navbar

Our website already looks pretty decent. We have a navigation bar in place, a footer placeholder, and various sections populated with some sample content. But we are not quite there yet. The website's overall user experience is still a bit edgy, and does not yet feel very refined. Take user navigation, for instance. While clicking on a navbar link, indeed does take the user to the correct section, the navbar disappears once we navigate across the sections. This means that the navbar loses its purpose. It no longer facilitates easy navigation across the different sections of our website. Instead, the user will need to scroll to the top of the page every time they wish to use the navbar. To make the navbar persistent, append `navbar-fixed-top` to the `class` attribute of our `nav` element:

```
<nav class="navbar navbar-myphoto navbar-fixed-top">
...
</nav>
```

Save, refresh, and scroll. Voila! Our navbar now remains fixed at the top of our page. The `navbar-fixed-top` works as follows:

- The element's position is set to `fixed`. This positions the element relative to the browser window (*not* relative to other elements), meaning that the element will remain in the same place, regardless of the positioning of other elements on the page.
- The element's `top` is set to 0. This means that the distance between the navbar and the top of the browser window is 0.

In addition to some minor margin and padding changes, `navbar-fixed-top` also changes the element's `z-index` to 1,030, therefore ensuring that the element will appear above all other elements on the page (that is, all elements that have a `z-index` of less than 1,030).

Did you know?

Did you know that, within web development, another term for persistency is *sticky*? For example, instead of asking "How can I make my navbar persistent?", you often hear people asking "How do I make my navbar *sticky*?".

Should you desire to fixate the navbar at the bottom of the page, you can use the `navbar-fixed-bottom` class. This class behaves in exactly the same way as the `navbar-fixed-top` class, except that, instead of setting the element's top to 0, it sets the `bottom` property to 0, thereby ensuring that the element resides at the bottom of the page.

If we wanted to quickly change the color of the navbar without wanting to write a whole bunch of custom rules, then we could apply the `navbar-*` and `bg-*` classes:

- `navbar-dark`: This is used to indicate that the navbar's foreground color should be adjusted to match a dark background. As such, the rule will apply a white foreground color to all navbar items.
- `navbar-light`: This is the opposite of the aforementioned `navbar-dark`, and applies a dark foreground color in order to support a light background.
- `bg-*`: This will set the background color to that of the desired context class (we will cover the various context classes later on in this chapter). For example, `bg-primary`, `bg-success`, and `bg-info`. `bg-inverse` mimics an inverted background, setting the background color to `#373a3c`.

Take a look at the following screenshot:

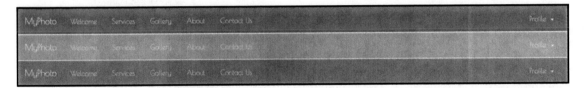

Figure 4.1: The MyPhoto navbar with three different context styles: pg-primary, bg-warning, and bg-danger.

Improving navigation using Scrollspy

Now that we have fixated the navbar at the top of the page, it will no longer disappear as the user scrolls down the page. But now we are faced with a new problem. As the user clicks on a navbar item, they have no way of telling which section of the site they are visiting, or whether the section has loaded successfully without actually examining the section's content. Wouldn't it be nice if the user could tell which section they are currently visiting by looking at the navbar? To this end, we would need to find a way of highlighting the navbar items based on the user's navigation. For example, if the user is browsing the **Services** section, then we would need to update the color of the **Services** navbar item.

Luckily, Bootstrap comes equipped with a plugin that allows us to automatically update the navbar items based on the user's navigation. Take a look at the following screenshot:

Figure 4.2: Currently, all navbar items are the same color – there is no way for the user to tell where on the page they are currently just by looking at the navbar itself.

Meet Scrollspy. Scrollspy allows us to automatically update navigation targets based on the user's current position within the page. In other words, Scrollspy allows us to denote scrollable areas within our page and update elements to denote when the user enters a specific scrollable area. It also allows us to add scroll animations to our page. We'll see more about this later.

Scrollspy is already included in our installed Bootstrap build, so there is no need for any additional downloads. The first thing that we must do is denote our scrollable area.

By adding `data-spy="scroll"` to the element that contains our contents, we are, in essence, telling Bootstrap to use anything contained within the given element as our scrollable area. Typically, `data-spy="scroll"` is added to the body element of our page:

```
<body data-spy="scroll">
...
</body>
```

The `data-spy` attribute is by far the most important attribute when using Scrollspy, as without it, Bootstrap wouldn't know what to do with the remainder of the Scrollspy instructions. It is also important to note that Scrollspy will only work with `container` elements whose position is relative.

Next, we must tell Scrollspy how to identify our `navbar` element. After all, how else will the plugin know where the navbar items that it has to update are located? It is important that you point to the parent element that contains the list of navbar items. If you point to any other element, the feature will not work. Before we can tell Scrollspy about our list of nav items, we must first be able to uniquely identify them. To do so, we will use our navbar's class name, `navbar`. Alternatively, we could assign our navbar an `id` by adding `id="navbar"` to our `navbar` element. We will then make Scrollspy aware of the navbar by using the `data-target` attribute:

```
<body data-spy="scroll" data-target=".navbar">
    <nav class="navbar navbar-fixed-top navbar-myphoto">
        <div class="collapse navbar-toggleable-xs" id="navigation">
            <ul class="nav nav-pills">
                ...
            <ul/>
```

```
        </div>
      </nav>
      ...
    </body>
```

Note that, when using the `data-target` attribute, class names must be preceded by a . (period), while each `id` must be preceded by # (hash).

Save and refresh. Now try to navigate between sections and observe the navbar's behavior. Items are automatically highlighted (see *Figure 4.3*) as you change position. Take a look at the following screenshot:

Figure 4.3: Navbar items are highlighted, depending on the user's current position within the page.

Customizing scroll speed

Great! Our navbar items are now automatically updated based on the user's scroll position. Easy, huh? But we're not quite done yet. The transition between sections actually feels quite rough. The page literally jumps from one section to another. Such a jerky movement is not very pleasing. Instead, we should improve the user experience of our website by making this transition between sections smoother. We can quite easily accomplish this by customizing the scroll speed of our page by using jQuery. The first step in this task involves automating the scroll, that is, forcing a scroll event to a target on the page using jQuery, without the user needing to actually perform a scroll operation. The second step involves defining the speed of such a scroll operation.

As it turns out, the developers behind jQuery already thought about both of these steps by providing us with the `animate` method. As its name implies, this method allows us to apply an animation to a given set of HTML elements. Furthermore, we can specify the duration of this animation (or use jQuery's default value). If you take a look at the jQuery documentation for animate (`http://api.jquery.com/animate/`), you will see that one of the possible parameters is `scrollTop`. Therefore, by writing `{scrollTop: target}` we can automatically scroll to `target` (`target` being the *target* location of the scroll).

Now, before we can apply our animation, we must ask ourselves on which element the animation should take effect. Well, the nesting of our HTML document takes the form of the following elements:

```
body
|__#welcome
|__#services
|__#gallery
|__#about
|__#contact
```

Furthermore, the scroll serves to navigate between elements. Therefore, it makes sense to apply the animation to the parent element of our HTML document:

```
$('body').animate({
    scrollTop: target
});
```

Great! So, we have told our browser to apply a scroll animation to the given target. But what exactly is the target? How do we define it? Well, our navbar items are anchor tags, and the anchor's href denotes the section to which an internal scroll should apply. Therefore, we would need to access the individual navbar's href target and then use this as the target for our scroll animation. Luckily, this too is easy to do using jQuery. We first need to add an event listener to each navbar item. Then, for each clicked anchor, we extract the element to which its href attribute refers. We then determine this element's offset and pass this offset to our scroll animation.

To add an event listener to an element, we use jQuery's on method and pass click as a parameter to denote that we want to capture an on-click event:

```
$("nav div ul li a").on('click', function(evt) {
});
```

Note how our selector only identifies anchor tags that are located within an unordered list inside a div. This ensures that only navigation menu items are being matched, as our markup should not contain any other anchor tags that are located inside list items belonging to a navigation element.

From within our event listener, we can access the object on which the click was performed using the `this` keyword. Thus, our clicked object will always be an anchor instance, and we can access the contents of its `href`. Specifically, we can access the string that follows the hash symbol within the `href`. To do this, all we have to write is `$(this).prop(hash)` or (better and more concise) `this.hash`

Remember that the string following the hash within a `href` identifies an internal element within the HTML document. We can therefore use the extracted string as a jQuery selector to get jQuery to retrieve the desired instance of the HTML element. All that we need to do then is use jQuery's `offset()` method to calculate our element's coordinates for us:

```
$("nav ul li a").on('click', function(evt) {
  var offset = $(this.hash).offset();
});
```

Voila! We are almost done! Let's piece it all together, wrap the code into a `script` tag, and place it into the `head` of our HTML document:

```
<script type="text/javascript">
    $(document).ready(function() {
        $("nav div ul li a").on('click', function(evt) {
            var offset = $(this.hash).offset();
            $('body').animate({
                scrollTop: offset.top
            });
        });
    });
</script>
```

Save the document and try it out in your browser. Our code executes correctly. But something still isn't quite right. Did you notice the odd flicker as you clicked on the navbar items? This is because the anchor tag on which we are clicking still tells the browser to jump to the specified internal element. At the same time, we also instruct our browser to animate a scroll to the element. To resolve this duplication, we have to prevent the on-click event from trickling down to the anchor tag once it reaches our event listener. To do this, we call `preventDefault` on the event:

```
$("nav div ul li a").on('click', function(evt) {
    evt.preventDefault();
    //...
});
```

Apply the changes, save, refresh, and try again. Great! Our custom scroll works! But there is one last annoyance. Clicking on the drop-down menu that launches our **Profile** and **Settings** modal dialogs. Did you notice how their anchor tags link to a plain hash symbol?

Let's deal with this corner case by checking whether jQuery's `offset()` method can successfully execute an offset. To do this, we must wrap our call to animate within an `if` statement, so that our final block of code is as follows:

```
<script type="text/javascript" >
    $(document).ready(function() {
        $("nav div ul li a").on('click', function(evt) {
            evt.preventDefault();
            var offset = $(this.hash).offset();
            if (offset) {
                $('body').animate({
                    scrollTop: offset.top
                })
            }
        });
    });
</script>
```

Icons

The customization of our `MyPhoto` navbar is coming along nicely. We now have a nice scroll animation in place as well as a set of navbar items that update themselves based on the user's scroll position. However, we are not quite there yet. The items in our **Profile** drop-down menu still looks quite plain. Wouldn't it be nice if we could use icons to increase each drop-down menu item's readability? Adding icons to controls and menus helps draw attention to important functionality while clearly outlining a control's intended purpose.

When it comes to icons, a popular choice among web developers is the Font Awesome icon library (`https://fortawesome.github.io/Font-Awesome/`) which is a free collection of over 500 icons that were made to be used with Bootstrap websites. Take a look at the following screenshot:

Figure 4.4: Examples of various Font Awesome icons.

To download the icon library, run a bower install as follows:

```
bower install components-font-awesome
```

Once the download completes, you will see that a new sub directory named `components-font-awesome` has been created inside your `bower_components` directory:

```
bower_components/
bootstrap/
components-font-awesome/
|___css/
|___fonts/
|___less/
|___scss/
```

Font Awesome icons ship as fonts. In order to be able to use the downloaded icons, all that you will need to do is include the Font Awesome style sheet that is located inside your `bower_components/components-font-awesome/css` directory. Insert the following link into the `head` of our HTML document:

```
<link rel="stylesheet" href="bower_components/components-font-awesome
/css/font-awesome.min.css" />
```

The complete `head` of our HTML document should now look as follows:

```
<head>
    <metacharset="UTF-8">
    <title>ch04</title>
    <link rel="stylesheet" href="bower_components/bootstrap/dist/css
    /bootstrap.min.css" />
    <link rel="stylesheet" href="styles/myphoto.css" />
    <link rel="stylesheet" href="bower_components/components-font-
    awesome/css/font-awesome.min.css" />
    <script src="bower_components/jquery/dist/jquery.min.js"></script>
    <script src="bower_components/bootstrap/dist/js/bootstrap.min.js">
        </script>
    <script type="text/javascript">
        // Smooth scroll JavaScript code here
    </script>
</head>
```

To use an icon, just apply the icon's class name to an HTML element. The class names for individual icons can be determined by looking at either the Font Awesome documentation, or by using GlyphSearch (`http://glyphsearch.com/`), a handy little search engine that lets you search for icons, preview them, and then copy their class name to use within your HTML document. It is important to note that each (Font Awesome) icon must be a child of a special class, The `fa` class. That is, to use an icon, you must first apply the `fa` class to the selected element, followed by the icon's name. For example, if your icon's class name is `fa-user`, then you would set your element's class attribute to `class="fa fa-user"`:

```
<span class="fa fa-user"></span>
```

Note that, while it is perfectly acceptable to apply a `fa` class to any HTML element, the convention for icons is to use the `<i>` element. That is:

```
<i class="fa fa-user"></i>
```

Having applied a `fa` class to our desired element, we can now style it just as we would any other element. For example, to change its color:

```
<i class="fa fa-user" style="color: red;"></i>
```

Take a look at the following screenshot:

Figure 4.5: Changing the color of a Font Awesome icon.

Now that we know how to include icons in our page, let's go ahead and customize our **Profile** drop-down menu so that the individual drop-down menu items contain both text and a descriptive icon. Feel free to select your own icons, however, appropriate choices for each item would be:

- `fa-user`: This is for **Profile**
- `fa-cog`: This is for **Settings**
- `fa-sign-out`: This is for **Logout**

To add the individual icons to our drop-down menu, simply create a new `<i>` in front of the menu item's text and apply the appropriate class:

```
<ul class="nav navbar-nav navbar-right">
    <li class="dropdown">
        <a href="#" class="dropdown-toggle" data-toggle="dropdown"
        role="button"
            aria-haspopup="true" aria-expanded="false">Profile <span
                class="caret"></span></a>
        <ul class="dropdown-menu">
            <li>
                <a href="#" data-toggle="modal" data-target="
                #profile-modal">
                    <i class="fa fa-user"></i> Profile
                </a>
            </li>
            <li>
                <a href="#" data-toggle="modal" data-target="
                #settings-modal">
                    <i class="fa fa-cogs"></i> Settings
                </a>
            </li>
            <li role="separator" class="divider"></li>
            <li>
                <a href="#">
                    <i class="fa fa-sign-out"></i> Logout
                </a>
            </li>
        </ul>
    </li>
</ul>
```

Take a look at the following screenshot:

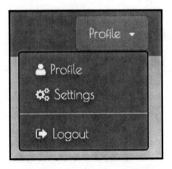

Figure 4.6: Our navbar's new drop-down menu sporting Font Awesome icons.

A note on icons in Bootstrap 3

Bootstrap 3 came with a large library of icons that range from symbols and objects to products. While the icons were provided by a third party (GLYPHICONS), they were free to use (for non-commercial purposes) and fully customizable. In this sense, the term customizable referred to the fact that they came embedded as fonts. This means that you could style them, just as you would with any other text. For example, you can change their color or size by applying CSS in the same way as you would to any other HTML element. Unfortunately, Bootstrap 4 no longer ships with icons.

Using and customizing alerts

Now that we know how to use icons, let's turn to a different topic, namely, alert boxes. Alert boxes are typically used to highlight an important event, or to emphasize an important message. As such, the purpose behind alerts is to provide a content area that immediately stands out, and therefore cannot be easily overseen by the user. For example, imagine that MyPhoto only supports browsers above certain versions. In such a case, a user who visits the site with an unsupported browser version should be notified that their browser is not supported. After all, the website may not function or display correctly when viewed with unsupported software. Bootstrap provides us with the alert class, which makes it very easy for us to implement this hypothetical scenario (the JavaScript for browser detection will be presented in Chapter 5, *Speeding Up Development Using jQuery Plugins*).

Bootstrap's alert comes with four contexts: **Success, Warning, Info,** and **Danger.** Each context class styles the element to which it is applied differently, depending on the intended message. See *Figure 4.7*, which lists the four default alert styles that come with Bootstrap:

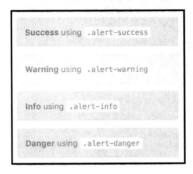

Figure 4.7: Bootstrap's four contextual alert classes: .alert-success, .alert-warning, .alert-info, and .alert-danger.

Let's go ahead and apply one of these styles to our new unsupported browser alert box. Go ahead and create a new div and set its class attribute to alert alert-danger:

```
<div class="alert alert-danger">
    <strong>Unsupported browser</strong> Internet Explorer 8 and
    lower are not supported by this website.
</div>
```

Now insert this alert div inside our **Welcome** section, below the jumbotron:

```
<div class="container-fluid myphoto-section bg-myphoto-welcome"
id="welcome">
    <div class="container">
        <div class="jumbotron">
            <h1>Welcome to MyPhoto</h1>
            <p>Photographs you can cherish!</p>
        </div>
        <div class="alert alert-danger">
            <strong class="alert-heading">Unsupported browser</strong>
            Internet Explorer 8 and lower are not supported by this
            website.
        </div>
    </div>
</div>
```

Save and refresh. Voila! We have just created our very first Bootstrap alert (see *Figure 4.8*). Take a look at the following screenshot:

Figure 4.8: Our first dangerous alert dialog.

But something isn't quite right. What if the user knows that their browser is outdated, but still wishes to continue viewing the contents of our **Welcome** section without the invasive alert? Could we provide a way for the user to acknowledge the message and then allow them to continue browsing without its invasive presence? The answer is yes. Bootstrap provides us with a very easy way to make alerts dismissible using the `data-dismiss` attribute:

```
<div class="alert alert-danger alert-dismissible">
    <a href="#" class="close" data-dismiss="alert" aria-label="close">
    &times;</a>
    <strong>Unsupported browser</strong> Internet Explorer 8
    and lower are not supported by this website.
</div>
```

This will add an **X** to the right side of our alert dialog. Adding the `alert-dismissible` class will align the **X** and have it inherit its color. Click this **X**, and see the alert disappear.

This is great. Users can now dismiss our alert. However, what happens when the user jumps straight into a different section of `MyPhoto`? Currently, the alert is placed inside our **Welcome** section. As such, users viewing other sections of our website will not necessarily be able to see the alert dialog. The solution is to adjust the position of our alert dialog so that it appears stuck to our page, regardless of the section that the user is currently in. How do we do this? First, we will need to take the alert outside of our **Welcome** section, and move it just below our navbar. This will make the alert hidden behind our fixed navbar. To make the alert visible below our navbar, we can simply offset the position of the alert from the top of the page using the CSS `margin-top` property. To then make the alert sticky, that is, fixed below the navbar regardless of which section the user is currently in, we use the CSS `position` property and set it to fixed. Lastly, we can adjust the left offset and width of our alert so that it is nicely indented from the left hand side of our page, and stretches horizontally across the page (note that, for the sake of keeping the sample code short and concise, we are applying inline styles to achieve this. However, as we will discover in Chapter 8, *Optimizing Your Website* we should normally avoid using inline styles whenever we can). Observe the following code:

```
<nav class="navbar navbar-myphoto navbar-fixed-top" role="navigation">
    <!-- Navbar markup -->
</nav>
    <div class="alert alert-danger alert-dismissible" style="position:
    fixed; margin-top: 4em; width: 90%;margin-left: 4em;">
    <a href="#" class="close" data-dismiss="alert" aria-label="close">
    &times;</a>
    <strong class="alert-heading">Unsupported browser</strong>
    Internet Explorer 8 and lower are not supported by this website.
</div>
```

Take a look at the following screenshot:

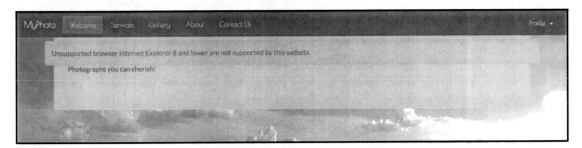

Figure 4.9: Our sticky alert dialog now stretches across the entire page and remains visible across the sections.

Great! Try scrolling down the page and observe how our alert remains fixed below the navbar. Let's add an icon:

```
<div class="alert alert-danger alert-dismissible" style="position:
fixed; margin-top: 4em; width: 90%;margin-left: 4em;">
    <a href="#" class="close" data-dismiss="alert" aria-label="close">&
    times;</a>
    <strong class="alert-heading"><i class="fa fa-exclamation"></i>
    Unsupported browser</strong>Internet Explorer 8 and lower are not
    supported by this website.
</div>
```

Our alert is already looking pretty decent. It is positioned nicely below our navbar, is dismissible, and sports a nice little icon. But it somehow doesn't look very dangerous, does it? How about we customize its colors a bit? For example, we could darken the background color slightly, and lighten the foreground color. But how would we go about doing this without modifying the Bootstrap source? Easy! Just apply the desired CSS properties using either an inline style, or, even better, apply it globally throughout our style sheet. Go ahead and open `styles/myphoto.css`. Insert the following CSS snippet, save, and then refresh the `MyPhoto` page:

```css
.alert-danger {
    background-color: #a94342;
    color: white;
}
```

The snippet that you just added to your myphoto.css file should be pretty self-explanatory: It applies a white foreground and a dark red background (*Figure 4.10*) to any element that has the class `alert-danger`. Consequently, this foreground and background color will apply to any alert dialog that uses the `alert-danger` context class. Congratulations! You just learned how to customize your first Bootstrap component!

Let's finish by tidying any inline styles that we created (we will talk more about inline styles in `Chapter 8`, *Optimizing Your Website*; for now just accept that you should avoid using inline styles whenever possible). Create a custom class, `alert-myphoto`, extract the inline styles into it, and add a `z-index` rule to ensure that our warning will appear above all other elements on the page:

```css
.alert-myphoto {
    background-color: #a94342;
    color: white;
    position: fixed;
    margin-top: 4em;
    width: 90%;
    margin-left: 4em;
    z-index: 3000;
}
```

Take a look at the following screenshot:

Figure 4.10: Our alert now with a white foreground and a darker background.

Under the hood

Bootstrap defines the background color for the individual context classes using the `$state-<context>-bg` variable, where context refers to one of the four Bootstrap contexts: **Success, Danger, Info**, or **Warning**. As such, you can globally override the default background color for a given alert by changing the value of `$state-<context>-bg` to your desired background color. For example, to make the background of the danger alert blue, you could write the following:

```
$state-danger-bg: blue
```

However, this is generally not recommended as it will change the background color for all danger alerts across your entire website.

Note that, when adding links to alerts, that you should apply the `alert-link` class to the link element. This will style the element to match the alert's context.

Creating a footer

At the moment, `MyPhoto` only contains a placeholder in place of a useful footer. Before `MyPhoto` goes live, it will desperately need a footer that should contain at least three pieces of information:

- A copyright notice
- A link to your website's terms and conditions
- A link to your website's **About** section

Let's go ahead and modify our footer to include these three pieces of information:

```
<footer class="footer">
    <p class="text-muted">&copy; MyPhoto Inc.</p>
    <p class="text-muted">Terms &amp;Conditions</p>
    <p class="text-muted">About Us</p>
</footer>
```

Now open `styles/myphoto.css` and insert the following CSS:

```
footer p {
    display: inline;
}
```

So, what exactly did we just do? We inserted our copyright notice, and some placeholder text for our **Terms and Conditions** and **About Us** link. We embedded each of these three texts inside a paragraph element and applied Bootstrap's `text-muted` context class. The `text-muted` class does precisely what its name implies. It attempts to mute anything containing text by setting the foreground color to `#777` (a very soft, light grey). Take a look at the following screenshot:

© MyPhoto Inc.   Terms & Conditions   About Us

Figure 4.11: Our footer text: Copyright notice, Terms & Conditions, and About Us

Save and refresh (see *Figure 4.11*). Our footer is already looking better, however, unfortunately the text is somewhat obtrusive. Go ahead and make it smaller:

```
<footer class="footer">
    <p class="text-muted"><small>&copy; MyPhoto Inc.</small></p>
    <p class="text-muted"><small>Terms &amp; Conditions</small></p>
    <p class="text-muted"><small>About Us</small></p>
</footer>
```

Now center the text by applying Bootstrap's `text-xs-center` context class (recall from Chapter 3, *Building the Layout* that the `text-xs-center` will center align text on viewports of size `xs` or wider):

```
<footer class="footer text-xs-center">
    <p class="text-muted"><small>&copy; MyPhoto Inc.</small></p>
    <p class="text-muted"><a href="#"><small>Terms &amp;
    Conditions</small>
    </a></p>
    <p class="text-muted"><a href="#"><small>About Us</small></a></p>
</footer>
```

Last but not least, we first space the individual paragraphs out by adding a left margin of 10 pixels to each paragraph, and then adjust the foreground color of our footer's links:

```
footer p {
    display: inline;
    margin-left: 10px;
}
footer a {
    color: inherit ;
}
```

© MyPhoto Inc.   Terms & Conditions   About Us

Figure 4.12: Our completed footer

Under the hood

Bootstrap's text alignment classes are just wrappers for the CSS text-align property. That is, the text-xs-center class is defined by one line only: text-align: center !important;. Likewise, text-xs-right and text-xs-left are represented by text-align: right !important and text-align: left !important. Other sizes are defined through CSS media queries. For example, the bootstrap.css file defines the text alignment classes for small viewports so that they only apply to viewports that are at least 544 pixels wide:

```
@media (min-width: 544px) {
    text-sm-left {
        text-align: left !important;
    }
    .text-sm-right {
        text-align: right !important;
    }
    .text-sm-center {
        text-align: center !important;
    }
}
```

Creating and customizing forms

At long last we are ready to move on to the final part of our landing page, the **Contact Us** form. Note that we will not be writing any of the actual JavaScript that transfers the contents of the **Contact Us** form to the server. Instead, we will learn how to use Bootstrap to lay out our form elements in an elegant and responsive manner.

Typically, **Contact Us** forms require at least three pieces of information from the user—the user's name (so that the recipient of the form data will know *who* they are talking to), the user's e-mail address (so that the recipient of the form data can *reply* to the user), and the actual message (what the user wants to send to the recipient). As such, we will be creating a form that will consist of three inputs—a name field, an e-mail address field, and a text area for the user to write their message.

Let's dig right into it. Start by creating an empty form below the **Contact Us** header:

```
<div class="container-fluid myphoto-section bg-myphoto-light"
id="contact">
    <div class="container">
        <div class="row">
            <h3>Contact Us</h3>
                <form>
                    <!--Our form will go here-->
                </form>
        </div>
    </div>
</div>
```

At the heart of Bootstrap's form layout is the `form-group` class. On its own, all this class does is set a 15 px margin. However, as we will see, combining the form group with form controls gives us a powerful way of controlling our form's appearance.

By default, Bootstrap lays out its form elements vertically. That is, each element is stacked above the other. Let's go ahead and add a `name` field to our form. Insert the following snippet in between our previously created form tags:

```
<div class="form-group">
    <label for="name">First and Lastname</label>
    <input type="name" class="form-control" id="name"
    placeholder="Name">
</div>
```

Save and hit refresh. As you can see, the label takes over the entire first row, with the `name` input field appearing on the second row (*Figure 4.13*). Note how we applied the `form-control` class to our `name` input field. This class is what styles our actual input element.

Among other things, Bootstrap sets its height (to exactly 34 px), pads it, sets the input's font size (to 14 px), and gives the element a nice inset effect by adjusting the border style, border color, and border radius. Removing this class from our input will result in just a simple, plain input box being displayed.

Now, what if we wanted slightly smaller form elements? Well, we could apply our own styles, for example, we could change the font size or height of our input element. However, Bootstrap provides us with `form-group-sm` and `form-group-lg`. The former reduces the height of nested form controls to 30 px, the font size to 12 px, and the line height to 1.5 mm. The `form-group-lg`, on the other hand, makes its containing form controls larger by increasing their font size to 18 px and their height to 46 px. Go ahead and apply either one to our form group. For example:

```
<div class="form-group-sm">
    <label for="name">Name</label>
    <input type="name" class="form-control" id="name"
    placeholder="Name">
</div>
```

Take a look at the following screenshot:

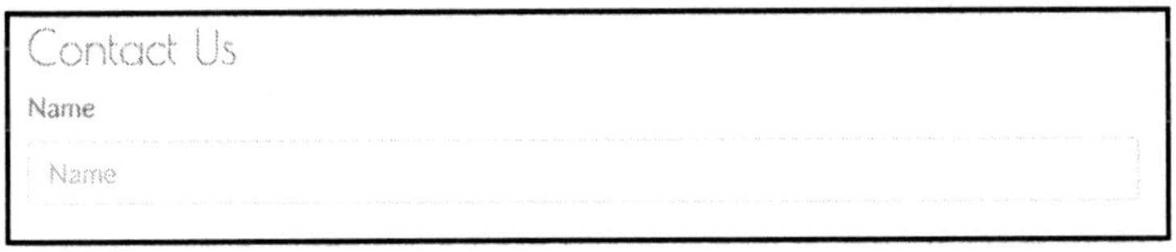

Figure 4.13: Our name input.

Great! We have created our first form. But note how (*Figure 4.13*) our name field stretches across the entire page, taking up a lot of valuable real estate. Seeing how users will certainly not need all this space for their names, you might wish to align the `label` and `name` input field. Luckily, Bootstrap makes this quite easy for us by offering horizontal form layouts and inline forms through the `form-inline` class. Applying it to our `form` element will change the display style of form controls and form groups contained within the form to `inline-block`. This will align the various components within your `form` element. Go ahead and apply it (see *Figure 4.14*):

```
<form class="form-inline">
    <div class="form-group-sm">
        <label for="name">Name</label>
        <input type="name" class="form-control" id="name"
        placeholder="Name">
    </div>
</form>
```

Take a look at the following screenshot:

Figure 4.14: Our vertical name form group.

This is much better. But we are not done quite yet. Try adding a second form group to the form. It will end up on the same line as our name form group. Furthermore, the input fields are now a bit too small to be of practical use. Try customizing them by combining the lessons that you learned in this chapter with the lessons you learned in Chapter 2, *Making a Style Statement.*

While we can save valuable space by aligning labels and input boxes, there is a second approach that we can take to combine input description with the actual input fields: Icons and placeholder texts (see *Figure 4.15*). The idea is that we combine icons and placeholder text to signify the expected input. The advantage behind this approach is that we will not be losing space to label elements.

First, let's remove the previously inserted label element and edit the input's placeholder attribute to contain the string Your name. Our name form group should now consist of a single input element:

```
<div class="form-group">
    <input type="text" class="form-control" placeholder="Your name">
</div>
```

Let's go ahead and duplicate this form group so that we now also have an input for our user's e-mail address:

```
<form>
    <div class="form-group">
        <input type="text" class="form-control" placeholder="Your
        name">
    </div>
    <div class="form-group">
        <input type="text" class="form-control" placeholder="Your email
        address">
    </div>
</form>
```

Now let's go ahead and select two Font Awesome icons that best describe the expected input. We recommend:

- A user symbol to indicate the user's name: `fa fa-user`
- An @ symbol to indicate the user's e-mail address: `fa fa-at`

Take a look at the following screenshot:

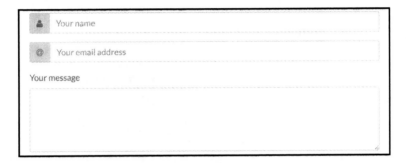

Figure 4.15: The finished Contact Us form: labels and placeholder text are combined to describe the expected input for a given input field.

To combine the input element with the icon, we first apply Bootstrap's `input-group` class to the form control. That is, our form control's `class` attribute should now be set to `class="form-group input-group"`. Next, we create the `<i>` tag for our Font Awesome icon, insert it before our input element, and then wrap the icon with a `span` element. We set the `span` class attribute to `class="input-group-addon"`:

```
<span class="input-group-addon"><i class="fa fa-user"></i></span>
```

Under the hood

The `input-group` class modifies the display, position, and `z-index` properties of a `form-control` element. In combination with an `input-group-addon`, this allows you to insert elements to the left or right of input elements.

Apply this to both the name and e-mail inputs and save. You should now see that the icons are aligned to the left of our input elements. To align them to the right, simply move the icon span *after* the input element:

```
<div class="form-group input-group">
    <input type="text" class="form-control" placeholder="Your email
    address">
    <span class="input-group-addon"><i class="fa fa-at"></i></span>
</div>
```

Our form is almost done. All that is left is to add a text area for our message (using the `textarea` element) and a **Send** button. To achieve the former, go ahead and create a new `form-group`. However, instead of the `form-group` containing an `input` box, add a `label` and a `textarea`. Just as with the `input` elements, the `textarea` should be a form control (so go ahead and set its class attribute to `form-control`):

```
<div class="form-group">
    <label for="name">Your message</label>
    <textarea class="form-control" rows="5" id="message"></textarea>
</div>
```

The last missing part of the puzzle is our **Send** button. Although we won't be writing the event listeners for our **Send** button, we will now explore the various Bootstrap context styles available for buttons. The parent class of any button is the `btn` class. In essence, the `btn` class adjusts the padding, margin, text alignment, font size, and weight as well as the border radius of any element that it is applied to. The seven context classes offered by Bootstrap are `btn-primary`, `btn-secondary`, `btn-success`, `btn-link`, `btn-info`, `btn-danger`, and `btn-warning` (see *Figure 4.16*). Take a look at the following screenshot:

Figure 4.16: The five Bootstrap button context styles. From left to right: Default, success, danger, info, and warning.

Let's go ahead and complete our form by inserting a `button` element and apply the `success` context class. Create a new form group below our text area. Inside the form group, create a button element and set its class to `btn btn-success`. Insert a nice icon and add some text to the button:

```
<div class="container-fluid myphoto-section bg-myphoto-light"
id="contact">
    <div class="container">
        <div class="row">
            <h3>Contact Us</h3>
            <form>
```

```
                    <div class="form-group input-group">
                        <span class="input-group-addon"><i class="fa
                        fa-user">
                        </i></span>
                        <input type="text" class="form-control"
                        placeholder="Your name">
                    </div>
                    <div class="form-group input-group">
                        <span class="input-group-addon"><i class="fa
                        fa-at">
                        </i></span>
                        <input type="text" class="form-control"
                        placeholder="Your email address">
                    </div>
                    <div class="form-group">
                        <label for="name">Your message</label>
                        <textarea class="form-control" rows="5"
                        id="message">
                        </textarea>
                    </div>
                    <div class="form-group">
                        <button class="btn btn-success">
                            <i class="fa fa-send-o"></i>
                            Send
                        </button>
                    </div>
                </form>
            </div>
        </div>
</div>
```

Last but not least, we can add some descriptive text to our **Contact Us** section. In this case, we will use placeholder text generated using `http://generator.lorem-ipsum.info/` (a useful tool if you ever require placeholder text for demo purposes):

```
<h3>Contact Us</h3>
<p>
    Lorem ipsum dolor sit amet, modo integre ad est, omittam temporibus
    ex sit,
    dicam molestie eum ne. His ad nonumy mentitum offendit, ea tempor
    timeam nec,
    doming latine liberavisse his ne. An vix movet dolor. Ut pri
    qualisque reprehendunt,
    altera insolens torquatos in per. Mei veri omnium omittam at,
    ea qui discere ceteros.
</p>
```

Take a look at the following screenshot:

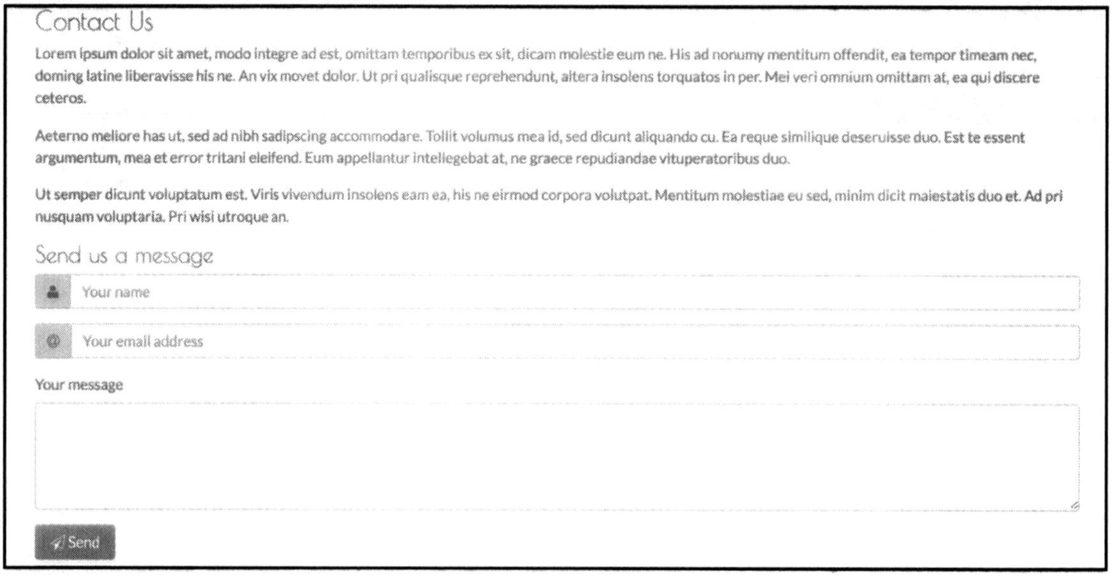

Figure 4.17: The Contact Us section along with the Send button.

While in the case of the preceding example the inputs are pretty explanatory, there may be inputs that require an explanation. As such, you can add descriptive text using the `form-text` class:

```
<p class="form-text">Some text describing my input.</p>
```

All that the `form-text` class does is set the element's display to block, and add a top margin of 0.25 rem to the element.

Furthermore, it should be noted that we wrapped both the **Contact Us** and **Send us a message** text inside `h3` and `h4` header tags. This is appropriate in this case, as the titles blend nicely with the content. However, for cases in which the title should stand out more, or should not blend with the content, one should use Bootstrap's display heading class `display-*`, where * denotes a number between 1 and 4. As with the header tags, the smaller the number, the bigger the font. The largest display class applies a font size of 6 rem to the target element, and decreases this by 0.5 rem for each successive display class (so, for example, `display-2` sets the font size to 5.5 rem). The display style definition also sets the font weight to 300. The *Figure 4.18* contrasts the use of `display-*` against the use of the HTML header tags. Take a look at the following screenshot:

Figure 4.18: Contrasting Bootstrap's display classes against the HTML header tags.

Increasing the font size and weight of paragraphs

In order to emphasize the text contained within paragraphs (as opposed to their headers), the lead class should be used. This class changes the font size to 1.25 rem and the font weight to 300.

Form validation

Although this book does not cover the server-side logic required to make this happen, we will need to implement one last essential stepping stone, client-side form validation. In other words, what is currently missing from our form, aside from the server-side code to send or store the actual message, is a way for us to validate the user's form input and to notify the user should they fill out the form incorrectly. One obvious solution is to identify what type of input the form fields require, and then to use either plain JavaScript or jQuery to check the contents of each field using regular expressions. Once an expression fails to match, we could then set the contents of a specific HTML element to contain an error message. However, do we really need to implement all this from scratch? The short answer is *no*. Form validation is a well explored area within web development. Consequently, there exist plenty of third-party JavaScript libraries that allow us to implement form validation quickly and with relatively little effort. As such, we will not be concerned with implementing the client-side validation logic as part of this book. Instead, a more noteworthy topic is Bootstrap's new validation styles. Unlike its predecessor, Bootstrap 4 comes with form validation styles, which greatly simplifies form development. Specifically, Bootstrap provides the has-success, has-warning, and has-danger validation classes, which are to be added to the parent element of input in order to indicate a specific context (*Figure 4.19*):

```
<div class="form-group input-group has-danger">
    <span class="input-group-addon"><i class="fa fa-at"></i></span>
    <input type="text" class="form-control" placeholder="Your email
    address">
</div>
```

Take a look at the following screenshot:

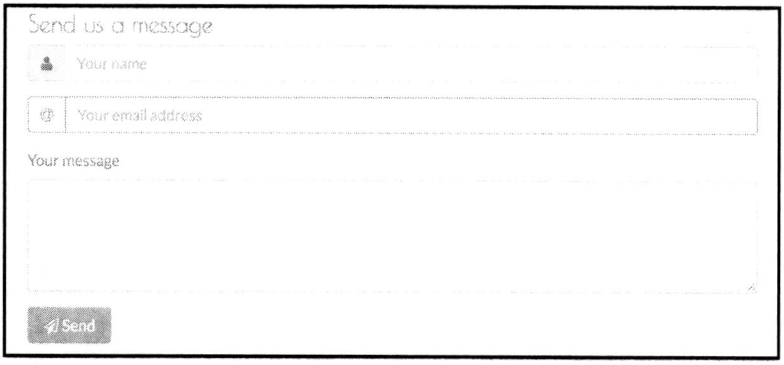

Figure 4.19: The has-danger context class applied to the form-group element containing our e-mail address input.

Adding the `form-control-*` to the input will cause a contextual icon to appear to the right-hand side of the input. The `*` denotes one of the three contexts—`danger`, `success`, or `warning`. So adding both `has-danger` to the `form-group` element and `form-control-danger` to the `input` element will cause the input to be highlighted using the danger context. A small icon, indicating failure, will appear to the right of the input:

```
<div class="form-group input-group has-danger">
    <span class="input-group-addon"><i class="fa fa-at"></i></span>
    <input type="text" class="form-control form-control-danger"
    placeholder="Your email address">
</div>
```

Progress indicators

Although unfitting of the context in which we are developing `MyPhoto`, progress indicators form an important part of many user interfaces. As such, it is worth pointing out that Bootstrap comes with some very nice styles for the `progress` element present in HTML5. Till date, the following classes are available:

- `progress`: This is for applying a default progress bar style.
- `progress-`: This is for applying context styles. Specifically, `progress-success`, `progress-info`, `progress-warning`, and `progress-danger`.
- `progress-striped`: This is for adding stripes to the progress bar, and `progress-animated` for animating the added stripes (note that currently animations are not supported by all browsers).

Since the `progress` element is not supported by Internet Explorer 9, Bootstrap also supplies the `progress-bar` class, which allows an element to be turned into a progress bar. The `progress-bar` requires the parent element to have the `progress` class applied to it.

Adding content using media objects

As you add more contents to your website or web application, you will notice that a large proportion of this content revolves around the text aligned next to an image. Indeed, text and image alignment form the basis from which most modern websites are built, and combining these two elements into a reusable component results in what are called **media objects** (*Figure 4.20*). Take a look at the following screenshot:

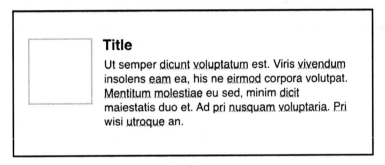

Title

Ut semper dicunt voluptatum est. Viris vivendum insolens eam ea, his ne eirmod corpora volutpat. Mentitum molestiae eu sed, minim dicit maiestatis duo et. Ad pri nusquam voluptaria. Pri wisi utroque an.

Figure 4.20: A media object refers to the combination of a title, text, and image element in such a way that they form a reusable entity.

Given how fundamental these media objects are to a website's content, it is of no surprise that Bootstrap 4 offers out-of-the-box support for them. Let's see how we can make use of Bootstrap's `media-object` to improve the appearance of our **About Us** section. One suggestion for improvement could be to add some profile information about one of the photographers at `MyPhoto`. To do so, go ahead and create a new `div` element, and assign it the `media` class. This identifies the element as a `media` object and gives the element a top margin of 15 px. To add a left aligned image of one of the `MyPhoto` photographers, create a new `div` element, set its class to `media-left` and create a nested image element to which the class `media-object` is applied. This ensures that the image is aligned to the left of our content, with appropriate padding (specifically, a `padding-right` of 10 px and a top vertical alignment). To add some biographical information about our photographer, we must use the `media-body` class. Create a second `div` inside the `media` element, assign it the `media-body` class, and add some text. Use a `header` element in conjunction with the `media-heading` class to create a title:

```
<div class="media">
    <div class="media-left">
        <img class="media-object" src="images/jason.jpg" alt="Jason">
```

```
        </div>
        <div class="media-body">
            <h4 class="media-heading">Jason</h4>
                Some text about Jason, our photographer. Aeterno meliore
                has ut, sed ad.
                Tollit volumus mea id, sed dicunt aliquando cu. Ea reque
                dmedsimilique deseruisse duo
                Est te essent argumentum, mea et error tritani eleifend.
                Eum appellantur intellegebat at, ne graece repudiandae
                vituperatoribus duo.
        </div>
    </div>
```

Take a look at the following screenshot:

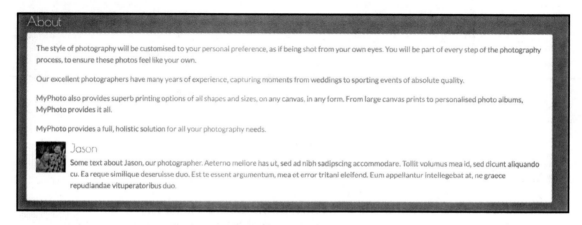

Figure 4.21: Using Bootstrap's media objects to add a photographer profile to MyPhoto's About Us section.

Instead of top aligning our `media` element, we could also:

- Middle align the `media` element using `media-left media-middle`.
- Bottom align the `media` element using `media-left media-bottom`.

 Note that, currently, Bootstrap 4 only supports left alignment (right alignment is not supported).

Of course, media elements do not need to appear on their own. Instead, they can be both nested and/or combined into lists. To nest a media element, simply place the child element inside the parent's body element (recall from our example above that body elements are denoted using the `media-heading` class).

Lists of media elements are created using the `media-list` class. Simply apply it to a list element (`ul` or `ol` tag), and use the `media` class in conjunction with the individual list items (`li` tags).

Figures

If requiring just a figure, and no media context, then Bootstrap's figure classes should be used. Although they do not fit into the current context of `MyPhoto`, Bootstrap's figure styling is a commonly used and important feature. As such, it is worth explaining the three classes that are to be used when creating a figure. The `figure` class sets the element's display to `inline-block`. This forces the element to behave just like inline elements, but also allows it to have a set width and height. The `figure-img` class should be applied to `img` elements within the `figure` element, adjusting their bottom margin and line height. Lastly, the `figure-caption` class is used to denote captions, and adjusts the font size (setting it to 90%) and the font color (setting it to #818a91). Observe the following code:

```
<figure class="figure">
    <img data-src="/img/example.png" class="figure-img">
    <figcaption class="figure-caption">Sample text.</figcaption>
</figure>
```

Quotes

There will be occasions in which you may want to display a famous quote or citation on your site. While an appropriate style for this would not be too difficult or time consuming to implement on your own, block quotes are a common enough scenario for the Bootstrap developers to have decided to take this too off your hands. Bootstrap 4, therefore, offers the `blockquote` for displaying quotes. The style rule for this class is not very complex. It merely adjusts the font size, bottom margin, and padding of the element to which it applies. It also adds a grey left-hand border to emphasize the element's contents. Let's go ahead and apply this class to an important motivational quote by one of the founders of `MyPhoto` that underpins the very foundations of the company (see *Figure 4.22*):

```
<blockquote class="blockquote">
    <p>I am very motivated today.</p>
```

```
            <footer class="blockquote-footer">The Founder,
                <cite >Times Magazine</cite>
            </footer>
        </blockquote>
```

Note how we not only display the quote itself, but also provide a source using the optional `blockquote-footer` class.

Take a look at the following screenshot:

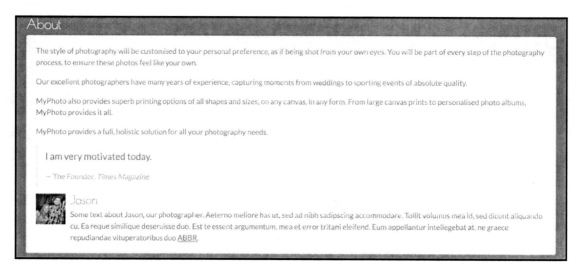

Figure 4.22: Using Bootstrap block quotes to cite the MyPhoto founder.

Instead of a left-hand border and left alignment, we can apply a right-hand border and align the source to the right using the reverse block quote class, `blockquote-reverse`:

```
        <blockquote class="blockquote blockquote-reverse">
            <p>I am very motivated today.</p>
            <footer class="blockquote-footer">The Founder,
                <cite >Times Magazine</cite>
            </footer>
        </blockquote>
```

All that `blockquote-reverse` does is set the CSS text align rule to right and adjust the padding and border properties accordingly.

Abbreviations

Just as with Bootstrap 3, Bootstrap 4 styles HTML's built-in `abbr` tag, which gives developers the ability to denote abbreviations. Denoting a piece of text as being an abbreviation will result in a small, dotted line being drawn underneath the text. As the user hovers over the text, the mouse pointer will change into a question mark. By setting the `title` attribute, a tool top will appear with the full `title` attribute's text content:

```
<abbr>ABBR</abbr>
```

And, just as with Bootstrap 3, the `initialise` class can be used in conjunction with the `abbr` tag in order to reduce the font size.

Summary

In this chapter we continued fleshing out the landing page of our demo project. We learned how to improve our website's navbar, and how to automate and customize our scroll speed. We used Bootstrap's Scrollspy plugin, and worked with and customized icons. This was followed by a discussion and practical examples of how to use and style custom Bootstrap alerts. Last but not least, we improved the footer for MyPhoto, learned how to create forms, discovered Bootstrap's media objects, and used Bootstrap's various content styles.

In the next chapter, Chapter 5, *Speeding Up Development Using jQuery Plugins*, we will bring this chapter's various new components to life. By learning how to apply third-party jQuery plugins, we will make MyPhoto interactive, and tie this chapter's various additions together to provide our site's visitors with a rich user experience.

5
Speeding Up Development Using jQuery Plugins

The previous chapter showed us how to style the content for `MyPhoto` and how to improve a website's overall appearance by using and customizing different Bootstrap components. We learned how to use Bootstrap's navbar, how to use icons, and how to customize a website's scrolling behavior using the Scrollspy plugin. In this chapter, we will emphasize the power of third-party plugins, introducing you to some essential third-party (and hence non-Bootstrap) plugins that will help speed up the development of the most common and mundane features. Building on the features implemented throughout the previous chapters, we will first teach you how to quickly and efficiently implement client-side browser detection using the jQuery browser plugin (`jquery.browser`). We will then improve the display of our tabular **Events** section by using pagination, first covering Bootstrap's pagination, and then showing you how to rapidly improve the default pagination feature using **bootpag**, Bootstrap's pagination plugin. Further improvements to our **Events** section will be made by adding images using Bootstrap Lightbox. Finally, staying within our tabular data display, we will improve the display of `MyPhoto`'s price list using jQuery DataTables.

To summarize, this chapter will cover the following:

- Browser detection using the jQuery browser plugin
- Improved pagination using bootpag
- Using Bootstrap Lightbox to display images
- Enhancing the display of tabular data using DataTables

Browser detection

Recall the hypothetical example from `Chapter 4`, *On Navigation, Footers, Alerts, and Content,* where `MyPhoto` only supports browsers above certain versions. To this end, we added a Bootstrap alert to our page, which notified visitors that their browser is not supported. Up until now, however, we had no way to actually identify which browser or browser version a `MyPhoto` visitor was using. Lacking any logic to hide and display the alert, the alert was visible regardless of whether or not the user's browser was actually supported by our website. Now the time has come for us to implement this missing logic.

Web browsers identify themselves by specifying their name and version information using a special field called **User-Agent**, which is part of the HTTP **Request Header** (see *Figure 5.1*). JavaScript allows users to access this field using the `window.navigator` property. This property contains the exact same string that is present in the **User-Agent** field of the HTTP **Request Header**. Therefore, to determine whether our visitor's browser is indeed supported, all that one needs to do is match the supported browser against the string presented by `window.navigator`. However, as can be seen from *Figure 5.1*, these strings are typically quite long and complex. As a result, matching different browsers can be tedious and prone to programming errors. Therefore, it is much better to use external resources that do this matching for us, and have been well tested, well documented, and are kept up to date. The popular, open source jQuery browser plugin (`https://github.com/gabceb/jquery-browser-plugin`) is one such resource that we can use. Let's go ahead and do just that! As usual, go ahead and fire up your console and install the plugin using Bower:

```
bower install jquery.browser
```

Once the installation is complete, you should see a new directory under `bower_components`:

`bower_components/jquery.browser`

Inside the `dist` folder, you should see two files, namely, `jquery.browser.js` and `jquery.browser.min.js`.

Take a look at the following screenshot:

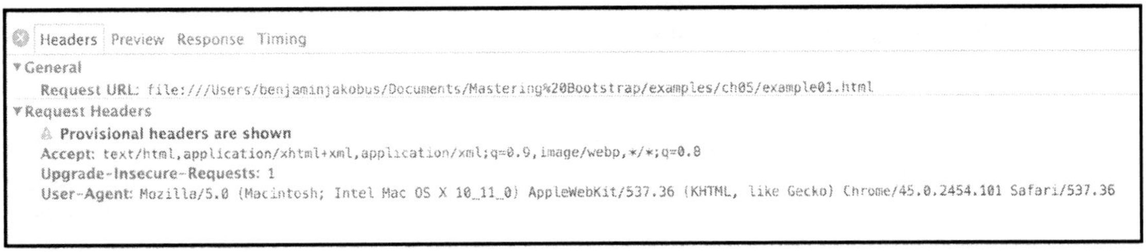

Figure 5.1: An example of a User-Agent string transmitted as part of the HTTP header when making a request.

If you can see the aforementioned files, then this means that `jquery.browser` has been successfully installed. Now, before we start using `jquery.browser`, we first need to work some more on our alert. The first thing that we will need to do is find a way of uniquely identifying it. Let's use the HTML `id` attribute for this purpose. Add the `id` attribute to our alert: `id="unsupported-browser-alert"`.

Next, we should tidy up our markup. Go ahead and open `css/myphoto.css` and move the inline styles for our alert into our style sheet.

As previously stated, we must eliminate inline styles at all costs. While we may, at times, apply inline styles to keep sample code snippets short, you should always try to avoid doing so outside the classroom.

This won't affect browser detection, but will simply allow us to keep our markup nice and tidy. Observe the following code:

```
#unsupported-browser-alert {
    position: fixed;
    margin-top: 4em;
    width: 90%;
    margin-left: 4em;
}
```

Generally, it is not a good idea to couple CSS rules with an `id`, as this is bad for reusability. But hold tight; we will talk more about this in `Chapter 6`, *Customizing Your Plugins*.

Since we only want the alert to display under certain conditions (namely, if the user is using a specific version of Internet Explorer), we should hide the `alert` `div` by default. Go ahead and add the following CSS to our `alert` styles:

```
display: none;
```

Save and refresh. The alert at the top of the page should now no longer be visible. Furthermore, our outermost `alert` `div` should now only contain `id` and `class` attributes:

```
<div class="alert alert-danger" id="unsupported-browser-alert">
    <a href="#" class="close" data-dismiss="alert" aria-label="close"
    >&times;</a>
    <strong class="alert-heading"><i class="fa fa-exclamation"></i>
    Unsupported browser</strong> Internet Explorer 8 and lower are
    not supported by this website.
</div>
```

Now it is finally time to start using our freshly installed jQuery plugin. Open the `MyPhoto` `index.html` file and include the minified `jquery.browser` JavaScript file within the `head` of the document:

```
<script
src="bower_components/jquery.browser/dist/jquery.browser.min.js">

</script>
Great. The head of our index.html should now look as follows:
<head>
    <meta charset="UTF-8">
    <title>ch05</title>
    <link rel="stylesheet" href="bower_components/bootstrap/dist/css
    /bootstrap.min.css" />
    <link rel="stylesheet" href="styles/myphoto.css" />
    <link rel="stylesheet" href="bower_components/components-
    font-awesome/css/font-awesome.min.css" />
    <script src="bower_components/jquery/dist/jquery.min.js"></script>
    <script src="bower_components/bootstrap/dist/js/bootstrap.min.js">
    </script>
    <script src=
    "bower_components/jquery.browser/dist/jquery.browser.min.js">
    </script>
    <script type="text/javascript">
        $( document ).ready(function() {
            $("nav ul li a").on('click', function(evt) {
                evt.preventDefault();
                var offset = $(this.hash).offset();
                if (offset) {
                    $('body').animate({
```

```
                    scrollTop: offset.top
                });
            }
        });
    });
    </script>
</head>
```

We are now ready to use `jquery.browser` to detect which browser the visitor is using. To this end, and as noted in the `jquery.browser` documentation, the following variables are are available:

- `$.browser.msie`: This is true if the website visitor is using Microsoft Internet Explorer.
- `$.browser.webkit`: This is true if the website visitor is using either Chrome, Safari, or Opera.
- `$.browser.version`: This shows the browser version (not type!) that the website visitor is using.

To add the logic that makes the alert visible, let us start with a general condition of whether or not the user is using Internet Explorer. We will move to a more specific condition later (whether the user is using a specific version of Internet Explorer). In other words, let us begin by making the browser alert visible only if the visitor's browser is identifying itself as Internet Explorer. The code for this is fairly straightforward. We simply check the `$.browser.msie` variable. If this variable evaluates to true, then we use jQuery to make our alert visible:

```
if ($.browser.msie) {
    $('#unsupported-browser-alert').show();
}
```

Now let us make our browser test more specific. We now want to test whether the visitor is using both Internet Explorer and whether the version of Internet Explorer (let's say version 8 and below) is unsupported by `MyPhoto`. To do so, we simply perform a second check using the `$.browser.version` variable. If the conditional evaluates to true, then the `show()` function is executed. The `show()` function modifies the display rule of an element to make it visible:

```
if ($.browser.msie && $.browser.version <= 8) {
    $('#unsupported-browser-alert').show();
}
```

Go ahead and insert this snippet into the `head` of our HTML document:

```
<script type="text/javascript">
    $( document ).ready(function() {
        $("nav ul li a").on('click', function(evt) {
            evt.preventDefault();
            var offset = $(this.hash).offset();
            if (offset) {
                $('body').animate({
                    scrollTop: offset.top
                });
            }
        });
        if ($.browser.msie && $.browser.version <= 7) {
            $('#unsupported-browser-alert').show();
        }
    });
</script>
```

Conditional comments with Internet Explorer

If you wished to target Internet Explorer only for specific portions of your markup, then you can use Microsoft's conditional comments with Internet Explorer. Other browsers that are not Internet Explorer will simply ignore these proprietary comments:

```
<!--[if IE 8]-->
    <insert IE specific markup here>
[endif]-->
```

Enhanced pagination using bootpag

In this section, we will learn both how to use Bootstrap's default pagination, and how to overcome its limitations quickly and with minimal effort. We will first populate the section with a set of sample events, and then group these events into pages in an effort to reduce the overall length of the section. In order to add a set of events to the **Events** section, replace the `<p>Lorem Ipsum</p>` markup in the `services-events` div with the following event placeholder text:

```
<h3>My Sample Event #1</h3>
<p>Lorem ipsum dolor sit amet, consectetur adipiscing elit.
Curabitur leo dolor,
fringilla vel lacus at, auctor finibus ipsum. Lorem ipsum dolor sit
amet,
```

```
consectetur adipiscing elit. Morbi quis arcu lorem. Vivamus elementum
convallis
enim sagittis tincidunt. Nunc feugiat mollis risus non dictum.
Nam commodo nec
sapien a vestibulum. Duis et tellus cursus, laoreet ante non,
mollis sem.
Nullam vulputate justo nisi, sit amet bibendum ligula varius id.</p>
```

Repeat this text three times so that we now have three sample events displaying on our page under the **Events** tab (see *Figure 5.2*). Add top padding and a left-hand margin of 2rem to the parent container to offset the events in an effort to make the section look less crowded:

```
#services-events .container {
    margin-left: 2rem;
    padding-top: 1rem;
}
```

Take a look at the following screenshot:

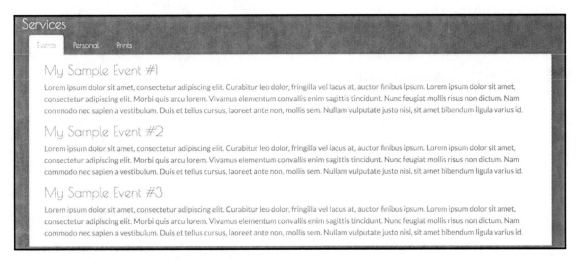

Figure 5.2: Three sample events displayed one below the other within our Events tab.

Hit save and refresh. Voila! This looks pretty good already, so why exactly would we want to display the events on separate pages? Well, as we begin adding more and more events, the events will appear below one another. As such, the **Events** section will grow indefinitely. Pagination is a clever way of avoiding this while allowing us to maintain the ability to list all MyPhoto events. Bootstrap offers a visually appealing pagination style (see *Figure 5.3*) that can be added to any section of your page by applying the pagination class to an unordered list element. The individual list items within this unordered list should have the `page-item` class applied to them. Applying this class simply sets the element's display property to `inline`. Applying the `pagination` class sets the display of the unordered list to `inline-block` and adjusts its margins. As such, in order to display pagination with 10 pages (for example's sake, we will carry on using 10 pages from now on), add the following markup after the `p` element of our third event (note how the active class is used on a list item to denote the currently selected page. The `pagination-lg` and `pagination-sm` classes can be used to increase or decrease the size of the pagination control):

```html
<ul class="pagination">
    <li class="page-item"><a class="page-link active"
    href="#">1</a></li>
    <li class="page-item"><a class="page-link" href="#">2</a></li>
    <li class="page-item"><a class="page-link" href="#">3</a></li>
    <li class="page-item"><a class="page-link" href="#">4</a></li>
    <li class="page-item"><a class="page-link" href="#">5</a></li>
    <li class="page-item"><a class="page-link" href="#">6</a></li>
    <li class="page-item"><a class="page-link" href="#">7</a></li>
    <li class="page-item"><a class="page-link" href="#">8</a></li>
    <li class="page-item"><a class="page-link" href="#">9</a></li>
    <li class="page-item"><a class="page-link" href="#">10</a></li>
</ul>
```

Pagination in Bootstrap 3

When it comes to pagination, the changes from Bootstrap 3 to Bootstrap 4 are not that drastic. The `pagination` class remains between the two versions. However, in Bootstrap 3, we did not explicitly need to specify which elements were pagination items and which elements were pagination links. As the `page-item` and `page-link` classes have only been introduced with Bootstrap 4, one could previously specify the pagination by simply creating an unordered list and applying the `pagination` class to it:

```html
<ul class="pagination">
    <li><a class="active" href="#">1</a></li>
    <li><a href="#">2</a></li>
    <li><a href="#">3</a></li>
</ul>
```

With the addition of the preceding markup, we have already reached the end of Bootstrap's default pagination capabilities. The implementation of the actual pagination is up to us. Specifically, this would involve the following:

- Grouping our events into pages.
- Detecting the currently active page.
- Toggling the visibility of the various pages depending on the page that is currently selected.

As our event grows beyond 10 pages, we would then be required to manually add both a new page and a new list item to the paginator. While implementing the logic for all this is not quite rocket science, it would be nice if we did not have to be concerned with reinventing a solution to such a well known user interface problem. Indeed, there exist plenty of third-party libraries to help us speed up the development of our events pagination.

One of the most popular libraries is `jQuery.bootpag`, a jQuery plugin that allows you to paginate your data. Unfortunately, bootpag (versions 1.0.7 and below) currently does not support Bootstrap 4 out of the box, and as such will require a little bit of tweaking. As with all libraries presented in this chapter, `jQuery.bootpag` is free to use, and its source code, as well as licensing information, is available on GitHub at `https://github.com/botmonster/jquery-bootpag`. Take a look at the following screenshot:

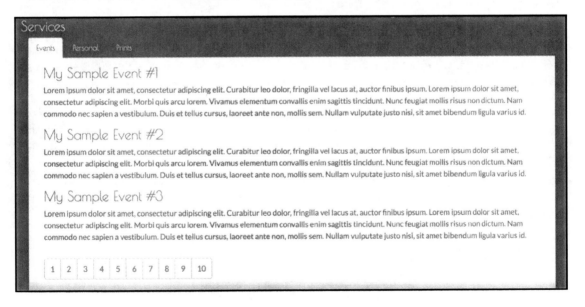

Figure 5.3: Bootstrap default pagination.

Unsurprisingly, the `bootpag` Bower package's name is also bootpag. Go ahead and install it:

```
bower install bootpag
```

Once installation is complete, you should see a directory named `bootpag` under your `bower_components` directory. Inside `bootpag/lib`, you should see the following files:

- `jquery.bootpag.js`
- `jquery.bootpag.min.js`

As always, we want to work with the minified version of our plugin, so go ahead and include `jquery.bootpag.min.js` within the `head` of our document:

```
<script
src="bower_components/bootpag/lib/jquery.bootpag.min.js"></script>
```

Before we can start using bootpag, we must understand that the plugin needs containers: one container in which to display the pagination control, and one container for displaying the content that is to be paginated. In other words, it requires one to divide the area of the **Events** section between the data that is to be displayed, and one to separate the controls with which the user navigates the data. As a user navigates the data using the pagination control, the content area will be updated with the new content, or, alternatively, the visibility of multiple containers will be toggled.

We will be using the latter approach. That is, we will first divide our events into pages, and then use an event listener on the pagination control to toggle the visibility of these various pages. To this end, we must now go ahead and modify our events in the **Services** section so that each of our events is contained within its own distinct page (that is, by using `div`).

Since our example consists of only three sample events, we will divide the events into two pages. The first page will contain **My Sample Event #1** and **My Sample Event #2**, while the second page will contain **My Sample Event #3**. We will use a `div` element to represent an individual page. Each page's `div` will consist of a unique `id`, the word `page`, followed by the page number. The pagination control will be added in after our last event. To do this, add an empty `div` for holding the pagination below the last of our pages. It should also be assigned a unique `id`:

```
<div class="row">
    <div id="page-1">
        <h3>My Sample Event #1</h3>
        <p>Lorem ipsum dolor sit amet, consectetur adipiscing elit.
        Curabitur leo dolor,
            fringilla vel lacus at, auctor finibus ipsum. Lorem ipsum
```

```
        dolor sit amet,
    consectetur adipiscing elit. Morbi quis arcu lorem. Vivamus
    elementum convallis
    enim sagittis tincidunt. Nunc feugiat mollis risus non dictum.
    Nam commodo nec
    sapien a vestibulum. Duis et tellus cursus, laoreet ante non,
    mollis sem.
    Nullam vulputate justo nisi, sit amet bibendum ligula varius
    id.
    </p>
    <h3>My Sample Event #2</h3>
    <p>Lorem ipsum dolor sit amet, consectetur adipiscing elit.
    Curabitur leo dolor,
       fringilla vel lacus at, auctor finibus ipsum. Lorem ipsum
       dolor sit amet,
    consectetur adipiscing elit. Morbi quis arcu lorem. Vivamus
    elementum convallis
    enim sagittis tincidunt. Nunc feugiat mollis risus non dictum.
    Nam commodo nec
    sapien a vestibulum. Duis et tellus cursus, laoreet ante non,
    mollis sem
    Nullam vulputate justo nisi, sit amet bibendum ligula varius
    id.
    </p>
</div>
<div id="page-2">
    <h3>My Sample Event #3</h3>
    <p>Lorem ipsum dolor sit amet, consectetur adipiscing elit.
    Curabitur leo dolor,
    fringilla vel lacus at, auctor finibus ipsum. Lorem ipsum
    dolor sit amet,
    consectetur adipiscing elit. Morbi quis arcu lorem. Vivamus
    elementum convallis
    enim sagittis tincidunt. Nunc feugiat mollis risus non dictum.
    Nam commodo nec
    sapien a vestibulum. Duis et tellus cursus, laoreet ante non,
    mollis sem.
    Nullam vulputate justo nisi, sit amet bibendum ligula varius
    id.
    </p>
</div>
<div id="services-events-pagination"></div>
</div>
```

Before we will be able to actually use our pagination control, we must inform `bootpag` of its container. We do so by calling the `bootpag` function on our element, passing a configuration object as a parameter that contains our desired page count (10 in our case). Insert the following code into the `head` of our HTML document:

```
$('#services-events-pagination').bootpag({
    total: 10
}).on("page", function(event, num){});
```

The `bootpag` function will render the control to the element with an `id` equal to `services-events-pagination`, but notice the `on` event listener with the `page` parameter. This is our event listener, which will invoke the code contained within the (currently empty) callback as the user uses the pagination control to change pages. However, before we can implement the page change logic that will toggle the visibility of our individual pages, we must first hide our pages. To this end, we must update our `myphoto.css` file.

Now, one obvious approach would be to add a style for each one of our individual pages, identifying them by their `id`. As our number of events grows, this will seriously bloat our style sheet, as you will be required to add a new CSS rule for each new page. A much neater approach would be to wrap our pages within their own container and then use CSS selectors to hide all pages (that is, `div` elements) within this content area. To achieve this, first wrap the pages inside a new `container div` and assign this `container` a unique id:

```
<div id="services-events-content">
    <div id="page-1">
    <h3>My Sample Event #1</h3>
    <p>...</p>
    <h3>My Sample Event #2</h3>
    <p>...</p>
    </div>
    <div id="page-2">
    <h3>My Sample Event #3</h3>
    <p>...</p>
    </div>
</div>
```

Did you know?

There is an easier way to implement the aforementioned code. You could use Bootstrap's `hide` class, and toggle it in the callback. Try solving this yourself!

Then we update our style sheet so that the individual page `div` elements held within this new `container` are hidden by default:

```
#services-events-content div
{
    display: none;
}
```

Save and hit refresh. All of our events should now be hidden.

Now all we need to do is implement the logic that makes our individual pages visible as the user navigates. To this end, we complete the currently empty callback function, so that it first hides all pages and only then displays the currently selected page. Hiding all the pages, instead of the previous page, makes our code much cleaner, as we require no logic to determine the previously selected page; instead, we just use a CSS selector to hide all `div` elements contained within our `services-events-content` container. The `bootpag` plugin informs us of the currently selected page number through the second parameter (here named `num`) passed to our callback function. As such, we can use this page number to construct the `id` of the `div` (page) that we wish to make visible:

```
$('#services-events-pagination').bootpag({
    total: 10
}).on("page", function(event, num){
    $('#services-events-content div').hide();
    var current_page = '#page-' + num;
    $(current_page).show();
});
```

Seeing how our style sheet hides all the pages, we should include a statement that makes the first page visible as the user first visits our page. To do this, simply add `$('#page-1').show();` to the `head` of our document, so that our code takes the following structure:

```
$('#page-1').show();
$('#services-events-pagination').bootpag({
    total: 10
}).on("page", function(event, num){
    // Pagination logic
});
```

Take a look at the following screenshot:

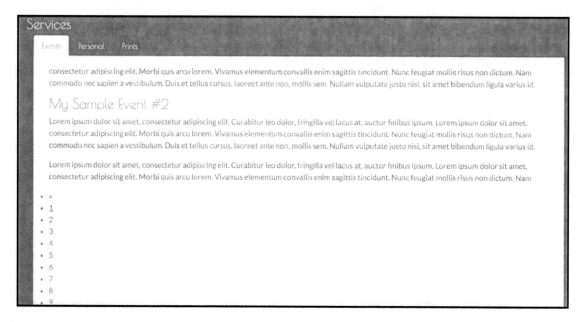

Figure 5.4: The display of the bootpag pagination controls is broken for Bootstrap 4. This is due to the changes to the pagination controls introduced by Bootstrap 4.

Hit save and refresh. While the pagination controls themselves are working, their display is broken (see *Figure 5.4*). This is due to the previously discussed changes to the pagination controls introduced by Bootstrap 4. Examining `jquery.bootpag.js`, we can see that the issue lies in constructing the pagination list items on line 130+. Observe the following code:

```
return this.each(function(){
    var $bootpag, lp, me = $(this),
        p = ['<ul class="', settings.wrapClass, ' bootpag">'];

    if(settings.firstLastUse){
        p = p.concat(['<li data-lp="1" class="', settings.firstClass,
        '"><a href="', href(1), '">', settings.first, '</a></li>']);
    }
    // ...
});
```

As the pagination items are being created for Bootstrap 3, the problem here lies with the fact that the code generating the items fails to apply the page-item and page-link classes. We can fix this easily enough. First, create a new folder, js, in our project root. Copy the jquery.bootpag.js file into this folder. Update the pagination markup generation logic so that the page-item and page-link classes are being applied to the list item and anchor elements:

```
return this.each(function(){
    var $bootpag, lp, me = $(this),
    p = ['<ul class="', settings.wrapClass, ' bootpag">'];

    if(settings.firstLastUse){
        p = p.concat(['<li data-lp="1" class="page-item ',
        settings.firstClass, '"><a class="page-link" href="', href(1),
        '">',
        settings.first, '</a></li>']);
    }
    if(settings.prev){
        p = p.concat(['<li data-lp="1" class="page-item ',
        settings.prevClass, '"><a class="page-link" href="', href(1),
        '">',
        settings.prev, '</a></li>']);
        }
    for(var c = 1; c <= Math.min(settings.total, settings.maxVisible);
    c++){
        p = p.concat(['<li class="page-item" data-lp="', c, '"><a
        class="page-link" href="', href(c), '">', c, '</a></li>']);
    }
    if(settings.next){
        lp = settings.leaps && settings.total > settings.maxVisible
        ? Math.min(settings.maxVisible + 1, settings.total) : 2;
        p = p.concat(['<li data-lp="', lp, '" class="page-item ',
        settings.nextClass, '"><a class="page-link" href="', href(lp),
        '">', settings.next, '</a></li>']);
    }
    if(settings.firstLastUse){
        p = p.concat(['<li data-lp="', settings.total, '" class=
        "page-item
        last"><a class="page-link" href="', href(settings.total),'">',
        settings.last, '</a></li>']);
    }
});
```

Finally, update the reference in the document head to point to our modified version of `bootpag`:

```
<script src="js/jquery.bootpag.js"></script>
```

Take a look at the following screenshot:

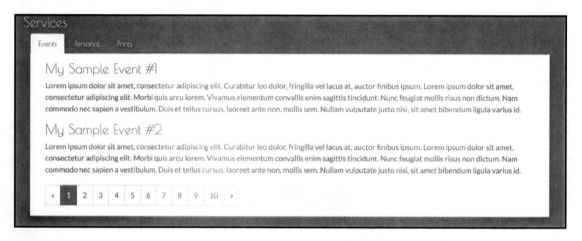

Figure 5.5: Pagination using our modified version of the bootpag plugin.

As you paginate to our second page, you will spot one issue: the last page may, at times, contain only one event (as is the case with **My Sample Event #3**), and the event descriptions differ in their lengths. Hence, there will be a height difference, which becomes apparent as the user switches pages. As a consequence, the pagination control `div` will move up and down (see *Figure 5.6*). Luckily, the fix for this is straightforward, and involves assigning our `event-services-content div` a fixed height of `15em`. Open the `myphoto.css` and add the following:

```
#services-events-content {
    height: 15em;
}
```

Take a look at the following screenshot:

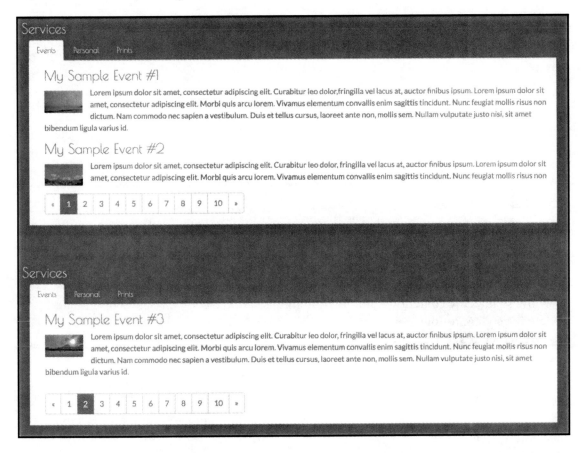

Figure 5.6: Notice the height difference between the two pages. Having a different number of events per page or listing events with differing descriptions will result in the container growing and shrinking.

Now that our `events` container is of a fixed height, we can be certain that the container will not shrink based on its content. As a result, the pagination control will remain fixed in its position. However, this raises one final issue, of long event descriptions. How can we deal with events that contain more text than is permissible by our `events` container? For example, consider the additional paragraph added to **My Sample Event #2** in *Figure 5.7*. As you can see, the pagination control is now rendered above the event description.

Any text exceeding our container's height is simply cut:

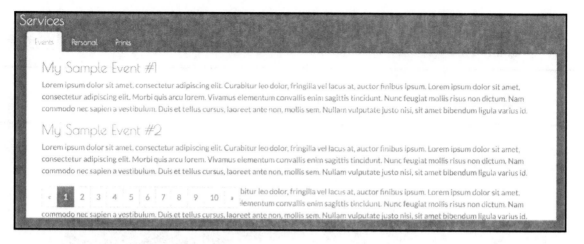

Figure 5.7: Display bug: Long event descriptions result in the pagination control being rendered above the event description. Any text exceeding our container's height is cut.

Once again, our fix is a simple one-liner, and involves setting the container's *Y*-axis overflow so that any content within the container is scrollable. Open `myphoto.css` and update the styling for our `services-events-content` container so that its `overflow-y` property is set to `scroll`:

```
#services-events-content {
    height: 15em;
    overflow-y: scroll;
}
```

Save and refresh. Voila!

Displaying images using Bootstrap Lightbox

One important feature missing from our **Events** section is the ability to include images that illustrate an event (or provide additional information). Sure, you can add images using the `img` tag, but that may not be very practical, as the image size will be limited by the container's dimensions.

In this section, we will demonstrate how we can overcome this limitation by allowing users to enlarge images as they click on them, without redirecting them away from our page. To this end, go ahead and embed one image with each event (see *Figure 5.8*). Each image should be aligned to the left of the event description, have a width of 80, and a height of 45:

```
<div id="page-1">
    <h3>My Sample Event #1</h3>
    <p>
        <img src="images/event1.jpg" align="left" width="80"
        height="45"/>
        Lorem ipsum dolor sit amet, consectetur adipiscing elit.
        Curabitur leo dolor,
        fringilla vel lacus at, auctor finibus ipsum. Lorem ipsum dolor
        sit amet,
        consectetur adipiscing elit. Morbi quis arcu lorem. Vivamus
        elementum convallis
        enim sagittis tincidunt. Nunc feugiat mollis risus non dictum.
        Nam commodo nec
        sapien a vestibulum. Duis et tellus cursus, laoreet ante non,
        mollis sem.
        Nullam vulputate justo nisi, sit amet bibendum ligula varius
        id.
    </p>
    <h3>My Sample Event #2</h3>
    <p>
        <img src="images/event2.jpg" align="left" width="80"
        height="45"/>
        Lorem ipsum dolor sit amet, consectetur adipiscing elit.
        Curabitur leo dolor,
        fringilla vel lacus at, auctor finibus ipsum. Lorem ipsum
        dolor sit amet,
        consectetur adipiscing elit. Morbi quis arcu lorem. Vivamus
        elementum convallis
        enim sagittis tincidunt. Nunc feugiat mollis risus non dictum.
        Nam commodo nec
        sapien a vestibulum. Duis et tellus cursus, laoreet ante non,
        mollis sem.
        Nullam vulputate justo nisi, sit amet bibendum ligula varius
        id.
    </p>
</div>
```

As you save the preceding markup and refresh the page, you will notice that the images are not very nicely aligned with the text. They appear somewhat squashed. We can improve their appearance by adding some spacing between the images, the text, and the top of the container. To do this, go ahead and add a top margin of 0.5em and a right margin of 1em to each image within our `services-events-content` container:

```
#services-events-content div img {
    margin-top: 0.5em;
    margin-right: 1em;
}
```

Did you know?
You can solve the aforementioned problem using a specific class (which may in fact be a neater solution). Try and improve these rules by yourself!

Take a look at the following screenshot:

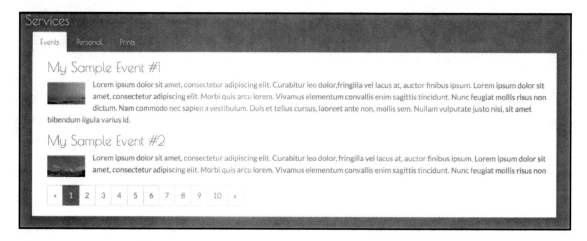

Figure 5.8: Sample images accompanying each event description. The images are left-aligned and have a dimension of 80 x 45.

One popular third-party library that allows users to enlarge the images embedded within the event description is Bootstrap Lightbox, available via GitHub at `https://github.com/jbutz/bootstrap-lightbox`. Unfortunately, the plugin is no longer maintained and ships with several unfixed bugs and usability issues. Upon downloading it, you will find that it does not immediately work out of the box. Luckily, DJ Interactive (`http://djinteractive.co.uk`) extended the original Bootstrap Lightbox through Lightbox for Bootstrap. Also available via GitHub (`https://github.com/djinteractive/Lightbox-for-Bootstrap`), the plugin is published under the Creative Commons Attribution 2.5 license. This means that the plugin is free for use under the condition that the author of the plugin is properly attributed.

Go ahead and download Lightbox for Bootstrap, and include both its JavaScript and CSS files within the `head` of our HTML document:

```
<script src="bower_components/lightbox-for-bootstrap
```

```
/js/bootstrap.lightbox.js"></script>
<link rel="stylesheet" href="bower_components/bootstrap-lightbox
/css/bootstrap.lightbox.css" />
```

Using the plugin to display our images within a lightbox fortunately requires hardly any modification to our existing markup. The only two steps to undertake are as follows:

1. Place our existing `img` element inside a container element that has a `thumbnail` class and `data-toggle` attribute.

2. Apply the `thumbnail` class and `data-target` attribute to our `img` element:

```
<p>
  <span class="thumbnails" data-toggle="lightbox">
      <img src="images/event1.jpg" align="left" width="80"
      height="45"
      class="thumbnail" data-target="images/event1.jpg"/>
  </span>
  Lorem ipsum dolor sit amet, consectetur adipiscing elit.
  Curabitur leo
  dolor,fringilla vel lacus at, auctor finibus ipsum. Lorem
  ipsum dolor sit amet,
  consectetur adipiscing elit. Morbi quis arcu lorem. Vivamus
  elementum convallis
  enim sagittis tincidunt. Nunc feugiat mollis risus non dictum.
  Nam commodo nec
  sapien a vestibulum. Duis et tellus cursus, laoreet ante non,
  mollis sem.
  Nullam vulputate justo nisi, sit amet bibendum ligula varius
  id.
</p>
```

The `data-target` attribute tells Lightbox for Bootstrap where our larger image is located. It is important to note that the `src` attribute of our image element has no effect on the image that will be displayed within the lightbox; only the `data-target` attribute determines this. As such, we could display a thumbnail, which then actually links to a different lightbox image (although this would make little sense and be grossly misleading). Unsurprisingly, the `data-toggle` attribute is used to identify the element that serves as the lightbox toggle, in our case, the toggle is our 80 x 45 image. However, it is important to note that toggles do not need to be image elements. Any element can become a lightbox toggle.

Last but not least, the `thumbnails` class serves as selectors for the `lightbox` plugin. Without them, the desired functionality would not work. Take a look at the following screenshot:

Figure 5.9: An enlarged image displayed using Lightbox for Bootstrap.

To summarize, our **Events** section should now look as follows:

```
<div class="container">
    <div class="row" style="margin: 1em;">
        <div id="services-events-content">
            <div id="page-1">
                <h3>My Sample Event #1</h3>
                <p>
                    <span class="thumbnails" data-toggle="lightbox">
                    <img src="images/event1.jpg" align="left"
                    width="80" height="45"
                    class="thumbnail" data-target="images/event1.jpg"/>
                </span>
                Lorem ipsum...
                </p>
                <h3>My Sample Event #2</h3>
                <p>
                    <span class="thumbnails" data-toggle="lightbox">
                        <img src="images/event2.jpg" align="left"
                        width="80" height="45"
                        class="thumbnail"
```

```
                        data-target="images/event2.jpg"/>
                    </span>  Lorem ipsum...
                </p>
            </div>
            <div id="page-2">
                <h3>My Sample Event #3</h3>
                <p>
                    <span class="thumbnails" data-toggle="lightbox">
                    <img src="images/event3.jpg" align="left"
                    width="80" height="45"
                    class="thumbnail" data-target="images/event3.jpg"/>
                    </span>
                    Lorem ipsum...
                </p>
            </div>
        </div>
        <div id="services-events-pagination"></div>
    </div>
</div>
```

Improving our price list with DataTables

With the **Events** section in place, it is time to move onto our price list that we built in
Chapter 2, *Making a Style Statement* and Chapter 3, *Building the Layout*. For the data that is
currently displayed, the existing table structure works perfectly fine. The prices are nicely
presented, and the table is not too crowded. However, what if MyPhoto were required to
display hundreds of prices (yes, this case may seem far fetched, but bear with it for
demonstration purposes)? Our existing table structure would far exceed its display
capacity; the columns would be too crowded and we would need to implement some form
of pagination to help keep the table organized. Of course, if you read the previous sections,
you will know how easy it is to implement pagination using a third-party plugin. However,
with hundreds or thousands of items, pagination will not be enough to make the website
usable. Users may require more advanced features, such as the ability to filter tabular data,
or the ability to search for a specific table item. Users may also desire the ability to adjust
the number of table items displayed per page. All these requirements are bound to make
our table implementation quite complex and challenging. However, once again, these user
requirements are common, well understood, and well studied. Because of this, there is an
excellent third-party library that we can use to enhance our MyPhoto price list. Meet
DataTables (https://www.datatables.net). DataTables is a jQuery plugin that includes
Bootstrap styles, and provides us with all of the previously mentioned features.

To use DataTables, you can either customize your own build via the DataTables website (they offer a neat download builder), or you can use Bower:

```
bower install DataTables
```

Once installed, you should find the following directory: `bower_components/DataTables`

Inside this directory, `media/` will contain both minified and un-minified JavaScript and CSS files, which we can include within the head of our document. Specifically, the directory will contain the normal jQuery plugin and styles, as well as the Bootstrap-specific styling:

- `dataTables.bootstrap.min.js`
- `jquery.dataTables.min.js`
- `dataTables.bootstrap.min.css`

Let's go ahead and incorporate the files:

```
<script src="bower_components/DataTables/media
/js/jquery.dataTables.min.js"></script>
<script src="bower_components/DataTables/media
/js/dataTables.bootstrap.min.js"></script>
<link rel="stylesheet" href="bower_components/DataTables/media
/css/dataTables.bootstrap.min.css" />
```

Before we can dive into our freshly included `dataTables`, we must reorganize our print sizes and prices. Go ahead and create a table, using the same dataset as before (however, for simplicity's sake, we can just display one price set):

```
<table id="services-prints-table">
    <thead>
        <tr>
            <th>Extra Large</th>
            <th>Large</th>
            <th>Medium</th>
            <th>Small</th>
        </tr>
    </thead>
    <tbody>
        <tr>
            <td>24x36  (€60)</td>
            <td>19x27  (€45)</td>
            <td>12x18  (€28)</td>
            <td>6x5  (€15)</td>
        </tr>
        <tr>
            <td>27x39  (€75)</td>
```

```
                <td>20x30 (€48)</td>
                <td>16x20 (€35)</td>
                <td>8x10 (€18)</td>
            </tr>
            <tr>
                <td>27x40 (€75)</td>
                <td>22x28 (€55)</td>
                <td>18x24 (€40)</td>
                <td>11x17 (€55)</td>
            </tr>
        </tbody>
    </table>
```

The preceding table is a standard HTML table with a `head` and a `body`. Save and refresh. Good, we now have a plain and simple table. Next, let's go ahead and style it. First, set the table to use the entire available space by setting its `width` to `100%`. Next, apply the following two Bootstrap classes: `table` and `table-striped`. The former class, `table`, applies a basic table styling to our table by adjusting the padding, line height, and vertical alignment. The latter class, `table-striped`, alternates the colors of our individual rows:

```
<table id="services-prints-table" class="table table-striped"
width="100%">
    <thead>
        <!-- Content here-->
    </thead>
    <tbody>
        <!--Content here-->
    </tbody>
</table>
```

To initialize the data table, we just need one line of code:

```
$('#services-prints-table').DataTable();
```

Save and refresh. Immediately, you will see that the table is flowing outside of our container. To solve this, wrap the table element into a `div`, and give this `div` a maximum width of `90%` (note that we are using inline styles for demonstration purposes only, and you should always try to avoid inline styles):

```
<div style="max-width: 90%;">
    <table id="services-prints-table" class="display">...</table>
</div>
```

Once again, save and hit refresh. Voila! Our table is displaying nicely (see *Figure 5.10*). Go ahead and play with it for a bit. Use the search box to filter specific table rows, or add more table rows and see how the table becomes magically pageable. You can even control the number of entries to display per page without any additional effort. Take a look at the following screenshot:

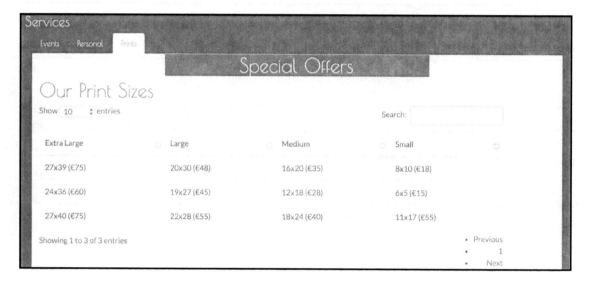

Figure 5.10: The non-Bootstrap variant of our DataTables price list. Note the broken pagination display.

Note how, just as with `bootpag`, the `dataTable` plugin applies Bootstrap 3 pagination styling. To make the plugin Bootstrap 4-compatible, first copy `dataTables.bootstrap.js` into the `js` folder (which we created when fixing `bootpag`) and navigate to line 63. The `switch` statement is what determines the list item classes to use. Immediately after the `switch` statement, add the following line:

```
btnClass += 'page-item table-page-item';
```

Furthermore, update line 109 (which generates the anchor element) to include the `page-link` class:

```
.append( $('<a>', {
    'class': 'page-link',
    'href': '#',
    'aria-controls': settings.sTableId,
    'data-dt-idx': counter,
    'tabindex': settings.iTabIndex
    } )
    .html( btnDisplay )
```

```
    )
```

Note how, along with the `page-item` class, we also added the `table-page-item` class, which we now define as follows:

```
.table-page-item {
    margin-left: 0.5rem;
}
```

Take a look at the following screenshot:

Figure 5.11: The fixed DataTable, complete with pagination controls and a Terms and Conditions Apply label.

To conclude this section, our complete price section should now look as follows:

```
<div class="container">
    <h1 class="hidden-md">Our Print Sizes</h1>
    <div style="max-width: 90%;">
        <table id="services-prints-table" class="table table-striped"
        width="100%">
            <thead>
                <tr>
                    <th>Extra Large</th>
                    <th>Large</th>
                    <th>Medium</th>
                    <th>Small</th>
                </tr>
            </thead>
            <tbody>
```

```
    <tr>
        <td>24x36 (€60)</td>
        <td>19x27 (€45)</td>
        <td>12x18 (€28)</td>
        <td>6x5 (€15)</td>
    </tr>
    <tr>
        <td>27x39 (€75)</td>
        <td>20x30 (€48)</td>
        <td>16x20 (€35)</td>
        <td>8x10 (€18)</td>
    </tr>
    <tr>
        <td>27x40 (€75)</td>
        <td>22x28 (€55)</td>
        <td>18x24 (€40)</td>
        <td>11x17 (€55)</td>
    </tr>
    </tbody>
    </table>
    </div>
</div>
```

Summary

In this chapter, we learned how to solve common user interface development requirements using third-party libraries. By improving various functionalities built out during the course of the previous chapters, we demonstrated how to detect a user's browser and its version using the jQuery browser plugin. We used the `bootpag` plugin to allow users to navigate data. Along with it, we enhanced the look and feel of our **Events** section using images and Lightbox for Bootstrap. We also looked at improving the usability of our price list using DataTables.

Armed with the knowledge of how to use popular and widely adopted third-party libraries, we are now ready to customize Bootstrap's jQuery plugins to suit our exact needs. Lets go to the next chapter!

6
Customizing Your Plugins

So far, we have built the `MyPhoto` demo page leveraging all that Bootstrap has to offer, customizing Bootstrap's themes and components, and using jQuery plugins along the way. In this chapter, we will be delving deep into Bootstrap's jQuery plugins with extensive customization via JavaScript and CSS.

We will take some of the plugins we have introduced into `MyPhoto`, take a look under the hood, and, step by step, we will customize them to meet the needs of our page. Plugins will be examined and extended throughout this chapter in an effort to not only make our page better, but to also build our knowledge of how jQuery plugins are built and behave within Bootstrap's ecosystem.

When we are comfortable with customizing Bootstrap's jQuery plugins, we will create a fully customized jQuery plugin of our own for `MyPhoto`.

Summarizing all of this, in this chapter we will globally do the following:

- Learn about the anatomy of a Bootstrap jQuery plugin
- Learn how to extensively customize the behavior and features of Bootstrap's jQuery plugins via JavaScript
- Learn how to extensively customize the styling of Bootstrap's jQuery plugins via CSS
- Learn how to create a custom Bootstrap jQuery plugin from scratch

Anatomy of a plugin

Bootstrap jQuery plugins all follow the same convention in how they are constructed. At the top level, a plugin is generally split across two files, a JavaScript file and a Sass file. For example, the Alert component is made up of `bootstrap/js/alert.js` and `bootstrap/scss/_alert.scss`. These files are compiled and concatenated as part of Bootstrap's distributable JavaScript and CSS files. Let us look at these two files in isolation to learn about the anatomy of a plugin.

JavaScript

Open up any JavaScript file in `bootstrap/js/src`, and you will see that they all follow the same pattern: an initial setup, a class definition, data API implementation, and jQuery extension. Let's take a detailed look at `alert.js`.

Setup

The `alert.js` file, written in ECMAScript 2015 syntax (also known as ES6, the latest (at the time of writing) standardized specification of JavaScript), first imports a utilities module:

```
import Util from './util'
```

A constant is then created, named `Alert`, which is assigned the result of an **Immediately Invoked Function Expression (IIFE)**:

```
const Alert = (($) => {
...
})(jQuery)
```

A `jQuery` object is being passed into a function for execution, the result of which will be assigned to the immutable `Alert` constant.

Within the function itself, a number of constants are also declared for use throughout the rest of the code. Declaring immutables at the beginning of the file is generally seen as best practice. Observe the following code:

```
const NAME               = 'alert'
const VERSION            = '4.0.0-alpha'
const DATA_KEY           = 'bs.alert'
const EVENT_KEY          = '.${DATA_KEY}'
const DATA_API_KEY       = '.data-api'
const JQUERY_NO_CONFLICT = $.fn[NAME]
```

```
const TRANSITION_DURATION = 150

const Selector = {
  DISMISS : '[data-dismiss="alert"]'
}
const Event = {
  CLOSE : 'close${EVENT_KEY}',
  CLOSED : 'closed${EVENT_KEY}',
  CLICK_DATA_API : 'click${EVENT_KEY}${DATA_API_KEY}'
}

const ClassName = {
  ALERT : 'alert',
  FADE : 'fade',
  IN : 'in'
}
```

The NAME property is the name of the plugin, and VERSION defines the version of the plugin, which generally correlates to the version of Bootstrap. DATA_KEY, EVENT_KEY, and DATA_API_KEY relate to the data attributes that the plugin hooks into, while the rest are coherent, more readable, aliases for the various values used throughout the plugin code. Following that is the class definition.

Immediately Invoked Function Expression

An Immediately Invoked Function Expression (IIFE or iffy) is a function which is executed as soon as it has been declared, and is known as a self-executing function in other languages. A function is declared as an IIFE by either wrapping the function in parentheses or including a preceding unary operator, and including a trailing pair of parentheses. Examples:

```
(function(args){ })(args)
```

```
!function(args){ }(args)
```

Class definition

Near the top of any of the plugin JS files, you will see a comment declaring the beginning of the class definition for that particular plugin. In the case of alerts, it is:

```
/**
 * -----------------------------------------------------------------
 -----
 * Class Definition
```

```
 *  -------------------------------------------------------------
 -----
 */
```

The class definition is simply the constructor of the base object, in this case, the `Alert` object:

```
class Alert {
    constructor(element) {
        this._element = element
    }
    ...
}
```

The convention with plugins is to use Prototypal inheritance. The `Alert` base object is the object all other `Alert` type objects should extend and inherit from. Within the class definition, we have the public and private functions of the `Alert` class. Let's take a look at the public `close` function:

```
close(element) {
    element = element || this._element
    let rootElement = this._getRootElement(element)
    let customEvent = this._triggerCloseEvent(rootElement)
    if (customEvent.isDefaultPrevented()) {
      return
    }

    this._removeElement(rootElement)
}
```

The `close` function takes an `element` as an argument, which is the reference to the DOM element the `close` function is to act upon. The `close` function uses the private function `_getRootElement` to retrieve the specific DOM element, and `_triggerCloseEvent` to reference the specific event to be processed. Finally, close calls `_removeElement`. Let's take a look at these private functions:

```
_getRootElement(element) {
    let selector = Util.getSelectorFromElement(element)
    let parent   = false

    if (selector) {
        parent = $(selector)[0]
    }

    if (!parent) {
        parent = $(element).closest(`.${ClassName.ALERT}`)[0]
    }
```

```
        return parent
    }
```

The _getRootElement tries to find the parent element of the DOM element passed to the calling function, in this case, close. If a parent does not exist, _getRootElement returns the closest element with the class name defined by ClassName.ALERT in the plugin's initial setup. This in our case is Alert. Observe the following code:

```
_triggerCloseEvent(element) {
    let closeEvent = $.Event(Event.CLOSE)
    $(element).trigger(closeEvent)
    return closeEvent
}
```

The _triggerCloseEvent also takes an element as an argument and triggers the event referenced in the plugin's initial setup by Event.CLOSE:

```
_removeElement(element) {
    $(element).removeClass(ClassName.IN)
    if (!Util.supportsTransitionEnd() ||
        !$(element).hasClass(ClassName.FADE)) {
      this._destroyElement(element)
      return
    }
    $(element)
        .one(Util.TRANSITION_END, $.proxy(this._destroyElement,
        this, element))
        .emulateTransitionEnd(TRANSITION_DURATION)
}
```

The _removeElement then carries out the removal of the rootElement safely and in accordance with the configuration in the element itself, or as defined in the plugin's initial setup, for example, TRANSITION_DURATION.

All core behaviors and functions of the plugin should be defined in the same manner as the close function. The class definition represents the plugin's essence.

After the public and private functions come the static functions. These functions, which are also private, are similar to what would be described as the plugin definition in Bootstrap 3. Observe the following code:

```
static _jQueryInterface(config) {
    return this.each(function () {
        let $element = $(this)
        let data = $element.data(DATA_KEY)
        if (!data) {
```

```
                data = new Alert(this)
                $element.data(DATA_KEY, data)
            }
            if (config === 'close') {
                data[config](this)
            }
        })
    }
    static _handleDismiss(alertInstance) {
        return function (event) {
            if (event) {
                event.preventDefault()
            }
            alertInstance.close(this)
        }
    }
}
```

The _jQueryInterface is quite simple. First, it loops through an array of DOM elements. This array is represented here by the this object. It creates a jQuery wrapper around each element and then creates the Alert instance associated with this element, if it doesn't already exist. _jQueryInterface also takes in a config argument. As you can see, the only value of config that _jQueryInterface is concerned with is 'close'. If config equals 'close', then the Alert will be closed automatically.

_handleDismiss simply allows for a specific instance of Alert to be programmatically closed.

Following the class definition, we have the data API implementation.

Data API implementation

The role of the data API implementation is to create JavaScript hooks on the DOM, listening for actions on elements with a specific data attribute. In alert.js, there is only one hook:

```
$(document).on(
    Event.CLICK_DATA_API,
    Selector.DISMISS,
    Alert._handleDismiss(new Alert())
)
$(document).on('click.bs.alert.data-api', dismiss,
Alert.prototype.close)
```

The hook is an on-click listener on any element that matches the dismiss selector.

When a click is registered, the `close` function of `Alert` is invoked. The dismiss selector here has actually been defined at the beginning of the file, in the plugin setup:

```
const Selector = {
    DISMISS : '[data-dismiss="alert"]'
}
```

Therefore, an element with the attribute `data-dismiss="alert"` will be hooked in, to listen for clicks. The `click` event reference is also defined in the setup:

```
const Event = {
    CLOSE           : 'close${EVENT_KEY}',
    CLOSED          : 'closed${EVENT_KEY}',
    CLICK_DATA_API  : 'click${EVENT_KEY}${DATA_API_KEY}'
}
```

`EVENT_KEY` and `DATA_API_KEY`, if you remember, are also defined here:

```
const DATA_KEY          = 'bs.alert'
const EVENT_KEY         = '.${DATA_KEY}'
const DATA_API_KEY      = '.data-api'
```

We could actually rewrite the API definition to read as follows:

```
$(document).on('click.bs.alert.data-api', '[data-dismiss="alert"]',
Alert._handleDismiss(new Alert()))
```

The last piece of the puzzle is the jQuery section, which is a new feature in Bootstrap 4. It is a combination of Bootstrap 3's plugin definition and a conflict prevention pattern.

jQuery

The jQuery section is responsible for adding the plugin to the global jQuery object so that it is made available anywhere in an application where jQuery is available. Let's take a look at the code:

```
$.fn[NAME]              = Alert._jQueryInterface
$.fn[NAME].Constructor  = Alert
$.fn[NAME].noConflict   = function () {
    $.fn[NAME] = JQUERY_NO_CONFLICT
    return Alert._jQueryInterface
}
```

The first two assignments extend jQuery's prototype with the plugin function. As `Alert` is created within a closure, the constructor itself is actually private. Creating the `Constructor` property on `$.fn.alert` allows it to be accessible publicly.

Then, a property of `$.fn.alert` called `noConflict` is assigned the value of `Alert._jQueryInterface`. The `noConflict` property comes into use when trying to integrate Bootstrap with other frameworks to resolve issues with two jQuery objects with the same name. If in some framework the Bootstrap `Alert` got overridden, we could use `noConflict` to access the Bootstrap `Alert` and assign it to a new variable:

```
$.fn.bsAlert = $.fn.alert.noConflict()
```

`$.fn.alert` is the framework version of `Alert`, but we have transferred the Bootstrap `Alert` to `$.fn.bsAlert`.

All plugins tend to follow the pattern of initial setup, class definition, data API implementation, and jQuery extension. To accompany the JavaScript, a plugin also has its own specific Sass style sheet.

Sass

Sass files for plugins aren't as formulaic as the corresponding JavaScript. In general, JavaScript hooks into classes and attributes to carry out a generally simple functionality. In a lot of cases, much of the functionality is actually controlled by the style sheet; the JavaScript simply adds and removes classes or elements under certain conditions. The heavy lifting is generally carried out by the Sass, so it is understandable that the Sass itself may not fit into a uniform pattern.

Let's take a look at `scss/_alert.scss`. The `_alert.scss` opens up with a base style definition. Most, but not all, plugins will include a base definition (usually preceded by a base style or base class comment). Defining the base styles of a plugin at the beginning of the Sass file is best practice for maintainability and helps anyone who might want to extend the plugin to understand it.

Following the base styles, the styles associated with, or responsible for, the functionality of the plugin are defined. In the case of alerts, the dismissible alert styles are defined. The only piece of functionality an alert has, besides being rendered on the page, is to be dismissed. This is where Alerts defines what should happen when the `close` class is applied to an Alerts element.

The Sass will also generally include an alternate style definition. The alternate styles generally align with Bootstrap's contextual classes, which we explored in Chapter 2, *Making a Style Statement*. Observe the following code:

```
// Alternate styles
//
// Generate contextual modifier classes for colorizing the alert.
.alert-success {
    @include alert-variant($alert-success-bg, $alert-success-border,
    $alert-success-text);
}
.alert-info {
    @include alert-variant($alert-info-bg, $alert-info-border,
    $alert-info-text);
}
.alert-warning {
    @include alert-variant($alert-warning-bg, $alert-warning-border,
    $alert-warning-text);
}
.alert-danger {
    @include alert-variant($alert-danger-bg, $alert-danger-border,
    $alert-danger-text);
}
```

As you can see, alert provides styles to correspond with the success, info, warning, and danger contexts. The variables used in the rules, such as $alert-danger-bg, are declared in _variables.scss. Declaring variables in a _variables.scss file is best practice, as otherwise maintenance would be supremely difficult. For instance, open up _variables.scss and see the definition for $alert-danger-bg:

```
$alert-warning-bg: $state-warning-bg !default;
```

The $state-warning-bg is another variable, but this variable is used for all form feedback and alert warning background variables. If we wanted to change the color that the warning context corresponds to, we would just need to change the value in one place:

```
$state-warning-bg: #fcf8e3 !default;
```

Beyond the base styles and, to an extent, the alternate styles, there is no real template for plugging in the Sass files.

The JavaScript file and the Sass file are the two ingredients that make a plugin work. Looking at the example from Chapter 4, *On Navigation, Footers, Alerts, and Content*, we can see the alert plugin in action:

```
<div class="alert alert-danger">
    <a href="#" class="close" data-dismiss="alert"
    aria-label="close">&times;</a>
    <strong class="alert-heading"><i class="fa fa-
    exclamation"></i> Unsupported browser</strong>
    Internet Explorer 8 and lower are not supported by this website.
</div>
```

Let's start customizing plugins.

Customizing plugins

While there are many plugins to customize, we will choose two that we have already come across in the previous chapters:

- Bootstrap's jQuery alert plugin
- Bootstrap's jQuery carousel plugin

Customizing Bootstrap's jQuery alert plugin

The alert plugin, as we have seen, is exceedingly simple. The alert is rendered on the page, displaying a message, and the only functionality it has is the ability to close and disappear when a user clicks on a certain element.

To demonstrate how to customize or extend a plugin, in this case alert, we are going to keep it very simple. We are going to add an extra bit of functionality, when a user clicks on a certain element, the alert will minimize. We also, obviously, want to give the user the ability to expand the alert when it is in its minimized state. To do this, we need to extend both the JavaScript and the styling of alert.

Before we get to the coding of the plugin functionality and styling, let's put together the markup for an alert on the MyPhoto page.

The markup

As an example use case, let's display an alert informing the user of a special offer. We will add our alert above the unsupported browser alert:

```
<div class="alert alert-info" style="position: fixed; margin-top:
4em; width: 90%;margin-left: 4em;">
    <a href="#" class="close" data-dismiss="alert"
    aria-label="close">&times;</a>
    <strong><i class="fa fa-exclamation"></i> Special Offer - </strong>
    <span>2 FOR 1 PRINTS TODAY ONLY WITH PROMO CODE <span style="font-
    style: italic">BOOTSTRAP</strong></span>
</div>
```

We're using Bootstrap's contextual information class, `alert-info`, to style the alert box, and we're following the same pattern as the unsupported browser alert. The special offer alert has inline styles applied, and the unsupported browser alert has styles linked to its id. Before we go any further, let's extract that out into a single class in `myphoto.css` for reusability and maintainability. Remove the `#unsupported-browser-alert` rules and add the following:

```
.alert-position {
    position: fixed;
    margin-top: 4em;
    width: 50%;
    margin-left: 25%;
    z-index: 10;
}
.alert-position #unsupported-browser-alert {
    display:none;
}
```

We've made some slight changes here. The alert will now have a hard-set `width` of 50% of the viewport and will be rendered 25% from the left. To make sure the alert is always rendered above any other content on the page, we set the `z-index` to 10. As long as no other elements have a higher `z-index`, then the alert will always be visible. Now, we remove the inline styles on the alert elements and add the `alert-position` class. We extend the class slightly for elements with the `unsupported-browser-alert` id to make sure it isn't displayed. Update the `alert` elements with the `alert-position` class:

```
<div class="alert alert-info alert-position">
```

Take a look at the following screenshot:

Figure 6.1: A modified alert used to display special promotions. Unlike the default alert, this alert has its width hard-set to 50% of the viewport and will be rendered 25% from the left.

Okay, great. We now have our special offers alert. Now let's add our `minimize` and `expand` elements. We want these elements to function and display similarly to the `close` element, so we can use the `close` element as a template. Observe the following code:

```
<a href="#" class="close" data-dismiss="alert"
aria-label="close">&times;</a>
<a href="#" class="close minimize" data-minimize="alert"
aria-label="minimize">_</a>
<a href="#" class="close expand" data-expand="alert"
aria-label="expand">+</a>
```

We have replicated the `close` element twice. We have added a `minimize` and `expand` class, while retaining the `close` element as we want to inherit everything the `close` class includes. We have added new data attributes—instead of `data-dismiss`, we have `data-minimize` and `data-expand`. These are the data attributes that the plugin will listen to. We then updated the `aria-label` with the appropriate names, and applied appropriate content inside the element—an underscore (_) to indicate minimization and a plus (+) to indicate expansion (see *Figure 6.2*). Take a look at the following screenshot:

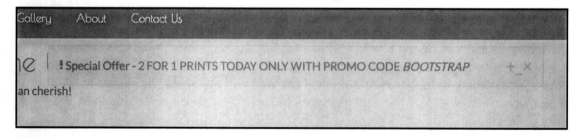

Figure 6.2: Our custom promotion alert with expand and minimize functionality

Besides the close button, we now have the expand and minimize buttons. We don't want to show the expand button when the alert is already expanded, and we don't want to show the minimize button when the alert is already minimized. As the alert is expanded by default, we'll add a `hidden-xs-up` class to the `expand` element. Recall that `hidden-xs-up` hides a given element for viewports that are xs or larger. That is, the element will be hidden for all viewports (`hidden-xs-up` is the equivalent of `hide` in Bootstrap 3). Observe the following code:

```
<a href="#" class="close" data-dismiss="alert"
aria-label="close">&times;</a>
<a href="#" class="close minimize" data-minimize="alert"
aria-label="minimize">_</a>
<a href="#" class="close expand hide" data-expand="alert"
aria-label="expand">+</a>
```

Take a look at the following screenshot:

Figure 6.3: Our custom promotion alert with the expand element hidden

Nice. The alert is starting to look the way we want it. With that, we are ready to customize the styling of the alert plugin.

Extending alert's style sheets

As we mentioned before, it is bad practice to modify Bootstrap's Sass files directly, due to maintenance issues. Instead, we are going to create our own style sheet—`styles/alerts.css`.

Before we create any new classes, we should extract any alert-related CSS from `myphoto.css` into this new style sheet in order to improve code maintainability. The only classes we have so far are `alert-danger` and `alert-position`. Place them into our new alert specific style sheet, and include the style sheet in our HTML. Be sure to include it after `bootstrap.min.css` and `myphoto.css`, to make sure the style rules in `alert.css` take priority. Observe the following code:

```
<link rel="stylesheet" href="bower_components/bootstrap/dist/css
/bootstrap.min.css" />
<link rel="stylesheet" href="styles/myphoto.css" />
<link rel="stylesheet" href="styles/alert.css" />
```

To create the ability to minimize and expand an alert, we actually do not need many style rules at all. In fact, we are going to use just one new class—`alert-minimize`. When a user clicks on the minimize button, the `alert-minimize` class will be applied to the root `alert` element. To expand it, the `alert-minimize` class will simply be removed.

Update `alert.css` with the following rules:

```css
.alert-minimize {
    width: 60px;
}
.alert-minimize * {
    display: none;
}
.alert-minimize.close {
    display: block;
}
```

The `alert-minimize` class will force a 60px element width. All descendants of the `alert-minimize` class will be given the display value of `none` so they do not appear on screen. To make sure the functional buttons are still visible, any element with the `close` class (remember we retained the `close` class for all our functional buttons in the alert) will be given the display value of `block`. Let's manually apply `alert-minimize` to our alert to see how it renders. Take a look at the following screenshot:

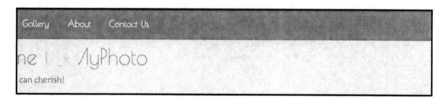

Figure 6.4: Our minimized custom promotion alert

Next up, let's remove the `alert-minimize` class and extend the alert plugin JavaScript to apply and remove the class dynamically.

Extending alert's functionality with JavaScript

As with extending the styles, to extend the JavaScript we could modify Bootstrap's `alert.js` directly, but, again, that is a bad idea in terms of maintainability. Instead, we are going to create a `js` directory in our project, and a file called `alert.js`. Include this file in your HTML, after `bootstrap.min.js`:

```html
<script
```

```
src="bower_components/bootstrap/dist/js/bootstrap.min.js"></script>
<script src="js/alert.js"></script>
```

The first thing we are going to do is to create an immediately invoked function, and add the function to the jQuery object:

```
+function ($) {
    'use strict';
    var Alert = $.fn.alert.Constructor;
}(jQuery);
```

The function assigns a variable Alert to the alert plugins prototype, which, as we saw earlier, is made available through the Constructor property.

With this reference to the Alert prototype, we can add our own functions to the prototype to handle minimizing and expanding an alert. Taking the close function we studied earlier, and with a few changes, let's create a function to minimize the alert:

```
Alert.prototype.minimize = function (e) {
    var $this = $(this)
    var selector = $this.attr('data-target')
    if (!selector) {
        selector = $this.attr('href')
        selector = selector && selector.replace(/.*(?=#[^\s]*$)/, '')
        // strip for ie7
    }
    $this.addClass('hidden-xs-up')
    $this.siblings('.expand').removeClass('hidden-xs-up')
    var $parent = $(selector)
    if (e) e.preventDefault()
    if (!$parent.length) {
        $parent = $this.closest('.alert')
    }
    $parent.trigger(e = $.Event('minimize.bs.alert'))
    if (e.isDefaultPrevented()) return
    $parent.addClass('alert-minimize')
}
```

The function is quite similar to the close function, so we will highlight the important differences. Line 15 and line 16 handle hiding the minimize button and showing the expand button, adding the hide class to the element that triggered the event, and removing the hide class from any sibling element with the expand class. Line 32 adds the alert-minimize class, which handles the shrinking of the Alert element, to the parent of the element that triggered the event. Essentially, the minimize function will shrink the alert, hide the minimize button, and show the expand button. Let's hook a listener up to this function.

We do this in the same way as the Bootstrap alert plugin links the data—dismiss the `click` event to the `close` function, adding the following to `alert.js`, below the `minimize` function definition:

```
$(document).on('click.bs.alert.data-api', '[data-minimize="alert"]',
Alert.prototype.minimize)
```

Now, an element with the `data-minimize` attribute with an `"alert"` value will call the `Alert.prototype.minimize` function on a `click` event. The `minimize` element in our special offers alert has this attribute. Open up `MyPhoto` and click the minimize button. Take a look at the following screenshot:

Figure 6.5: Our minimized custom promotion alert – note the expand and close buttons

Excellent. Our minimize button and functionality are wired up correctly to shrink our special offers alert and replace the minimize button with an expand button when clicked.

The last thing we need to do now is make sure the user can expand the alert when they click on the expand button. To do this, we follow the same steps as we did for the minimize functionality. Let's add an `expand` function to the `Alert` prototype:

```
Alert.prototype.expand = function (e) {
    var $this = $(this)
    var selector = $this.attr('data-target')
    if (!selector) {
        selector = $this.attr('href')
        selector = selector && selector.replace(/.*(?=#[^\s]*$)/, '')
        // strip for ie7
    }
    $this.addClass('hidden-xs-up')
    $this.siblings('.minimize').removeClass('hide')
    var $parent = $(selector)
    if (e) e.preventDefault()
    if (!$parent.length) {
        $parent = $this.closest('.alert')
    }
    $parent.trigger(e = $.Event('expand.bs.alert'))
    if (e.isDefaultPrevented()) return
    $parent.removeClass('alert-minimize')
```

```
    }
```

The differences between the `expand` and `minimize` functions are very small, so small that it probably makes sense for them to be encapsulated into one function. However, for the sake of simplicity, we will keep the two functions separate. Essentially, the actions of `minimize` are reversed. The `hidden-xs-up` class is again applied to the element triggering the event, the `hide` class is removed from any sibling with the `minimize` class, and the `alert-minimize` class is removed from the parent element. Simple and effective. Now, we just need to hook up a `click` event on an element with the `data-expand` attribute set to `alert` to the `expand` method. Observe the following code:

```
$(document).on('click.bs.alert.data-api', '[data-expand="alert"]',
Alert.prototype.expand)
```

That's it. With our extension to the alert plugin, when a user clicks expand in the minimized state, the alert reverts back to its initial expanded state and the expand button is replaced by the minimize button. Our users now have the ability to reduce the screen real estate our alert covers, but are still able to retrieve the information from the alert at a later stage if needed.

While these alert customizations are relatively simple, they do provide a strong example of how to extend a plugin's functionality and teach principles that can be applied to more complex extensions.

Customizing Bootstrap's jQuery carousel plugin

`MyPhoto` uses Bootstrap's carousel as a gallery to display sample images. The carousel is a very neat component, allowing the user to cycle through images. We are going to add some new functionality to the carousel plugin. Specifically, we are going to implement the ability to surface a larger version of the image in a modal window when there is a `click` event on a carousel slide. We will be using Bootstrap's modal plugin to surface the modal, and we will dynamically pass the image source and carousel caption from the markup of the slide to the modal. First, let's write the markup.

The markup

The only thing we really need to do in the markup is create a modal element, and reference that modal in the carousel's slide elements, so as to link them together. First, let's create the modal. We only want a bare-bones modal here—an image, a close button, and a title. We've seen how to create modals before, so let's just add the markup we need to our HTML. We will add it just above the `carousel` element:

```
<div class="modal fade carousel-modal" id="carousel-modal"
tabindex="-1" role="dialog">
    <div class="modal-dialog">
        <div class="modal-content">
            <div class="modal-header">
                <button type="button" class="close" data-dismiss
                ="modal" aria-label="Close"><span aria-hidden=
                "true">&times;</span></button>
                <h4 class="modal-title"></h4>
            </div>
            <div class="modal-body">
                <img>
            </div>
        </div>
    </div>
</div>
```

We have created a very simple modal here. We added a `carousel-modal` class to the parent element for any styles we may need to apply, and we attributed `carousel-modal` as the `id` for the modal. We have an empty `modal-title` element, which we will populate dynamically. Most interestingly, we have an empty `img` tag in the `modal-body` element. It isn't often that you see an `img` tag with no `src` attribute, but our extension will create this attribute dynamically. We could, of course, have created a different modal for each image, but that wouldn't scale, and it just wouldn't be interesting!

That's our simple modal window declared. Great. Now we just need to reference the modal in our slides. On each `img` element within the carousel, simply add a `data-modal-picture` attribute with the value `#carousel-modal`. Observe the following code:

```
<div class="carousel-inner" role="listbox">
    <div style="height: 400px" class="carousel-item active">
        <img data-modal-picture="#carousel-modal"
        src="images/brazil.png">
        <div class="carousel-caption">
            Brazil
        </div>
    </div>
    <div style="height: 400px" class="carousel-item">
```

```
    <img data-modal-picture="#carousel-modal"
    src="images/datsun.png">
    <div class="carousel-caption">
        Datsun 260Z
    </div>
  </div>
  <div style="height: 400px" class="carousel-item">
      <img data-modal-picture="#carousel-modal"
      src="images/skydive.png">
      <div class="carousel-caption">
          Skydive
      </div>
  </div>
</div>
```

The `data-modal-picture` attribute is the `data-attribute` we are going to hook our on-click listener to, in the very same way that alert hooked into `data-dismiss`. Let's set up our carousel plugin extension and wire all this together.

Extending carousel's functionality with JavaScript

Just like with our alert extension, we will create a new JS file for the carousel extension. Create a `js/carousel.js` file and include the file on the `MyPhoto` page:

```
<script src="js/carousel.js"></script>
```

Again, we want to create an IIFE and assign the carousel constructor to a variable we can work with. Observe the following code:

```
+function ($) {
    'use strict';
    var Carousel = $.fn.carousel.Constructor;
}(jQuery);
```

From our markup, we know what `data-attribute` we want to listen to—`data-modal-picture`. Observe the following code:

```
+function ($) {
    'use strict';
    var Carousel = $.fn.carousel.Constructor;
    $(document).on('click.bs.carousel.data-api', '[data-modal-
    picture]', Carousel.prototype.zoom)
}(jQuery);
```

Notice that, unlike with alert, we are not referencing any particular value for the `data-modal-picture` attribute. We will be using the attribute value to identify which modal to use, so of course we want the plugin to be flexible enough to handle more than one modal id. We have also defined which function we want to call when the event is triggered—`Carousel.protoype.zoom`. Let's create that function:

```
Carousel.prototype.zoom = function () {
    var $this = $(this)
    var $src = $this.attr('src')
    var $title = $this.next('.carousel-caption').text()
    var $modal = $this.attr('data-modal-picture')
    var $modalElement = $.find($modal)
    $($modalElement).find('.modal-body').find('img').attr('src', $src)
    $($modalElement).find('.modal-title').text($title)
    $($modal).modal('show')
}
```

First, as before, we create a jQuery wrapper of the element that triggers the event. Next, we use the `attr` method to find the value of the element's `src` attribute. We then use the `next` method to find the next `carousel-caption` element, and assign the inner text of that element to `$title`. We need these to dynamically update the blank modal.

Next, we grab the value of the `data-modal-picture` element, which we then use as a reference to find the modal we want to use to render our picture. We use the `find` method to first find the `modal-body` of this element, then the nested image element. We then create an `src` attribute on this element, passing in a reference to the source of the slide's image element. Similarly, we inject the caption of the slide into the modal's `title` element.

Finally, we use the modal API to show the modal. Take a look at the following screenshot:

Figure 6.6: Our modal showing an enlarged version of a slide image

The modal is now surfacing. The dynamic title is working well, too. The dynamic image is getting applied and loaded. Perfect, except that the entire thing looks terrible. But that's nothing a bit of CSS can't fix.

Extending carousel's style sheets

Thanks to our forward thinking, we already have the `carousel-modal` class applied to the modal parent element. We just need to set some rules.

As this modal is directly related to our carousel plugin extension, we will create a CSS file explicitly for handling styling born out of our extension. Create `styles/carousel.css` and include the file in our page:

```
<link rel="stylesheet" href="bower_components/components-font-
awesome/css/font-awesome.min.css" />
<link rel="stylesheet" href="styles/alert.css" />
<link rel="stylesheet" href="styles/carousel.css" />
```

There are two things wrong that we need to address. First, the modal is too narrow. We want it to be almost the full width of the page. Observe the following code:

```
.carousel-modal.modal-dialog {
    width: 95%;
}
```

Now, if an element has the `modal-dialog` class and its parent has the `carousel-modal` class, it will have have 95% of the available horizontal screen real estate. Take a look at the following screenshot:

Figure 6.7: Our modal showing an enlarged version of a slide image with applied changes

Now, we just need to make sure the image doesn't breech the borders of the modal. The fix here is simple. We will just give any `img` element that is a descendent of a `carousel-modal` element a width of `100%`, so that it will only take up the width explicitly available to it. Observe the following code:

```
.carousel-modal img {
    width: 100%;
}
```

Take a look at the following screenshot:

Figure 6.8: Our modal showing an enlarged version of a slide image, with the image fitting the modal

Much better. Our customization is complete. We have surfaced a modal on a `click` event from the carousel, passed data from the `carousel` component into the `modal` component, and rendered the image successfully. Very neat.

Now that we have successfully customized two of Bootstrap's jQuery plugins, let's build a plugin from scratch.

Writing a custom Bootstrap jQuery plugin

Following the patterns that we have seen in `alert.js` and `carousel.js`, we are going to build our own plugin. Of course, before we start coding, we need to understand what we want to build.

The idea – the A11yHCM plugin

The A11yHCM plugin, depending on your background and experience, may give you a clue about what we want to build. **A11y** is the accepted shorthand for **Accessibility**, or **Web Accessibility**. W3C defines web accessibility as follows:

> *"Web accessibility means that people with disabilities can use the web. More specifically, web accessibility means that people with disabilities can perceive, understand, navigate, and interact with the web, and that they can contribute to the web. Web accessibility also benefits others, including older people with changing abilities due to aging."*
>
> —`https://www.w3.org/WAI/intro/accessibility.php`

HCM is an acronym for an accessibility-related term: **High Contrast Mode**. HCM, in its simplest form, modifies the colors on a display to help visually impaired users view content.

However, different tools for enabling HCM may render differently, and some web pages may not actually improve the experience of a visually impaired user in HCM. Let's take a look at a couple of examples of `MyPhoto` in HCM, using two different tools.

First, we will use Mac OS X El Capitan's built-in high contrast options, **Invert colors** and **Increase contrast**:

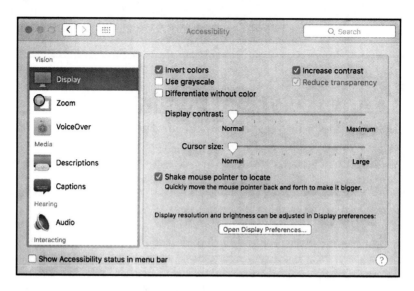

Figure 6.9: Mac OS X El Capitan's built-in Accessibility settings

With the **Invert colors** and **Increase contrast** settings enabled, MyPhoto is displayed quite differently:

Figure 6.10: Viewing MyPhoto with the Invert Colors and Increase Contrast Accessibility settings enabled on Mac OS X El Capitan, with the About navbar link in a focused state

Let's take a look at another tool—Google Accessibility's High Contrast Chrome plugin (`https://chrome.google.com/webstore/detail/high-contrast/djcfdncoelnlbldjfhinnj lhdjlikmph?hl=en`).

With the High Contrast Chrome plugin installed, a high contrast button is added to Google Chrome:

Figure 6.11: The High Contrast button in Chrome, which appears after installing Google Accessibility's High Contrast Chrome plugin

Let's see how `MyPhoto` displays with this High Contrast plugin enabled:

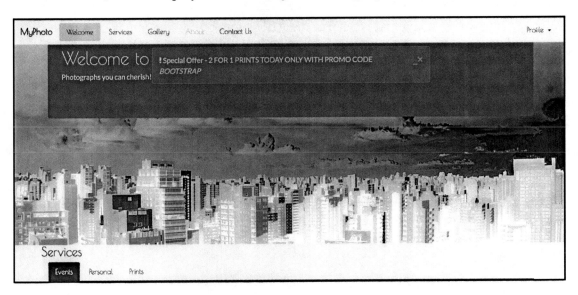

Figure 6.12: Viewing MyPhoto using Google's Accessibility High Contrast Chrome Plugin, with the 'About' navbar link in a focused state

The result of using the High Contrast Chrome plugin is similar to OS X's built-in high contrast options, but there are slight differences. For instance, the background color of our **Services** section and our special offers alert changes between the different tools.

At least one element of our page is clearly poor when displayed in HCM—the focused state of our navigation links. In HCM, the focused state of our navigation links, in this case the **Welcome** link, is practically illegible.

So what can we do here, without actually changing our default styles? The first thing that comes to mind is to simply check whether the display is in HCM and apply the appropriate styling, either through JavaScript or CSS. Unfortunately, high contrast may be applied in different ways by different tools, different browsers, different operating systems, and different devices. Programmatically, it may be very hard, or even impossible, to always recognize when your page is being displayed in HCM.

Time for plan B. Rather than figure out programmatically when a page is being viewed in high contrast, let's allow the user to simply tell us when they are viewing the page in HCM. Plan B is what our A11yHCM plugin is going to allow us to do.

The a11yHCM.js file

The first thing we are going to do is define the API. Before building a plugin, it is wise to figure out how you want developers to interact with it. By doing this, you will be able to understand exactly what you are trying to build before writing a single line of code.

The fundamental functionality of our plugin is to enable a style sheet to be dynamically loaded and removed from a page based on the occurrence of a specific event. So, we need two things:

- An event to trigger the JS
- The path to the style sheet that is to be loaded

We can use a `data-attribute` to act as the trigger, just as we did with the other plugins, and use it to pass the path of a CSS file. We want the `data-attribute` to be unique to our plugin, so we must use an appropriate `data-attribute` postfix. Let's try something like the following:

```
<div class="allyhcm" data-a11yhcm="path/to/css">High Contrast Mode
</div>
```

Nice and succinct. There isn't anything else we need right now, so we will get to writing our JavaScript. Our plugin's JavaScript code is going to live in `js/a11yhcm.js`. Let's set up our skeleton; just like we have seen before, we want it immediately invoked and added to our page's `jQuery` object. We want to create an on-click listener for any element with the `data-a11yhcm` attribute, but we need to declare which function it triggers. As we want this plugin to dynamically load and remove a style sheet, we will call our `function` toggle as it toggles HCM on and off. We also want to add a `VERSION` constant:

```
+function ($) {
    'use strict';
```

```
// A11YHCM CLASS DEFINITION
// ========================
var A11yHCM = function (element, options) {
$(element).on('click', '[data-a11yhcm]', this.toggle)
}
A11yHCM.VERSION = '1.0.0'
}(jQuery);
```

Next, we want to add the plugin definition. As explained earlier, the plugin definition creates an instance of the plugin for each DOM element with the a11yhcm class. Observe the following code:

```
// A11YHCM PLUGIN DEFINITION
// =========================
function Plugin(option) {
return this.each(function () {
    var $this = $(this)
    var data = $this.data('bs.a11yhcm')
    if (!data) $this.data('bs.a11yhcm', (data = new A11yHCM(this)))
    if (typeof option == 'string') data[option].call($this)
    })
}
var old = $.fn.a11yhcm
$.fn.a11yhcm = Plugin
$.fn.a11yhcm.Constructor = A11yHCM
```

We'd better not forget the noConflict function to help resolve namespace collisions.

```
// A11YHCM NO CONFLICT
// ===================
$.fn.a11yhcm.noConflict = function () {
    $.fn.a11yhcm = old
    return this
}
```

Now we're getting to the fun part. Before we get into coding the functionality, we must declare our API. We know we want to use the data-a11yhcm attribute as our trigger (and to pass data to our plugin), and to use the toggle function that we declared in the constructor. Observe the following code:

```
// A11YHCM DATA-API
// ================
$(document).on('click.bs.allyhcm.data-api', '[data-a11yhcm]',
A11yHCM.prototype.toggle)
```

We also want to make sure our plugin definition is called for all elements with the `data-a11yhcm` attributes. Add this to the `data` API:

```
$(window).on('load', function () {
    $('[data-a11yhcm]').each(function () {
        var $a11yhcm = $(this)
        Plugin.call($a11yhcm, $a11yhcm.data())
    })
})
```

Okay, now all we need to do is write the `toggle` function! Let's discuss our approach. The first thing we need to do is get the reference to the style sheet to be loaded from the `data-a11yhcm` attribute. Observe the following code:

```
A11yHCM.prototype.toggle = function (e) {
    var $this = $(this)
    var styleSheet = $this.attr('data-a11yhcm')
}
```

Easy. Then, we need to figure out the current state. Are we in HCM or not? We could separate the functionality into on and off functions, hiding and showing the options in the UI as appropriate, much like our alert expand and minimize customizations. But let's try to keep the API and DOM manipulation to a minimum. Instead, we can simply check to see whether the `link` tag with the high contrast style sheet is present in the DOM. To do that, we need a way of being able to select the `link` tag. We will do this by adding the `link` tag with a unique id—`bs-a11yhcm`. Let's update `toggle` with a check to see if the element exists. If it does, use jQuery to remove it; if it doesn't, we will use jQuery to append it to the head of the DOM:

```
if(document.getElementById('bs-a11yhcm'))
    $('#' + $this.styleSheetID).remove()
else {
    var styleSheetLink = '<link href="' + styleSheet + '"
rel="stylesheet" id="bs-a11yhcm"/>'
    $('head').append(styleSheetLink)
}
```

That is pretty much it! Let's do one more thing. What if, by some chance, there is already another element on the page, unrelated to A11yHCM, with the `id` value of `bs-a11yhcm`? Rather than forcing a developer to change their page to suit the plugin, we will do the right thing and allow the developer to pass in a custom value for the `id`. The `toggle` function will check to see if an `a11yhcm-id` attribute exists; if it does, A11yHCM will use that value as the `id` for the `link` tag. In that case, an element using A11yHCM could look like:

```
<div class="allyhcm" data-a11yhcm="path/to/css" a11yhcm-
```

```
    id="customId">High Contrast Mode</div>
```

Let's update the `toggle` function to reflect this. We will add the default value for the `id` as a property of A11yHCM:

```
var A11yHCM = function (element) {
    this.$element = $(element)
}
A11yHCM.VERSION = '1.0.0'
A11yHCM.DEFAULTS = {
    styleSheetID : 'bs-a11yhcm'
}
A11yHCM.prototype.toggle = function (e) {
    var $this = $(this)
    var styleSheet = $this.attr('data-a11yhcm')
if ($this.attr('a11yhcm-id'))
    $this.styleSheetID = $this.attr('a11yhcm-id')
  else
    $this.styleSheetID = A11yHCM.DEFAULTS.styleSheetID
  if (document.getElementById($this.styleSheetID))
    $('#' + $this.styleSheetID).remove()
else {
    var styleSheetLink = '<link href="' + styleSheet + '"
    rel="stylesheet" id="' + $this.styleSheetID + '"/>'
    $('head').append(styleSheetLink)
  }
}
```

Okay, that's it. That looks like all the JavaScript we're going to need to make A11yHCM work the way we envisaged. Now, let's put it into practice by adding the markup.

The markup

The first thing we have to do is make sure the JavaScript for the A11yHCM plugin is loaded. Include the JS file in the head of the page, after `bootstrap.min.js` and `jquery.min.js`. Observe the following code:

```
<script src="bower_components/jquery/dist/jquery.min.js">
</script>
<script src="bower_components/bootstrap/dist/js/bootstrap.min.js">
</script>
<script src="js/alert.js"></script>
<script src="js/carousel.js"></script>
<script src="js/a11yhcm.js"></script>
```

Let's add the new **High Contrast Mode** option to the **Profile** drop-down. We will also include a contrast icon from Font Awesome, and we want to load `styles/myphoto-hcm.css`:

```html
<li class="nav-item dropdown pull-xs-right">
    <a href="#" class="nav-link dropdown-toggle" data-toggle=
    "dropdown" role="button"
    aria-haspopup="true" aria-expanded="false">
    Profile <span class="caret"></span>
</a>
<div class="dropdown-menu dropdown-menu-right">
    <a class="dropdown-item" href="#" data-toggle="modal"
    data-target="#profile-modal">
        Profile
    </a>
    <a class="dropdown-item" href="#" data-toggle="modal"
    data-target="#settings-modal">
        Settings
    </a>
    <div class="dropdown-divider"></div>
    <a class="dropdown-item" href="#">
        Logout
    </a>
    <a class="dropdown-item a11yhcm" href="#" data-a11yhcm=
    "styles/myphoto-hcm.css">
        <i class="fa fa-adjust"></i> High Contrast Mode
    </a>
    </div>
</li>
```

Take a look at the following screenshot:

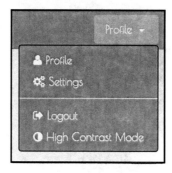

Figure 6.13: The new High Contrast Mode menu item

Great. Now, of course, when we click on **High Contrast Mode** we won't able to see any visual changes as we haven't actually created `styles/myphoto-hcm.css`. But if we inspect the DOM, we should be able to see the CSS file referenced in the head. Take a look at the following screenshot:

```
<script src="js/carousel.js"></script>
<script src="js/a11y-hcm.js"></script>
▶ <script type="text/javascript">…</script>
<link href="styles/myphoto-hcm.css" rel="stylesheet" id="bs-a11yhcm">
</head>
```

Figure 6.14: The High Contrast Mode style sheet dynamically added by the High Contrast Mode button

Click the **High Contrast Mode** button again, and the `link` element should be removed. Take a look at the following screenshot:

```
<script src="js/alert.js"></script>
<script src="js/carousel.js"></script>
<script src="js/a11y-hcm.js"></script>
▶ <script type="text/javascript">…</script>
</head>
```

Figure 6.15: The High Contrast Mode style sheet dynamically removed by the High Contrast Mode butto

Great. Our plugin is working. Let's pass in a non-default value to be used as the id for the `link` element, to make sure that is also working as expected.

```
<a href="#" class="a11yhcm" data-a11yhcm="styles/myphoto-hcm.css"
a11yhcm-id="myphoto-hcm">
```

Take a look at the following screenshot:

```
<script src="js/alert.js"></script>
<script src="js/carousel.js"></script>
<script src="js/a11y-hcm.js"></script>
▶ <script type="text/javascript">…</script>
<link href="styles/myphoto-hcm.css" rel="stylesheet" id="myphoto-hcm">
</head>
```

Figure 6.16: The High Contrast Mode style sheet dynamically added by the High Contrast Mode button, with a custom id attribute

Perfect. All functionality is working just like we wanted. Now, let's get to the CSS!

Adding some style

First, we're going to write the style sheet for A11yHCM, and, for good measure, we are going to write `myphoto-hcm.css`, to make our navigation more useful in **High Contrast Mode**.

Create a `styles/a11yhcm.css` file and include it in the `head` of our page:

```
<link rel="stylesheet" href="bower_components/components-font-
awesome/css/font-awesome.min.css" />
<link rel="stylesheet" href="styles/alert.css" />
<link rel="stylesheet" href="styles/carousel.css" />
<link rel="stylesheet" href="styles/a11yhcm.css" />
```

All we are going to do here is toggle the `a11yHCM` element to indicate whether it is `disabled` or `enabled`. We're simply going to add a checkmark when it is `enabled`. We will need a little bit of JavaScript too, to add and remove the `enabled` class to our element. First, let's write the CSS:

```
.a11yhcm.enabled::after {
  content: '√'
}
```

This rule simply appends a checkmark to the end of any content within an element with both the `a11yhcm` and `enabled` class applied, using the `after` pseudo-class. Let's update `a11yHCM.js` to add and remove the `enabled` class:

```
if (document.getElementById($this.styleSheetID)) {
    $('#' + $this.styleSheetID).remove()
    $this.removeClass('enabled')
}
else {
    var styleSheetLink = '<link href="' + styleSheet + '"
    rel="stylesheet" id="' + $this.styleSheetID + '"/>'
    $('head').append(styleSheetLink)
    $this.addClass('enabled')
}
```

Let's check it out. Click on the **High Contrast Mode** button:

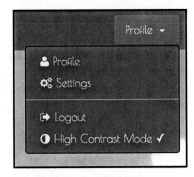

Figure 6.17: The checkmark is applied to the menu item to indicate when High Contrast Mode is enabled

Great. We now have a visual indicator for when **High Contrast Mode** is enabled. The checkmark might not be suitable for every design, but the rules can always be extended!

Now, let's get to fixing our navigation.

Create `styles/myphoto-hcm.css` and copy over the classes related to the hover, focus, and active states of the navigation from `myphoto.css`:

```css
.navbar-myphoto .navbar-nav > li > a:hover {
    background-color: #504747;
    color: gray;
}
.navbar-myphoto .navbar-nav > li > a:focus {
    background-color: #504747;
    color: gray;
}
.navbar-myphoto .navbar-nav > li.active > a {
    background-color: #504747;
    color: gray;
}
.navbar-myphoto .dropdown-menu > a {
    color: white;
    background-color: #504747;
}
.navbar-myphoto .dropdown-menu > a:hover {
    color: gray;
    background-color: #504747;
}
.navbar-myphoto .dropdown-menu > a:focus {
    color: gray;
    background-color: #504747;
}
```

```
.navbar-myphoto .dropdown-menu > .active > a:focus {
    color: gray;
    background-color: #504747;
}
```

We want these states to be very clear in **High Contrast Mode**. For full effect, we will use the color blue. But hang on, before you go changing all the `color` properties to blue. The high contrast tools we're using are inverting the colors, so we need the inverse of blue, that is, yellow. Observe the following code:

```
.navbar-myphoto .navbar-nav > li > a:hover {
    background-color: #504747;
    color: yellow;
}
.navbar-myphoto .navbar-nav > li > a:focus {
    background-color: #504747;
    color: yellow;
}
.navbar-myphoto .navbar-nav > li.active > a {
    background-color: #504747;
    color: yellow;
}
.navbar-myphoto .dropdown-menu > li > a:hover {
    background-color: #504747;
    color: yellow;
}
.navbar-myphoto .dropdown-menu > li > a:focus {
    background-color: #504747;
    color: yellow;
}
.navbar-myphoto .dropdown-menu > li > .active > a:focus {
    background-color: #504747;
    color: yellow;
}
```

Enable high contrast on your browser or OS, then click **High Contrast Mode** on the MyPhoto page to see the results. Take a look at the following screenshot:

Figure 6.18: Viewing MyPhoto using Google's Accessibility High Contrast Chrome Plugin, with the 'About' navbar link in a focused state and with MyPhoto's High Contrast Mode enabled

The UI is now much clearer, and all thanks to our custom-built A11yHCM jQuery plugin. There is a lot more to do to make this page fully accessible, but it's a start.

Summary

In this chapter, we have discovered quite a bit about Bootstrap's jQuery plugins but, most importantly, we put what we learned into practice. We now have an understanding of the structure of a plugin, from its JavaScript to its CSS and HTML.

Using what we learned, we extended the alert plugin, adding the ability to minimize and expand it together with a simple API. We then leveraged the modal plugin to extend the carousel plugin to surface larger versions of carousel images. Again, we achieved this through a simple API .

We put everything that we learned from building the alert and carousel plugin together to build our very own custom plugin, A11yHCM. A11yHCM dynamically loads CSS at the user's command. Putting this use case in the context of a visually impaired user, we were able to understand how useful a plugin like this might be.

In the following chapter, we will discover how to integrate some popular third-party plugins and libraries into Bootstrap to enhance the overall user experience of MyPhoto.

7
Integrating Bootstrap with Third-Party Plugins

In this chapter, we are going to discover how to integrate some popular plugins and libraries into Bootstrap to enhance the user experience of MyPhoto.

We will identify new features or improvements we want to make to MyPhoto, introduce libraries to help us achieve those goals, and figure out how these can be gracefully integrated within our existing architecture.

This chapter will focus on the integration of three popular plugins and libraries, namely, Salvattore, Animate.css, and Hover. These libraries will allow us to improve the overall user experience of MyPhoto, creating a much more polished look and feel.

To summarize, this chapter will help us:

- Learn how to leverage Salvattore to add more flexibility to Bootstrap's grid system
- Learn how to leverage Animate.css to easily add CSS3 animations to a Bootstrap page
- Learn how to leverage Hover to easily add hover effects to a Bootstrap page

Building a testimonial component with Salvattore

`MyPhoto` does a good job of boasting about the services on offer and the quality of those services. However, a user may want to read some feedback from the previous customers. To do this, we're going to add a `testimonials` component to our page as a new tab in the `services` component. The **Testimonials** tab will display some positive feedback from the users. Let's add that new tab to our list of tabs:

```
<li class="nav-item">
    <a href="#services-testimonials" class="nav-link"
    data-toggle="tab">Testimonials</a>
</li>
```

Next, we want to add some content. Let's use Bootstrap's grid system to display the testimonials in four neat rows of three columns. Add the following code below the `services-prints` markup:

```
<div role="tabpanel" class="tab-pane" id="services-testimonials">
    <div class="container">
        <div class="row myphoto-testimonial-row">
            <div class="col-xs-3 myphoto-testimonial-column">
                <h6>Debbie</h6>
                <p>Great service! Would recommend to friends!</p>
            </div>
            <div class="col-xs-3 myphoto-testimonial-column">
                <h6>Joey</h6>
                <p>5 stars! Thanks for the great photos!</p>
            </div>
            <div class="col-xs-3 myphoto-testimonial-column">
                <h6>Jack & Jill</h6>
                <p>So happy with how the photos turned out!
                Thanks for capturing the memories of our day!</p>
            </div>
            <div class="col-xs-3 myphoto-testimonial-column">
                <h6>Tony</h6>
                <p>Captured our Cup final win! Great stuff!</p>
            </div>
        </div>
        <div class="row myphoto-testimonial-row">
            <div class="col-xs-3 myphoto-testimonial-column">
                <h6>Anne</h6>
                <p>Really high quality prints!</p>
            </div>
            <div class="col-xs-3 myphoto-testimonial-column">
```

```
            <h6>Mary</h6>
            <p>Made a stressful event much easier!
            Absolute professionals!</p>
        </div>
    </div>
    <div class="row myphoto-testimonial-row">
        <div class="col-xs-3 myphoto-testimonial-column">
            <h6>Oscar</h6>
            <p>Declared their greatness, exhibited greatness.</p>
        </div>
        <div class="col-xs-3 myphoto-testimonial-column">
            <h6>Alice</h6>
            <p>Wonderful! Exactly as I imagined they would
            turn out!
            </p>
        </div>
        <div class="col-xs-3 myphoto-testimonial-column">
            <h6>Nick</h6>
            <p>Perfectly captured the mood of our gig.
            Top notch.</p>
        </div>
    </div>
</div>
</div>
```

We have added three rows with varying amounts of columns. Each column includes the name of a user and the associated testimonial. As we want a maximum of four columns in a row, we have given each column the `col-xs-3` class so that the column takes up three of the 12 columns in the Bootstrap grid system. We have also given each column an additional `myphoto-testimonial-column` class for specific styling, and each row a `myphoto-testimonial-row` class. Add the following rules to `myphoto.css`:

```css
.myphoto-testimonial-row {
    margin-right : 5px;
}
.myphoto-testimonial-column
{
    border: 1px solid black; background-color: #FFFFFF;
    padding: 10px;
    margin: 5px;
    max-width: 23%;
}
```

We have given some extra spacing to our testimonials. To make up for the extra spacing, we set a `max-width` property of `23%` as opposed to the `25%` declared by `col-xs-3`, and overrode the default `margin-right` property of the `row` class of `-15px` to `5px`. We also included a `black` border and solid white background. Let's check out our results:

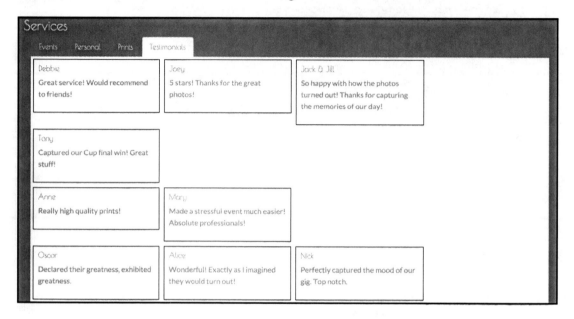

Figure 7.1: A Testimonials tab is created using Bootstrap's grid system

Okay, cool. We have our **Testimonials** tab and our positive testimonies from users. However, it looks kind of ugly. The contents of the columns are of varying lengths, which makes the spacing visually awkward. Take the distance between Joey's testimony on the first row and Mary's on the second. Wouldn't it be nice if we could decrease this distance? From column to column across individual rows, the spacing is uniform and looks good. Wouldn't it be nice if we could achieve this uniformity vertically, too? Unfortunately, Bootstrap's grid system is not flexible enough to make the vertical spacing uniform while allowing for varying heights of columns. However, we can achieve this with a popular library called Salvattore.

Introducing Salvattore

Salvattore (`http://salvattore.com/`) is a JavaScript library that allows for more flexible grid system definitions. For instance, with the help of Salvattore, we can define grid system rules that will allow three rows of four columns, but the position of each column is relative to the height of the corresponding column in the preceding row. Salvattore is a pure JavaScript library, meaning that it doesn't depend on any other library (such as jQuery) to work.

Let's add Salvattore to our project. Download Salvattore using Bower:

```
bower install salvattore
```

Then, make sure to include it in our markup, at the bottom of the page. Including the JavaScript file at the bottom of our page is the suggested practice by Salvattore as it needs the DOM to be loaded before it takes effect:

```
<footer class="footer text-center">
    <p class="text-muted">
        <small>&copy; MyPhoto Inc.</small>
    </p>
    <p class="text-muted text-center">
        <a href="#">
            <small>Terms &amp; Conditions</small>
        </a>
    </p>
    <p class="text-muted">
        <a href="#">
            <small>About Us</small>
        </a>
    </p>
</footer>
<script src="bower_components/salvattore/dist/
salvattore.min.js"></script>
```

Next, we need to rewrite our `testimonials` grid to work with Salvattore. One big difference between how we constructed the grid initially and how we need to construct it for Salvattore, is that we won't be grouping the testimonials by row; Salvattore will do the grouping for us.

Currently, we have the following:

```
<div class="row myphoto-testimonial-row">
    <div class="col-xs-3 myphoto-testimonial-column">
        <h6>Anne</h6>
        <p>Really high quality prints!</p>
```

```
        </div>
        <div class="col-xs-3 myphoto-testimonial-column">
            <h6>Mary</h6>
            <p>Made a stressful event much easier! Absolute
            professionals!</p>
        </div>
    </div>
</div>
```

Here, we are creating a row, and then constructing the columns within that row. That is not how Salvattore works. Let's rewrite our grid. This time, we will simply be listing the testimonials:

```
<div role="tabpanel" class="tab-pane" id="services-testimonials">
    <div class="container">
        <div class="myphoto-testimonial-grid" data-columns>
            <div>
                <h6>Debbie</h6>
                <p>Great service! Would recommend to friends!</p>
            </div>
            <div>
                <h6>Anne</h6>
                <p>Really high quality prints!</p>
            </div>
            <div>
                <h6>Oscar</h6>
                <p>Declared their greatness, exhibited greatness.</p>
            </div>
            <div>
                <h6>Joey</h6>
                <p>5 stars! Thanks for the great photos!</p>
            </div>
            <div>
                <h6>Mary</h6>
                <p>Made a stressful event much easier! Absolute
                professionals!</p>
            </div>
            <div>
                <h6>Alice</h6>
                <p>Wonderful! Exactly as I imagined they would
                turn out!</p>
            </div>
            <div>
                <h6>Jack & Jill</h6>
                <p>So happy with how the photos turned out! Thanks for
                capturing the memories of our day!</p>
            </div>
            <div>
                <h6>Nick</h6>
```

```
                    <p>Perfectly captured the mood of our gig.
                    Top notch.</p>
            </div>
            <div>
                    <h6>Tony</h6>
                    <p>Captured our Cup final win! Great stuff!</p>
            </div>
        </div>
    </div>
</div>
```

Okay, so that's quite a change. Let's talk through the important pieces. As mentioned earlier, we are now simply listing testimonials rather than grouping them by row. We no longer have our `row` wrapper elements. We have added a parent `div` wrapper around all the testimonials, with the `myphoto-testimonial-grid` class. As we are no longer referencing Bootstrap's grid system, each column entry no longer has the `col-xs-3` class and we have also removed the `myphoto-testimonial-column` classes. The final thing we need to do with the markup is add a `data-columns` attribute to the parent `grid` element. Observe the following code snippet:

```
<div id="myphoto-testimonial-grid" data-columns>
```

The `data-columns` attribute is the hook Salvattore needs to know which elements to act upon. All we need to do now is add some CSS.

Open up `myphoto.css` and add the following:

```
.myphoto-testimonials-grid[data-columns]::before {
    content: '4 .column.size-1of4';
}
.column {
    float: left;
}
.size-1of4 {
    width: 25%;
}
```

So, what's happening here? First, we are using the `before` pseudo-selector to define how many columns we want and the classes we want applied. In this case, we want four columns and to apply the `column` class and the `size-1of4` class. The `column` class makes sure any column elements are rendered as close to the left of the element's `container` element as possible, and any elements with the `size-1of4` class are to only take up a quarter of the available space. If we planned on only having three columns, then we could define and apply a `size-1of3` class with a rule to only take up `33.333%` of the available space, and so on. Salvattore will split the testimonials into four groups, as evenly as possible, and apply the classes defined by `.myphoto-testimonials-grid[data-columns]::before` to the column groups. For instance, in our example, the first group of columns has the following markup:

```
<div class="myphoto-testimonial-grid" data-columns="4">
    <div class="column size-1of4">
        <h6>Debbie</h6>
        <p>Great service! Would recommend to friends!</p>
    </div>
    ...
    <div>
        <h6>Mary</h6>
        <p>Made a stressful event much easier! Absolute
        professionals!</p>
    </div>
    <div>
        <h6>Tony</h6>
        <p>Captured our Cup final win! Great stuff!</p>
    </div>
</div>
...
```

Let's see how this renders:

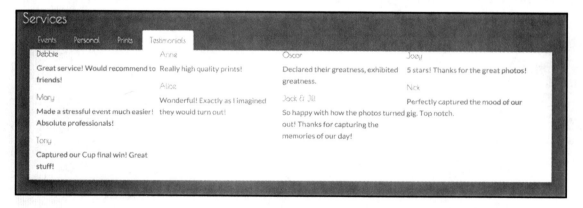

Figure 7.2: The unstyled testimonials, created using Salvattore

Great! Now all we need to do is add some styling!

The first thing that we want to do is create some space between the top and the content. As you can see, the top of the panel is very close to the list tab. We have a parent class for our `grid`, `myphoto-testimonial-grid`, that we can leverage. Add the following style rules:

```
.myphoto-testimonial-grid {
    padding-top : 30px ;
}
```

Take a look at the following screenshot:

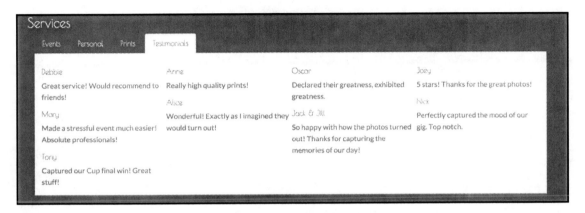

Figure 7.3: The unstyled testimonials, created using Salvattore with a top padding of 30px

Next up, we want to make the testimonials distinguishable. For this, we'll leverage the `myphoto-testimonial-column`. Remove any previous rules for this class and add the following:

```
.myphoto-testimonial-column {
    padding: 10px;
    border: 1px solid #000000;
    margin: 5px;
}
```

We have simply created a border around the element, added an internal spacing of `10px` between the element contents and its border, and lastly, we have created a margin of `5px` between each of the elements. Add the `myphoto-testimonial-column` class to each of our `testimonial` elements:

```
<div class="myphoto-testimonial-grid" data-columns>
    <div class="myphoto-testimonial-column">
        <h6>Debbie</h6>
        <p>Great service! Would recommend to friends!</p>
    </div>
```

```
<div class="myphoto-testimonial-column">
    <h6>Anne</h6>
    <p>Really high quality prints!</p>
</div>
<div class="myphoto-testimonial-column">
    <h6>Oscar</h6>
    <p>Declared their greatness, exhibited greatness.</p>
</div>
<div class="myphoto-testimonial-column">
    <h6>Joey</h6>
    <p>5 stars! Thanks for the great photos!</p>
</div>
<div class="myphoto-testimonial-column">
    <h6>Mary</h6>
    <p>Made a stressful event much easier! Absolute
    professionals!</p>
</div>
<div class="myphoto-testimonial-column">
    <h6>Alice</h6>
    <p>Wonderful! Exactly as I imagined they would
    turn out!</p>
</div>
<div class="myphoto-testimonial-column">
    <h6>Jack & Jill</h6>
    <p>So happy with how the photos turned out! Thanks
    for capturing the memories of our day!</p>
</div>
<div class="myphoto-testimonial-column">
    <h6>Nick</h6>
    <p>Perfectly captured the mood of our gig. Top notch.</p>
</div>
<div class="myphoto-testimonial-column">
    <h6>Tony</h6>
    <p>Captured our Cup final win! Great stuff!</p>
</div>
</div>
```

That's a little better. Now we can at least differentiate each of the testimonials from one another (see *Figure 7.4*). Compare this with the testimonial component we built using just Bootstrap's grid system; the visual improvements are obvious. We have a much more natural, flowing visual now, compared to the clunky, almost awkward, original visual.

Now, let's see how we can leverage Bootstrap's grid system to ease the use of Salvattore.

Take a look at the following screenshot:

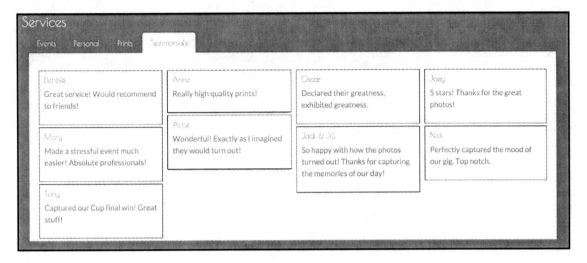

Figure 7.4: The testimonials arranged using Salvatorre and with some custom styling

Integrating Salvattore with Bootstrap

In our example, we created two new classes to lay out our Salvattore grid, namely, `column`, which just applies `float: left`, and `size-1of4`, which just sets a width of `25%` on the element. Doesn't Bootstrap already provide these classes? Of course it does.

In fact, our `col-**-**` classes all have the `float: left` property, and they all manage the width of our column. Let's use these classes instead!

First, we need to figure out which `col-**-**` class we want to use. We always want four horizontal columns with a width of 25%. Bootstrap's grid system is split into 12, so we want each of our columns to take up three column spaces; `col-xs-3` fulfils those requirements. Let's rewrite the `.myphoto-testimonial-grid[data-columns]`:

```
.myphoto-testimonial-grid[data-columns]::before {
    content: '4 .col-xs-3';
}
```

We have replaced the classes to be applied to the `column` groups with Bootstrap's `col-xs-3` class. Let's take a look at the results (see *Figure 7.5*):

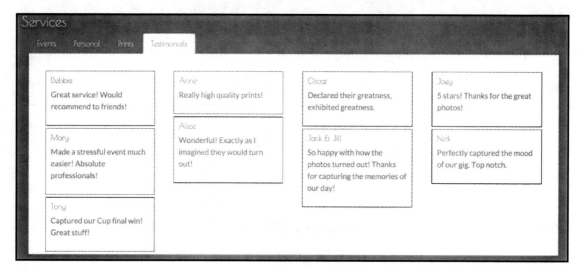

Figure 7.5: Using Bootstrap's col-**-** class to render the testimonials grid (note the additional padding)

Our `col-xs-3` class has added some extra padding that we don't really want in this scenario. Let's create a new class, `myphoto-testimonial-group`, to override the padding:

```
.myphoto-testimonial-group {
    padding: 0px;
}
```

We also need to make sure that the following class is applied to the `columns` groups:

```
.myphoto-testimonial-grid[data-columns]::before {
    content: '4 .col-xs-3.myphoto-testimonial-group';
}
```

Take a look at the following screenshot:

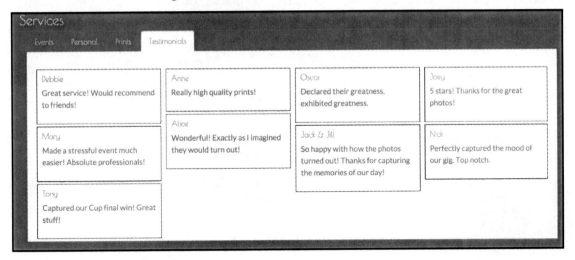

Figure 7.6: Using Bootstrap's col-**-** class together with the myphoto-testimonial-grid class to render the testimonials grid (note the reduced padding)

The content property

The content property is used to add content to a given element. For example, the rule `span::before {content: 'Hello World'; }` will insert the text "`Hello World`" before the content within any `span` element on the page. Similarly, the rule `span::before {content: 'Hello World'; }` inserts the text "`Hello World`" after the content within any `span` element on the page. It is important to note that the `content` property can only be used in conjunction with either the `after` or `before` selector.

Great! Our Salvattore grid is now powered by Bootstrap's grid system! This is quite important, as we now know how to use the flexibility and simplicity of Salvattore's grid system without having to worry about all the nitty-gritty work Bootstrap solves with its own grid system.

Let's animate. Animate.css (`https://daneden.github.io/animate.css/`) is a cross-browser, pure CSS library that provides a huge number of easy-to-use classes to add animations to a page. That is, the library has zero dependencies and can be layered upon any web page.

Adding Animate.css to MyPhoto

As it's a pure CSS library, integrating Animate.css with MyPhoto is exceedingly simple. First, use Bower to download Animate.css:

```
bower install animate.css
```

Next, include the library in the head of MyPhoto, after the other CSS includes:.

```
<link rel="stylesheet"
href="bower_components/bootstrap/dist/css/bootstrap.min.css" />
<link rel="stylesheet" href="styles/myphoto.css" />
...
<link rel="stylesheet"
href="bower_components/DataTables/media/css/dataTables.
bootstrap.min.css" />
<link rel="stylesheet"
href="bower_components/animate.css/animate.min.css" />
```

To make sure we are set up correctly, let's add an animation to the body of our web page. To use any of the classes provided by Animate.css, we must include the animated class on the element:

```
<body data-spy="scroll" data-target=".navbar" class="animated">
```

If we take a look at `animate.min.css`, we will see that all selectors depend on the `animated` class to be defined and the `animated` class itself provides the base animation rules:

```
.animated {
    -webkit-animation-duration: 1s;
    animation-duration: 1s;
    -webkit-animation-fill-mode: both;
    animation-fill-mode: both
}
.animated.hinge {
    -webkit-animation-duration:2s;
    animation-duration:2s
}
```

To apply the animation itself is just as simple. Add the desired class to the element. To make MyPhoto fade in, we just need to apply the `fadeIn` class to the `body` element:

```
<body data-spy="scroll" data-target=".navbar" class="animated
fadeIn">
```

If you fire up the page, you should see the page slowly fade in as it renders. If you do not see this animation, make sure you have the correct path to `animate.min.css` in the head.

Now that we have Animate.css added to our project and working, let's add some emphasis to some of the core elements in our site.

Bouncing alerts

`MyPhoto` has a special offers alert in a prominent position on the page. However, it may still not grab the attention of the user initially. We need to focus the attention of the user immediately on the alert and add some emphasis. We need to tell the user that this is something they should read.

Animate.css has a range of `bounce` classes which are great for grabbing the attention of a user. We have a selection of 11 bounce classes here: `bounce`, `bounceIn`, `bounceInDown`, `bounceInLeft`, `bounceInRight`, `bounceInUp`, `bounceOut`, `bounceOutDown`, `bounceOutLeft`, `bounceOutRight`, and `bounceOutUp`.

We're going to go with the `bounceIn` class, which gives a throbber-like behavior. To get the `bounceIn` effect, add the `animated` and `bounceIn` classes to the special offers alert element:

```
<div class="alert alert-info alert-position animated bounceIn">
    <a href="#" class="close" data-dismiss="alert" aria-label=
    "close">&times;</a>
    <a href="#" class="close minimize" data-minimize="alert"
    aria-label="minimize">_</a>
    <a href="#" class="close expand hide" data-expand="alert"
    aria-label="expand">+</a>
    <strong>
        <i class="fa fa-exclamation"></i> Special Offer -
    </strong>
    <span>2 FOR 1 PRINTS TODAY ONLY WITH PROMO CODE
        <span style="font-style: italic">BOOTSTRAP</span>
    </span>
</div>
```

The alert should now be animated. Animate.css also provides an infinite animation option, where the animation will be infinitely repeated. To use this option, simply add the `infinite` class to the element:

```
<div class="alert alert-info alert-position animated bounceIn
    infinite">
```

Now, the `bounceIn` effect will be infinitely repeated. However, it does not look great as the element actually transitions from hidden to visible during the animation, so this transition is also looped. This is a great example of how the `infinite` class does not play well with all animations. A more infinite-friendly animation is `pulse`, which offers a similar effect. Replace the `bounceIn` class with the `pulse` class:

```
<div class="alert alert-info alert-position animated pulse infinite">
```

Great, the special offers alert now animates infinitely, with a gentle pulse to gain the attention of the user. However, if we want this applied to all alerts, then we need to apply it to all alerts individually. In this scenario, if there is a design change and, for instance, we want to change the animation, we would again have to change them all individually. Let's manage it centrally, instead, by extending the Alert jQuery plugin by adding further customizations to the `js/alert.js` file we created in Chapter 6, *Customizing Your Plugins*.

So, what do we want to do? On page load, we want to add `animate.css` classes to our `alert` elements. First, let's add our `on load` listener to our IIFE. Add this directly after `$(document).on('click.bs.alert.data-api', '[data-expand="alert"]', Alert.prototype.expand)`:

```
$(window).on('load', function () {
})
```

Next, we need a hook for our plugin. Let's use a `data-*` attribute, as is the general practice with Bootstrap jQuery plugins. We will call it `data-alert-animate`. Any element to which we want these classes applied will already have the `data-alert-animate` attribute. Our plugin will loop through each of these elements, applying the relevant classes:.

```
$(window).on('load', function() {
    $('[data-alert-animate]').each(function() {
    })
})
```

In our markup, let's update the special offers alert element to remove the `animate.css` classes and add the `data-alert-animate` attribute:

```
<div class="alert alert-info alert-position" data-alert-animate>
```

We want to add three classes to the `data-alert-animate` elements: `animated`, `pulse`, and `infinite`. Let's update the plugin to apply these classes to each `data-alert-animate` element:

```
$(window).on('load', function() {
    $('[data-alert-animate]').each(function() {
        $(this).addClass('animated pulse infinite')
```

```
        })
    })
```

Now, the markup will be dynamically transformed on page load, adding the `animated`, `pulse` and `infinite` classes:

```
▼ <div class="alert alert-info alert-position animated pulse infinite" data-alert-animate>
    <a href="#" class="close" data-dismiss="alert" aria-label="close">×</a>
    <a href="#" class="close minimize" data-minimize="alert" aria-label="minimize">_</a>
    <a href="#" class="close expand hide" data-expand="alert" aria-label="expand">+</a>
  ▶ <strong>...</strong>
  ▶ <span>...</span>
  </div>
```

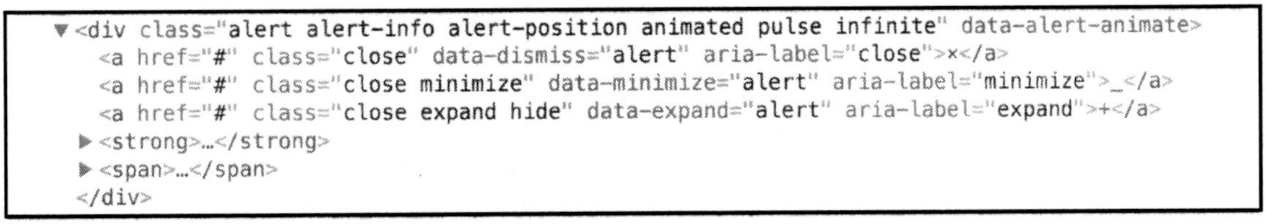

Figure 7.7: By examining the page source inside our browser, we can see the dynamically transformed markup: Our alert now has the animated, pulse, and infinite classes applied to it

Great, but it isn't exactly extensible. Our plugin does not allow for these classes to be overridden via the `data-alert-animate` attribute. Let's fix this by defining a default animation, using `pulse infinite`, but allowing a developer to override the animation via the `data-alert-animate` attribute. Update the `on load` function as follows:

```
$(window).on('load', function() {
    $('[data-alert-animate]').each(function() {
        var defaultAnimations = 'animated pulse infinite'
        var $animations = $(this).attr('data-alert-animate')
        if ($animations) {
            $(this).addClass('animated ' + $animations)
        } else {
            $(this).addClass(defaultAnimations)
        }
    })
})
```

Now, we are defining a `defaultAnimations` variable from `animated`, `pulse` and `infinite`. We then check if the `data-alert-animate` attribute has any value; if it has, add the classes referenced plus the `animated` class. If not, simply apply the classes defined in `defaultAnimations`.

Loading `MyPhoto` as-is, we should still see the `animated`, `pulse`, and `infinite` classes applied. However, the alert looks a little awkward, as it renders in a static state before the animation takes effect. To make the behavior of the alert more natural, let's make it invisible until `Alert.js` adds the animation classes. Add a new class, `hide-before-animated`, to `myphoto.css`:

```
.hide-before-animated {
    visibility: hidden;
}
.hide-before-animated.animated {
    visibility: visible;
}
```

The `hide-before-animated` class simply sets the `visibility` of the element to `hidden`, unless the `animated` class is also present on the element, in which case `visibility` is set to `visible`. As the `data-alert-animate` attribute adds the `animated` class to an element, the element will be invisible until the element is ready. Add the `hide-before-animated` class to the `class` attribute of the special offers alert element and reload the page to see the results:

```
<div class="alert alert-info alert-position hide-before-
animated" data-alert-animate>
```

Let's update our special offers alert element to override the `pulse` and `infinite` values with just the `bounceIn` class:

```
<div class="alert alert-info alert-position" data-alert-
animate="bounceIn">
```

Now, we should see just the `animated` and `bounceIn` classes applied to the element:

```
▼ <div class="alert alert-info alert-position animated bounceIn" data-alert-animate="bounceIn">
    <a href="#" class="close" data-dismiss="alert" aria-label="close">×</a>
    <a href="#" class="close minimize" data-minimize="alert" aria-label="minimize">_</a>
    <a href="#" class="close expand hide" data-expand="alert" aria-label="expand">+</a>
  ▶ <strong>…</strong>
  ▶ <span>…</span>
  </div>
```

Figure 7.8: By examining the page source inside our browser, we can see how only the animated and bounceIn classes have now been applied to our alert

Perfect. Now, via a neat little `data-attribute`, we can initiate a default animation for our alerts, and override that animation if need be.

Another nice use of these animations is to add a natural feel to the rendering of elements that may initially be hidden. Let's apply this idea to the **Testimonials** tab we created earlier in this chapter.

Animating a Salvattore grid

The `testimonials` component is a very simple grid built with Salvattore. While it is a neat grid, we want to make it a little flashier. Let's simply add an animation from Animate.css, the `fadeIn` class, so that, when the **Testimonial** tab is open, the grid appears to fade into view:

```
<div class="myphoto-testimonial-grid animated fadeIn" data-columns>
```

When a user clicks on the **Testimonials** tab, the tab panel will open and then the grid will fade into view.

We can go a bit further and actually apply an animation to the `column` groups, to induce optimal motion sickness. In `myphoto.css`, we already leverage the `data-columns` attribute to allow Salvattore to create the column groups for the grid and apply the appropriate style:

```
.myphoto-testimonial-grid[data-columns]::before {
    content: '4 .col-xs-3.myphoto-testimonial-group';
}
```

We can make the columns bounce into view by simply extending this rule to include the `animated` and `bounceIn` classes:

```
.myphoto-testimonial-grid[data-columns]::before {
    content: '4 .col-xs-3.myphoto-testimonial-
    group.animated.bounceIn';
}
```

Now, when the tab is opened, the whole grid fades in while the column groups also have a bounce effect. A little crass, but effective. The resulting markup for the component should look like the following:

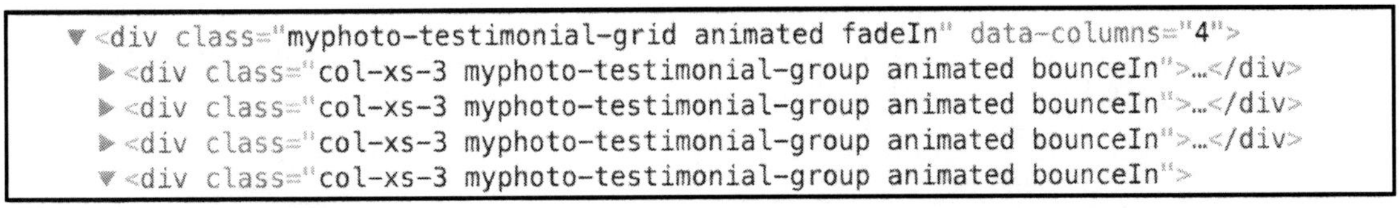

```
▼<div class="myphoto-testimonial-grid animated fadeIn" data-columns="4">
  ▶<div class="col-xs-3 myphoto-testimonial-group animated bounceIn">…</div>
  ▶<div class="col-xs-3 myphoto-testimonial-group animated bounceIn">…</div>
  ▶<div class="col-xs-3 myphoto-testimonial-group animated bounceIn">…</div>
  ▼<div class="col-xs-3 myphoto-testimonial-group animated bounceIn">
```

Figure 7.9: By examining the page source inside our browser, we can see that the testimonial grid now has bounce and fade effects applied to it

As far as Animate.css goes, that is all there is. A nice, simple, and elegant library for providing nice, simple, and elegant animations. For a full list of effects, take a look at the Animate demo website at `https://daneden.github.io/animate.css/`.

Next, we are going to take a look at a complementary library, Hover.

Hover

Hover, `http://ianlunn.github.io/Hover/`, is a neat, pure CSS library that provides transition effects. Adhering to the *"Do one thing, do one thing well"* approach, Hover only concerns itself with hover transitions, as you may have guessed from the name. Hover comes baked in with a huge array of transitions and provides easy integration with CSS, Less, and Sass.

Hover breaks these transitions into seven distinct groups:

- 2D transitons
- Background transitions
- Icons, by leveraging Font Awesome icons
- Border transitons
- Shadow and glow transitions, simulating 3D transitions
- Speech bubbles
- Curls

Throughout this section, we will touch on a number of these different groups. An extensive list of the transitions is available on the Hover website. Before we get to that, let's add Hover to MyPhoto.

Adding Hover to MyPhoto

Add Hover to `MyPhoto` via Bower:

```
bower install Hover
```

Within the `bower_components` directory, there should now be a `Hover` directory. We will reference the minified CSS straight into our markup. Add the following `link` tag in the head of the `MyPhoto` HTML, below the existing CSS references:

```
<link rel="stylesheet" href="bower_components/Hover/css/
hover-min.css" />
```

Let's add a Hover transition to make sure everything is in working order.

Making the navbar grow

As a quick test to make sure we have completed setting up of Hover correctly, let's apply some Hover transitions to the `MyPhoto` navbar.

Using Hover transitions is even simpler than Animate.css. We simply add one class to the element, and voila, a Hover transition is applied. As you will notice, all Hover classes are prefixed with `hvr-` to help avoid conflicts with other style sheets on the page.

We're going to spice up our `nav-link` links with one of the border transitions from Hover: `hvr-underline-from-center`. The `hvr-underline-from-center` class renders an underline on a given element, which grows from the center of the element. Let's add this to our five `nav-link` links:

```
<ul class="nav nav-pills">
    <li class="nav-item"><a class="nav-link hvr-underline-from-
    center" href="#welcome">Welcome</a></li>
    <li class="nav-item"><a class="nav-link hvr-underline-from-
    center" href="#services">Services</a></li>
    <li class="nav-item"><a class="nav-link hvr-underline-from-
    center" href="#gallery">Gallery</a></li>
    <li class="nav-item"><a class="nav-link hvr-underline-from-
    center" href="#about">About</a></li>
    <li class="nav-item"><a class="nav-link hvr-underline-from-
    center" href="#contact">Contact Us</a></li>
    <li class="nav-item dropdown pull-xs-right">
        ...
    </li>
</ul>
```

Take a look at the following screenshot:

Figure 7.10: A border transition temporarily added to our navigation menu items.
As the user hovers over one of the navigation links, they receive a clear visual cue.

Now, when a user hovers on one of our navigation links, they get a nice indicator providing a clear visual aid.

Awesome Hover icons

As previously mentioned, Hover has a range of icon effects. Hover leverages the Font Awesome library, to render icons, which Hover then animates. Hover provides a range of different effects, but each effect actually only applies to one icon. All these effects are prefixed with `hvr-icon-<effect name>`. Open `bower_components/hover/css/hover.css` and check out the `hvr-icon-bob:before` class:

```
.hvr-icon-bob:before {
    content: "\f077";
    position : absolute;
    right: 1em;
    padding: 0 1px;
    font-family: FontAwesome;
    -webkit-transform: translateZ(0);
    transform: translateZ(0);
}
```

Using the pseudo-selector `before`, `hvr-icon-bob` is creating an element with `content: \f077`, which relates to the icon specified by that id in Font Awesome, as the `font-family` is set to `FontAwesome`. Taking a look at `FontAwesome.css`, we can see that `\f077` represents the `fa-chevron-up` class. As you can see, the icon is hardcoded into the class, so we can only ever use `hvr-icon-bob` with the upward chevron icon, unless we override the `content` rule of that class. The `transform` properties with the value of `translateZ()` are used to make the transition smoother, as it creates a new stacking context. The new stacking context forces rendering of the animation to the GPU, creating a smoother transition.

Let's see `hvr-icon-bob` in action by updating the **Profile** drop-down button, replacing the `caret` class with the `hvr-icon-bob` class. Replace the **Profile** button markup with the following:

```
<a href="#" class="nav-link" data-toggle="dropdown" role="button"
    aria-haspopup="true" aria-expanded="false">
    <span class="hvr-icon-bob">Profile</span>
</a>
```

Take a look at the following screenshot:

Figure 7.11: An inverted chevron that moves up and down as the user hovers over it

When a user hovers over the icon, the icon will animate up and down. Great! Well, except that it is upside down and misaligned. Let's fix that. In `myphoto.css`, we will override the content property of `hvr-icon-bob` with `\f078`, which is the `fa-chevron-down` class, and we will vertically align it correctly:

```
.hvr-icon-bob :before {
    content: "\f078";
}
.hvr-icon-bob {
    vertical-align: top;
}
```

We also need to ensure that `myphoto.css` is loaded after Hover:

```
<link rel="stylesheet" href="bower_components/bootstrap/dist/css
/bootstrap.min.css" />
<link rel="stylesheet" href="bower_components/Hover/css/hover-min.css"
/>
```

Take a look at the following screenshot:

Figure 7.12: An animated chevron facing down

Better! However, this approach can easily become a maintenance nightmare. There are other approaches to managing Hover icon classes so they're more usable. For instance, we could use specific classes to determine which icon to display. Add the `.myphoto-chevron-down` selector to the `hvr-icon-bob:before` rule in `myphoto.css`:

```
.myphoto-chevron-down.hvr-icon-bob:before {
    content: "\f078";
}
```

Refresh the page, and the upwards chevron will be displayed again.

But, if we add the `myphoto-chevron-down` class to the element, the downward chevron will be rendered:

```
<span class="myphoto-chevron-down hvr-icon-bob">Profile</span>
```

The approach described here makes using the Hover icon animations far more maintainable, and adds much more context than just using `hvr-icon-bob`, which just describes the animation and not the icon. We could also simply use the actual `FontAwesome` classes to describe the behavior, but Font Awesome also provides display rules that may not be in line with how Hover designed these classes to work.

Salvattore Hover

We can also use Hover to improve a user's interaction with our Salvattore-powered `testimonials` component. The `testimonials` component already leverages Animate.css to add an interesting transition when rendering the grid, but we can use Hover to add an interesting transition when a user actually interacts with it.

The grid is quite flat and fails to grab the user's attention once loaded. The individual columns also fail to gain focus. To solve this, we can use Hover to increase the size of the column when a user hovers on the column. One of the classes provided by Hover is `hvr-grow-shadow`, which adds a hover state to an element that expands the column and adds a `drop-shadow`, but doesn't affect the other columns or rows within the grid. All we need to do here is add `hvr-grow-shadow` to each `testimonial` column:

```
<div class="myphoto-testimonial-grid animated fadeIn" data-columns>
    <div class="myphoto-testimonial-column hvr-grow-shadow">
        <h6>Debbie</h6>
        <p>Great service! Would recommend to friends!</p>
    </div>
    <div class="myphoto-testimonial-column hvr-grow-shadow">
        <h6>Anne</h6>
        <p>Really high quality prints!</p>
    </div>
    <div class="myphoto-testimonial-column hvr-grow-shadow">
        <h6>Oscar</h6>
        <p>Declared their greatness, exhibited greatness.</p>
    </div>
    <div class="myphoto-testimonial-column hvr-grow-shadow">
        <h6>Joey</h6>
        <p>5 stars! Thanks for the great photos!</p>
    </div>
    <div class="myphoto-testimonial-column hvr-grow-shadow">
        <h6>Mary</h6>
        <p>Made a stressful event much easier! Absolute
        professionals!</p>
    </div>
    <div class="myphoto-testimonial-column hvr-grow-shadow">
        <h6>Alice</h6>
```

```
                <p>Wonderful! Exactly as I imagined they would turn out!</p>
        </div>
        <div class="myphoto-testimonial-column hvr-grow-shadow">
                <h6>Jack & Jill</h6>
                <p>So happy with how the photos turned out! Thanks for
                capturing the memories of our day!</p>
        </div>
        <div class="myphoto-testimonial-column hvr-grow-shadow">
                <h6>Nick</h6>
                <p>Perfectly captured the mood of our gig. Top notch.</p>
        </div>
        <div class="myphoto-testimonial-column hvr-grow-shadow">
                <h6>Tony</h6>
                <p>Captured our Cup final win! Great stuff!</p>
        </div>
    </div>
```

Take a look at the following screenshot:

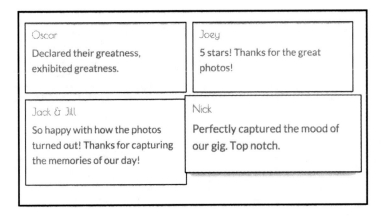

Figure 7.13: After applying the hvr-grow-shadow class, hovering over an individual testimonial will cause it to "grow" without effecting the rest of the grid

Now, when a user hovers over a column, the individual column *grows*, without affecting the rest of the grid. One of the cool things about Hover is that all the classes play nicely with each other, following the cascading nature of CSS. No JavaScript magic, just pure CSS. To see an example of this, we will add another Hover class. This one is from the range of Hover background transition classes, `hvr-sweep-to-top`. The `hvr-sweep-to-top` class animates a change in the background color with a fill effect from the bottom to the top. Let's add `hvr-sweep-to-top` to the testimonial columns:

```
        <div class="myphoto-testimonial-grid animated fadeIn" data-columns>
            <div class="myphoto-testimonial-column hvr-grow-shadow
            hvr-sweep-to-top">
```

```
      <h6>Debbie</h6>
      <p>Great service! Would recommend to friends!</p>
  </div>
  <div class="myphoto-testimonial-column hvr-grow-shadow
  hvr-sweep-to-top">
      <h6>Anne</h6>
      <p>Really high quality prints!</p>
  </div>
  <div class="myphoto-testimonial-column hvr-grow-shadow
  hvr-sweep-to-top">
      <h6>Oscar</h6>
      <p>Declared their greatness, exhibited greatness.</p>
  </div>
  <div class="myphoto-testimonial-column hvr-grow-shadow
  hvr-sweep-to-top">
      <h6>Joey</h6>
      <p>5 stars! Thanks for the great photos!</p>
  </div>
  <div class="myphoto-testimonial-column hvr-grow-shadow
  hvr-sweep-to-top">
      <h6>Mary</h6>
      <p>Made a stressful event much easier! Absolute
      professionals!</p>
  </div>
  <div class="myphoto-testimonial-column hvr-grow-shadow
  hvr-sweep-to-top">
      <h6>Alice</h6>
      <p>Wonderful! Exactly as I imagined they would turn out!</p>
  </div>
  <div class="myphoto-testimonial-column hvr-grow-shadow
  hvr-sweep-to-top">
      <h6>Jack & Jill</h6>
      <p>So happy with how the photos turned out! Thanks for
      capturing the memories of our day!</p>
  </div>
  <div class="myphoto-testimonial-column hvr-grow-shadow
  hvr-sweep-to-top">
      <h6>Nick</h6>
      <p>Perfectly captured the mood of our gig. Top notch.</p>
  </div>
  <div class="myphoto-testimonial-column hvr-grow-shadow
  hvr-sweep-to-top">
      <h6>Tony</h6>
      <p>Captured our Cup final win! Great stuff!</p>
  </div>
</div>
```

Take a look at the following screenshot:

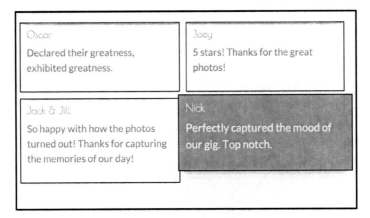

Figure 7.14: After applying the hvr-grow-shadow and hvr-sweep-to-top classes, hovering over an individual testimonial will cause it to "grow" and change color

Now we have both the expanded columns, with a drop-shadow, along with the fill effect provided by the `hvr-sweep-to-top` class. As we have seen, Hover provides very simple to use but very elegant transitions to add an extra layer of interaction for users. Being pure CSS, Hover is also exceedingly simple to integrate with most libraries and frameworks.

Summary

In this chapter, we have learned how to integrate third-party JavaScript and CSS libraries with our Bootstrap website, through Salvattore, Animate.css, and Hover.

We have been able to leverage Salvattore to add extra flexibility to Bootstrap's native grid system. We have also seen how to integrate Animate.css to add interesting transitions to `MyPhoto`, while integrating heavily with both Bootstrap and Salvattore. To improve the user experience of `MyPhoto`, we have seen how to leverage Hover, which has allowed us to provide improved visual cues to the user.

While Bootstrap provides a great amount of functionality out-of-the-box, using narrowly focused libraries such as Salvattore, Animate.css, and Hover can really improve the look and feel of a website.

Let's move on to Chapter 8, in which we will learn how to optimize `MyPhoto`.

8

Optimizing Your Website

Loosely put, *website optimization* refers to the activities and processes that improve your website's user experience and visibility while reducing the costs associated with hosting your website. In his book *Website Optimization*, Andrew B. King summarizes this notion succinctly with the question: *"How do we make our website better?"* (*Website Optimization*, Andrew B. King, O'Reilly). As such, the topic has been the sole subject of entire books, and a single chapter barely touches the tip of the iceberg. The topic is one of many facets, ranging from server-side optimization, search engine optimization, pay-per-click optimization, and client-side optimization. In this chapter, we will only discuss the latter. That is, we will be improving the loading and rendering time of `MyPhoto`. Specifically, this chapter is concerned with:

- Speeding up the loading time of our `MyPhoto index.html`
- Automating the tasks that achieve this objective

By the end of this chapter, you will understand the essential techniques behind client-side optimization. Within the context of `MyPhoto` you will therefore learn how to:

- Reduce the overall number of HTTP requests required to render our web page
- Automatically remove unused CSS rules
- Make our JavaScript and CSS files smaller (commonly referred to as minification)
- Automate the various optimization tasks
- Optimize CSS rules

CSS optimization

Before we even consider compression, minification, and file concatenation, we should think about the ways in which we can simplify and optimize our existing style sheet without using third-party tools. Of course, we should have striven for an optimal style sheet to begin with, and in many aspects we did. However, our style sheet still leaves room for improvement. Some of these improvements we have ignored on purpose within the previous chapters, as they would have detracted from the chapter's intended purpose. However, as this chapter is concerned with optimizing the client-side code of a web page, the time has come to talk a little about general tips and practices that will help you keep your style sheets small and your rules short. We will address each of these tips and practices in turn.

Inline styles

If, after reading this chapter, you only remember one thing, then please let it be the following: inline styles are bad. Period. Avoid using them whenever possible. Why? Because not only will they make your website impossible to maintain as the website grows, they also take up precious bytes as they force you to repeat the same rules over and over. Consider the following markup for our **Gallery** section:

```
<div class="carousel-inner" role="listbox">
    <div style="height: 400px" class="carousel-item active">
        <img data-modal-picture="#carouselModal" src=
        "images/brazil.png">
        <div class="carousel-caption">
            Brazil
        </div>
    </div>
    <div style="height: 400px" class="carousel-item">
        <img data-modal-picture="#carouselModal" src=
        "images/datsun.png">
        <div class="carousel-caption">
            Datsun 260Z
        </div>
    </div>
    <div style="height: 400px" class="carousel-item">
        <img data-modal-picture="#carouselModal" src=
        "images/skydive.png">
        <div class="carousel-caption">
            Skydive
        </div>
    </div>
</div>
```

Notice how the rule for defining a gallery item's height, `style="height: 400px"`, is repeated three times, once for each of the three gallery items. That's an additional 21 characters (or 21 bytes assuming that our document is UTF-8) for each additional image. Multiplying 3 * 21 gives us 63 bytes. And 21 more bytes for every new image that you want to add to the **Gallery**. Not to mention that, if you ever want to update the `height` of the gallery images, you will need to manually update the `style` attribute for every single image. The solution is of course to replace the inline styles with an appropriate class. Let's go ahead and define an `img` class that can be applied to any carousel image:

```
.carousel-item {
    height: 400px;
}
```

Now let's go ahead and remove the style rules:

```
<div class="carousel-inner" role="listbox">
    <div class="carousel-item active">
        <img data-modal-picture="#carouselModal" src=
        "images/brazil.png">
        <div class="carousel-caption">
            Brazil
        </div>
    </div>
    <div class="carousel-item">
        <img data-modal-picture="#carouselModal" src=
        "images/datsun.png">
        <div class="carousel-caption">
            Datsun 260Z
        </div>
    </div>
    <div class="carousel-item">
        <img data-modal-picture="#carouselModal" src=
        "images/skydive.png">
        <div class="carousel-caption">
            Skydive
        </div>
    </div>
</div>
```

Great! Not only is our CSS now easier to maintain, we also shaved 29 bytes off our website (the original inline styles required 63 bytes; our new class definition, however, requires only 34 bytes). Yes, this does not seem like much, especially in the world of high-speed broadband. But remember, your website will grow, and every byte adds up.

There are several more inline styles spread around our HTML document. Go ahead and fix them before moving on to the next section.

Long identifier and class names

The longer your strings, the larger your files. It's a no-brainer. As such, long identifier and class names naturally increase the size of your web page. Of course, extremely short class or identifier names tend to lack meaning, and therefore will make it more difficult (if not impossible) to maintain your page. As such, one should strive for an ideal balance between length and expressiveness (we will be covering a handy little tool that will provide you with the benefits of both later on in this chapter). Of course, even better than shortening identifiers, is to remove them altogether. One handy technique for removing these is to use hierarchical selection. Take our events pagination code. For example, we are using the services-events-content identifier within our pagination logic as follows:

```
$('#services-events-pagination').bootpag({
    total: 10
}).on("page", function(event, num){
    $('#services-events-content div').hide();

    var current_page = '#page-' + num;
    $(current_page).show();
});
```

To denote the services content, we broke the name of our identifier into three parts, namely, services, events, content. Our markup is as follows:

```
<div id="services-events-content">
    <div id="page-1">
        <h3>My Sample Event #1</h3>
        ...
    </div>
</div>
```

Let's try and get rid of this identifier altogether by observing two characteristics of our **Events** section:

- The services-events-content is an indirect descendent of a div with the id services-events. This id we cannot remove, as it is required for the menu to work.
- The element with the id services-events-content is itself a div. If we were to remove its id, we could also remove the entire div.

As such, we do not need a second identifier to select the pages that we wish to hide. Instead, all that we need to do is select the `div` within the `div` that is within the `div` that is assigned the `id` `services-events`. How do we express this as a CSS selector? Easy. Use `#services-events div div div`. And as such, our pagination logic is updated as follows:

```
$('#services-events-pagination').bootpag({
    total: 10
}).on("page", function(event, num){
    $('#services-events div div div').hide();
    var current_page = '#page-' + num;
    $(current_page).show();
});
```

Save and refresh. What's that? As you clicked on a page, the pagination control disappeared. That is because we are now hiding all `div` elements that are two `div` elements down from the element with the `id` `services-events`. Move the pagination control `div` outside its parent element. Our markup should now look as follows:

```
<div class="tab-content bg-myphoto-light">
    <div role="tabpanel" class="tab-pane active" id=
    "services-events">
        <div class="container">
            <div class="row" style="margin: 1em;">
                <div id="page-1">
                    <h3>My Sample Event #1</h3>
                    ...
                    <h3>My Sample Event #2</h3>
                    ...
                </div>
                <div id="page-2">
                    <h3>My Sample Event #3</h3>
                    ...
                </div>
            </div>
            <div id="services-events-pagination"></div>
        </div>
    </div>
</div>
```

Save and refresh. That's better! Last but not least, let us update `myphoto.css`. Take the following code:

```
#services-events-content div {
    display: none;
}
#services-events-content div img {
```

```
      margin-top: 0.5em;
    margin-right: 1em;
}
#services-events-content {
    height: 15em;
    overflow-y: scroll;
}
```

Replace this code with:

```
#services-events div div div {
    display: none;
}
#services-events div div div img {
    margin-top: 0.5em;
    margin-right: 1em;
}
#services-events div div div {
    height: 15em;
    overflow-y: scroll;
}
```

That's it, we have simplified our style sheet and saved some bytes in the process!

Shorthand rules

According to, the Mozilla Developer Network (shorthand properties, Mozilla Developer Network, `https://developer.mozilla.org/en-US/docs/Web/CSS/Shorthand_properties`, accessed November 2015), shorthand properties are:

> *"CSS properties that let you set the values of several other CSS properties simultaneously. Using a shorthand property, a Web developer can write more concise and often more readable style sheets, saving time and energy."*
>
> — *Mozilla Developer Network, 2015*

Unless strictly necessary, we should never be using longhand rules. When possible, shorthand rules are always the preferred option. Besides the obvious advantage of saving precious bytes, shorthand rules also help increase your style sheet's maintainability. For example, `border: 20px dotted #FFF` is equivalent to three separate rules:

```
border-style: dotted;
border-width: 20px;
border-color: #FFF;
```

Grouping selectors

Organizing selectors into groups will arguably also save some bytes. Consider lines 80 to 93 in `myphoto.css`:

```
.navbar-myphoto .dropdown-menu > a:hover {
    color: gray;
    background-color: #504747;
}
.navbar-myphoto .dropdown-menu > a:focus {
    color: gray;
    background-color: #504747;
}
.navbar-myphoto .dropdown-menu > .active > a:focus {
    color: gray;
    background-color: #504747;
}
```

Notice how each of the three selectors contains the same declarations. That is, the `color` and `background-color` properties are set to the exact same values for each selector. To prevent us from repeating these declarations, we should simply group them (reducing the code from 274 characters down to 181 characters):

```
.navbar-myphoto .dropdown-menu > a:hover,
.navbar-myphoto .dropdown-menu > a:focus,
.navbar-myphoto .dropdown-menu > .active > a:focus {
    color: gray;
    background-color: #504747;
}
```

Voilà! We just saved 93 bytes! (assuming UTF-8 encoding).

Rendering times

When optimizing your style rules, the number of bytes should not be your only concern. In fact, it comes secondary to the rendering time of your web page. CSS rules affect the amount of work that is required by the browser to render your page. As such, some rules are more expensive than others. For example, changing the color of an element is cheaper than changing its margin. The reason for this is that a change in color only requires your browser to draw the new pixels. While drawing itself is by no means a cheap operation, changing the margin of an element requires much more effort. Your browser needs to both re-calculate the page layout and also draw the changes. Optimizing your page's rendering times is a complex topic, and as such beyond the scope of this book.

However, we recommend that you take a look at `http://csstriggers.com/`. This site provides a concise overview of the costs involved when updating a given CSS property.

Did you know?

Udacity now offers a free online course on *Browser Rendering Optimization*. Head over to `https://www.udacity.com` for more. We cannot recommend the course highly enough!

Minifying CSS and JavaScript

Once you have improved the `MyPhoto` style rules so they're as compact, efficient, and maintainable as possible, it is time to look into minification. Minification is the process of removing redundant characters from a file, without altering the actual information contained within it. In other words, minifying our `myphoto.css` file will reduce its overall size, while leaving the actual CSS style rules intact. This is achieved by stripping out any whitespace characters within our file. Stripping out whitespace characters has the obvious result that our CSS is now practically unreadable and impossible to maintain. As such, minified style sheets should only be used when serving a page (that is, during production), and not during development.

Clearly minifying your style sheet manually would be an incredibly time-consuming (and hence pointless) task. Therefore, there exist many tools that will do the job for us. One such tool is `npm minifier`. Visit `https://www.npmjs.com/package/minifier` for more.

Let's go ahead and install it:

```
sudo npm install -g minifier
```

Once installed, we can minify our style sheet by typing the following command:

```
minify path-to-myphoto.css
```

Here `path-to-myphoto.css` represents the path to our `MyPhoto` style sheet. Go ahead and execute the command. Once minification is complete, you should see the message **Minification complete**. A new CSS file (`myphoto.min.css`) will have been created inside the directory containing the `myphoto.css` file. The new file should be 3,358 bytes. Our original `myphoto.css` file is 3,945 bytes. Minifying our style sheet just reduced the number of bytes to send by roughly 15%!

Go ahead and update the `head` of our HTML document to reference the new, minified style sheet:

```
<link rel="stylesheet" href="styles/myphoto.min.css" />
```

It is worth noting that, aside from CSS minification, minifier also allows you to minify JavaScript files. For example, to minify our `alert.js` file, simply type:

```
minify path-to-alert.js
```

Once again, as soon as the minification is complete, you should see the message **Minification complete**. Similar to before, a new file (`alert.min.js`) will have been created inside the directory containing the `alert.js` file.

Introducing Grunt

The minifier that we used in the previous section greatly reduced the size of our style sheet and JavaScript files, and also helped reduce the overall number of requests required to render `MyPhoto`. However, using it has one downside—every time that you make a change to either your CSS or JavaScript code during development, you are required to rerun the tool. This greatly slows down development and can even cause frustration and hair tearing. (Just imagine forgetting to run the minifier, thinking that you ran it, and not seeing your changes appear. You are likely to blame your code as opposed to your forgetfulness.) Therefore, would it not be nice if we could minify and concatenate our files automatically every time that we make a change to our source code?

Meet **Grunt**: The JavaScript Task Runner (`http://gruntjs.com/`). As implied by its name, Grunt is a tool that allows us to automatically run any set of tasks. Grunt can even *wait* while you code, and pickup changes made to your source code files (CSS, HTML, or JavaScript) and then execute a preconfigured set of tasks every time that you save your changes. This way you are no longer required to manually execute a set of commands in order for your changes to take effect.

Let's go ahead and install Grunt:

```
npm install grunt --save-dev
```

Before we can start using run with `MyPhoto`, we need to tell Grunt:

- What tasks to run. That is, what to do with the input (the input being our `MyPhoto` files) and where to save the output.
- What software is to be used to execute the tasks.

- How to name the tasks, so that we can invoke them when required.

With this in mind, we create a new JavaScript file (assuming UTF-8 encoding), called `Gruntfile.js`, inside our project root. We will also need to create a JSON file, called `package.json`, also inside our project root. Our project folder should have the following structure (note how we created one additional folder, `src`, and moved our source code and development assets inside it):

```
src
|__bower_components
|__images
|__js
|__styles
|__index.html
Gruntfile.js
package.json
```

Open the newly created `Gruntfile.js` and insert the following function definition:

```
module.exports = function(grunt) {
    grunt.initConfig({
        pkg: grunt.file.readJSON("package.json")
    });
};
```

As you can see, this is plain, vanilla JavaScript. Anything that we need to make Grunt aware of (such as the Grunt configuration) will go inside the `grunt.initConfig` function definition. Adding the configuration outside the scope of this function will cause Grunt to ignore it.

Now open `package.json` and insert the following:

```
{
    "name": "MyPhoto",
    "version": "1.0",
    "devDependencies": {
    }
}
```

The preceding code should be self-explanatory. The `name` property refers to the project name, `version` refers to the project's version, and `devDependencies` refers to any dependencies that are required (we will be adding to those in a while).

Great, now we are ready to start using Grunt!

Minification and concatenation using Grunt

The first thing that we want Grunt to be able to do is minify our files. Yes, we already have minifier installed, but remember that we want to use Grunt so that we can automatically execute a bunch of tasks (such as minification) in one go. To do so, we will need to install the `grunt-contrib-cssmin` package (a Grunt package that performs minification and concatenation. Visit `https://github.com/gruntjs/grunt-contrib-cssmin` for more information.):

```
npm install grunt-contrib-cssmin --save-dev
```

Once installed, inspect `package.json`. Observe how it has been modified to include the newly installed package as a development dependency:

```
{
    "name": "MyPhoto",
    "version": "0.1.0",
    "devDependencies": {
        "grunt": "^0.4.5",
        "grunt-contrib-cssmin": "^0.14.0"
    }
}
```

We must tell Grunt about the plugin. To do so, insert the following line inside the function definition within our `Gruntfile.js`:

```
grunt.loadNpmTasks("grunt-contrib-cssmin");
```

Our `Gruntfile.js` should now look as follows:

```
module.exports = function(grunt) {
    grunt.initConfig({
        pkg: grunt.file.readJSON("package.json")
    });
    grunt.loadNpmTasks("grunt-contrib-cssmin");
};
```

As such, we still cannot do much. The preceding code makes Grunt aware of the `grunt-contrib-cssmin` package (that is, it tells Grunt load it). In order to be able to use the package to minify our files, we need to create a Grunt task. We need to call this task `cssmin`:

```
module.exports = function(grunt) {
    grunt.initConfig({
        pkg: grunt.file.readJSON("package.json"),
        "cssmin": {
```

```
                    "target": {
                        "files": {
                            "src/styles/myphoto.min.css":
                            ["src/styles/*.css"]
                        }
                    }
                }
            });
            grunt.loadNpmTasks("grunt-contrib-cssmin");
    };
```

Whoa! That's a lot of code at once. What just happened here? Well, we registered a new task called `cssmin`. We then specified the target, that is, the input files that Grunt should use for this task. Specifically, we wrote:

```
    "src/styles/myphoto.min.css": ["src/styles/*.css"]
```

The property `name` here is being interpreted as denoting the output, while the property `value` represents the input. We are therefore in essence saying something along the lines of: *"In order to produce* `myphoto.min.css` *use any files ending with the file extension* `css` *within the* `src/styles` *directory".*

Go ahead and run the Grunt task by typing:

grunt cssmin

Upon completion, you should see output along the lines of:

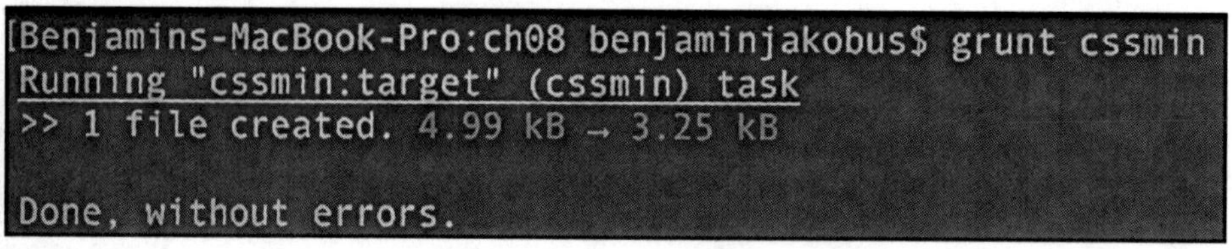

```
[Benjamins-MacBook-Pro:ch08 benjaminjakobus$ grunt cssmin
Running "cssmin:target" (cssmin) task
>> 1 file created. 4.99 kB → 3.25 kB

Done, without errors.
```

Figure 8.1: The console output after running cssmin

The first line indicates that a new output file (`myphoto.min.css`) has been created, and that it is **3.25 kB** in size (down from the original **4.99 kB**). The second line is self-explanatory; that is, the task executed successfully, without any errors.

Now that you know how to use `grunt-contrib-cssmin`, go ahead and take a look at their documentation for some nice extras!

Running tasks automatically

Now that we know how to configure and use Grunt to minify our style sheets, let us turn our attention to task automation. That is, how we can execute our Grunt minification task automatically as soon as we make changes to our source files. To this end, we will learn about a second Grunt package, called `grunt-contrib-watch` (`https://github.com/gruntjs/grunt-contrib-watch`). As with `contrib-css-min`, this package can be installed using npm:

```
npm install grunt-contrib-watch --save-dev
```

Open `package.json` and verify that `grunt-contrib-watch` has been added as a dependency:

```
{
    "name": "MyPhoto",
    "version": "0.1.0",
    "devDependencies": {
        "grunt": "^0.4.5",
        "grunt-contrib-cssmin": "^0.14.0",
        "grunt-contrib-watch": "^0.6.1"
    }
}
```

Next, tell Grunt about our new package by adding `grunt.loadNpmTasks('grunt-contrib-watch');` to `Gruntfile.js`. Furthermore, we need to define the `watch` task by adding a new empty property called `watch`:

```
module.exports = function(grunt) {
    grunt.initConfig({
        pkg: grunt.file.readJSON("package.json"),
        "cssmin": {
            "target":{
                "files": {
                    "src/styles/myphoto.min.css":
                    ["src/styles/*.css", "src/styles!*.min.css"]
                }
            }
        },
        "watch": {
        }
    });
    grunt.loadNpmTasks("grunt-contrib-cssmin");
    grunt.loadNpmTasks("grunt-contrib-watch");
};
```

Now that Grunt loads our newly installed `watch` package, we can execute the command `grunt watch`. However, as we have not yet configured the task, Grunt will terminate with:

```
Benjamins-MacBook-Pro:ch08 benjaminjakobus$ grunt watch
Running "watch" task
Waiting...
```

Figure 8.2: The console output after running the watch task

The first thing that we need to do, is tell our `watch` task what files to actually "watch". We do this by setting the `files` property, just as we did with `grunt-contrib-cssmin`:

```
"watch": {
    "target": {
        "files": ["src/styles/myphoto.css"],
    }
}
```

This tells the `watch` task to use the `myphoto.css` located within our `src/styles` folder as input (it will only watch for changes made to `myphoto.css`).

Note that in reality, you would want to be watching all CSS files inside `styles/`; however to keep things simple, let's just watch `myphoto.css`.

Go ahead and execute `grunt watch` again. Unlike the first time that we ran the command, the task should not terminate now. Instead, it should halt with the message **Waiting....** Go ahead and make a trivial change (such as removing a whitespace) to our `myphoto.css` file. Then save this change. Notice how the terminal output is now:

```
Benjamins-MacBook-Pro:ch08 benjaminjakobus$ grunt watch
Running "watch" task
Waiting...
>> File "src/styles/myphoto.css" changed.
```

Figure 8.3: The console output after running the watch task

Great! Our `watch` task is now successfully listening for file changes made to any style sheet within `src/styles`. The next step is to put this achievement to good use. That is, we need to get our `watch` task to execute the minification task that we created in the previous section. To do so, simply add the `tasks` property to our `target`:

```
"watch": {
    "target": {
        "files": ["src/styles/myphoto.css"],
        "tasks": ["cssmin"]
    }
}
```

Once again, run `grunt watch`. This time, make a visible change to our `myphoto.css` style sheet. For example, you could add an obvious rule such as `body {background-color: red; }`. Observe how, as you save your changes, our `watch` task now runs our `cssmin` task:

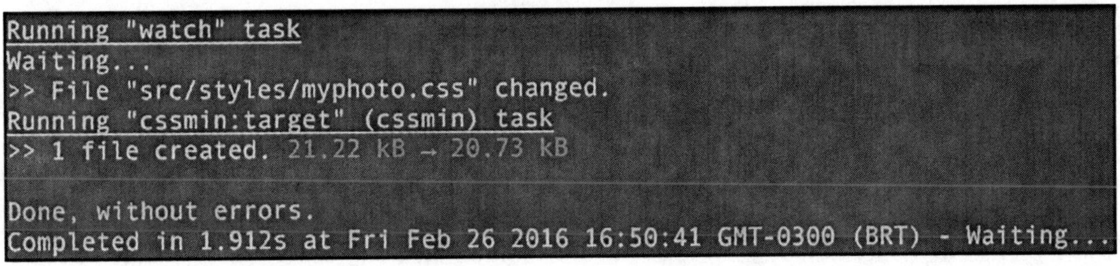

```
Running "watch" task
Waiting...
>> File "src/styles/myphoto.css" changed.
Running "cssmin:target" (cssmin) task
>> 1 file created. 21.22 kB → 20.73 kB

Done, without errors.
Completed in 1.912s at Fri Feb 26 2016 16:50:41 GMT-0300 (BRT) - Waiting...
```

Figure 8.4: The console output after making a change to the style sheet that is being watched

Refresh the page in your browser and observe the changes. Voilà! We now no longer need to run our minifier manually every time we change our style sheet.

Stripping our website of unused CSS

Dead code is never good. As such, whatever the project that you are working on may be, you should always strive to eliminate code that is no longer in use, as early as possible. This is especially important when developing websites, as unused code will inevitably be transferred to the client, and hence result in additional, unnecessary, bytes being transferred (although maintainability is also a major concern).

Programmers are not perfect, and we all make mistakes. As such, unused code or style rules are bound to slip past us during development and testing. Consequently, it would be nice if we could establish a safeguard to ensure that at least no unused style makes it past us into production. And this is where grunt-uncss fits in. Visit https://github.com/addyosmani /grunt-uncss for more.

UnCSS strips any unused CSS from our style sheet. When configured properly, it can therefore be very useful to ensure that our production-ready website is as small as possible. Let's go ahead and install UnCSS:

```
sudo npm install grunt-uncss –save-dev
```

Once installed, we need to tell Grunt about our plugin. Just as in the previous sub-sections, update the Gruntfile.js by adding the line grunt.loadNpmTasks('grunt-uncss'); to our Grunt configuration. Next, go ahead and define the uncss task:

```
"uncss": {
    "target": {
        "files": {
            "src/styles/output.css": ["src/index.html"]
        }
    }
},
```

In the preceding code, we specified a target consisting of the file index.html. This index.html will be parsed by Uncss. The class and id names used within it will be compared to those appearing in our style sheets. Should our style sheets contain selectors that are unused, then those are removed from the output. The output itself will be written to src/styles/output.css.

Let's go ahead and test this. Add a new style to our myphoto.css that will not be used anywhere within our index.html. For example:

```
#foobar {
    color: red;
}
```

Save and then run:

```
grunt uncss
```

Upon successful execution, the terminal should display output along the lines of:

```
[Benjamins-MacBook-Pro:ch08 benjaminjakobus$ grunt uncss
Running "uncss:target" (uncss) task
ReferenceError: Can't find variable: $

    file:///Users/benjaminjakobus/Desktop/ch08/src/index.html:34
File src/styles/output.css created: 298.19 kB → 29.69 kB

Done, without errors.
```

Figure 8.5: The console output after executing our uncss task

Go ahead and open the generated output.css file. The file will contain a concatenation of all our CSS files (including Bootstrap). Go ahead and search for #foobar. Find it? That's because UnCSS detected that it was no longer in use and removed it for us.

Now, we successfully configured a Grunt task to strip our website of the unused CSS. However, we need to run this task manually. Would it not be nice if we could configure the task to run with the other watch tasks? If we were to do this, the first thing that we would need to ask ourselves is, how do we combine the CSS minification task with UnCSS? After all, grunt watch would run one before the other. As such, we would be required to use the output of one task as input for the other. So how would we go about doing this?

Well, we know that our cssmin task writes its output to myphoto.min.css. We also know that index.html references myphoto.min.css. Furthermore, we also know uncss receives its input by checking the style sheets referenced in index.html. We therefore know that the output produced by our cssmin task is sure to be used by our uncss as long as it is referenced within index.html.

In order for the output produced by uncss to take effect, we would therefore need to reconfigure the task to write its output into myphoto.min.css. We would then need to add uncss to our list of watch tasks, taking care to insert the task into the list after cssmin. However, this leads to a problem: running uncss after cssmin will produce an un-minified style sheet. Furthermore, it also requires the presence of myphoto.min.css. However, as myphoto.min.css is actually produced by cssmin, the sheet will not be present when running the task for the first time. We therefore need a different approach. We will need to use the original myphoto.css as input to uncss, which then writes its output into a file called myphoto.min.css.

Our `cssmin` task then uses this file as input, minifiying it as discussed previously. Since `uncss` parses the style sheet references in `index.html`, we would need to first revert our `index.html` to reference our development style sheet, `myphoto.css`. Go ahead and do just that. Replace the line: `<link rel="stylesheet" href="styles/myphoto.min.css" />` with: `<link rel="stylesheet" href="styles/myphoto.css" />`.

Processing HTML

For the minified changes to take effect, we now need a tool that replaces our style sheet references with our production-ready style sheets. Meet `grunt-processhtml`. Visit `https://www.npmjs.com/package/grunt-processhtml` for more.

Go ahead and install it using the following command:

```
sudo npm install grunt-processhtml --save-dev
```

Add `grunt.loadNpmTasks('grunt-processhtml');` to our `Gruntfile.js` to enable our freshly installed tool.

While `grunt-processhtml` is very powerful, we will only cover how to replace style sheet references. We therefore recommend that you read the tool's documentation to discover further features.

In order to replace our style sheets with `myphoto.min.css`, we wrap them inside special `grunt-processhtml` comments:

```html
<!-- build:css styles/myphoto.min.css -->
    <link rel="stylesheet" href="bower_components/bootstrap/
    dist/css/bootstrap.min.css" />
    <link href='https://fonts.googleapis.com/css?family=Poiret+One'
    rel='stylesheet' type='text/css'>
    <link href='http://fonts.googleapis.com/css?family=Lato&
    subset=latin,latin-ext' rel='stylesheet' type='text/css'>
    <link rel="stylesheet" href="bower_components/Hover/css/
    hover-min.css" />
    <link rel="stylesheet" href="styles/myphoto.css" />
    <link rel="stylesheet" href="styles/alert.css" />
    <link rel="stylesheet" href="styles/carousel.css" />
    <link rel="stylesheet" href="styles/a11yhcm.css" />
    <link rel="stylesheet" href="bower_components/components-
    font-awesome/css/font-awesome.min.css" />
    <link rel="stylesheet" href="bower_components/lightbox-for
    -bootstrap/css/bootstrap.lightbox.css" />
    <link rel="stylesheet" href="bower_components/DataTables/
```

```
            media/css/dataTables.bootstrap.min.css" />
        <link rel="stylesheet" href="resources/animate/animate.min.css" />
    <!-- /build -->
```

Note how we reference the style sheet that is meant to replace the style sheets contained within the special comments on the first line, inside the comment:

```
    <!-- build:css styles/myphoto.min.css -->
```

Last, but not least, add the following task:

```
    "processhtml": {
        "dist": {
            "files": {
                "dist/index.html": ["src/index.html"]
            }
        }
    },
```

Notice how the output of our `processhtml` task will be written to `dist`. Test the newly configured task through the command `grunt processhtml`.

The task should execute without errors:

```
[Benjamins-MacBook-Pro:ch08 benjaminjakobus$ grunt processhtml
Running "processhtml:dist" (processhtml) task

Done, without errors.
```

Figure 8.6: The console output after executing the processhtml task

Open `dist/index.html` and observe how, instead of the 12 `link` tags, we only have one:

```
    <link rel="stylesheet" href="styles/myphoto.min.css">
```

Next, we need to reconfigure our `uncss` task to write its output to `myphoto.min.css`. To do so, simply replace the output path `'src/styles/output.css'` with `'dist/styles/myphoto.min.css'` inside our `Gruntfile.js` (note how `myphoto.min.css` will now be written to `dist/styles` as opposed to `src/styles`). We then need to add `uncss` to our list of `watch` tasks, taking care to insert the task into the list after `cssmin`:

```
        "watch": {
            "target": {
                "files": ["src/styles/myphoto.css"],
                "tasks": ["uncss", "cssmin", "processhtml"],
```

```
                "options": {
                    "livereload": true
                }
            }
        }
```

Next, we need to configure our `cssmin` task to use `myphoto.min.css` as input:

```
"cssmin": {
    "target": {
        "files": {
            "dist/styles/myphoto.min.css":
            ["src/styles/myphoto.min.css"]
        }
    }
},
```

Note how we removed `'src/styles!*.min.css'`, which would have prevented `cssmin` from reading files ending with the extension `min.css`.

Running `grunt watch` and making a change to our `myphoto.css` file should now trigger the `uncss` task and then the `cssmin` task, resulting in console output indicating the successful execution of all tasks. That is, the console output should indicate that first `uncss`, `cssmin`, and then `processhtml` were successfully executed. Go ahead and check `myphoto.min.css` inside the `dist` folder. You should see how:

- The CSS file contains an aggregation of all our style sheets
- The CSS file is minified
- The CSS file contains no unused style rules

However, you will also notice that the `dist` folder contains none of our assets—neither images, Bower components, nor our custom JavaScript files. As such, you will be forced to copy any assets manually. Of course, this is less than ideal. So let's see how we can copy our assets to our `dist` folder automatically.

The dangers of using UnCSS

UnCSS may cause you to lose styles that are applied dynamically. As such, care should be taken when using this tool. Take a closer look at the `MyPhoto` style sheet and see whether you spot any issues. You should notice that our style rules for overriding the background color of our navigation pills was removed. One potential fix for this is to write a dedicated class for gray nav pills (as opposed to overriding them with the Bootstrap classes).

Deploying assets

To copy our assets from `src` into `dist` we will use `grunt-contrib-copy`. Visit `https://github.com/gruntjs/grunt-contrib-copy` for more on this. Go ahead and install it:

```
sudo npm install grunt-contrib-copy –save-dev
```

Once installed, enable it by adding `grunt.loadNpmTasks('grunt-contrib-copy');` to our `Gruntfile.js`. Then configure the `copy` task:

```
"copy": {
    "target": {
        "files": [
            {
                "cwd": "src/images",
                "src": ["*"],
                "dest": "dist/images/",
                "expand": true
            },
            {
                "cwd": "src/bower_components",
                "src": ["*"],
                "dest": "dist/bower_components/",
                "expand": true
            },
            {
                "cwd": "src/js",
                "src": ["*"],
                "dest": "dist/js/",
                "expand": true
            },
        ]
    }
},
```

The preceding configuration should be self-explanatory. We are specifying a list of copy operations to perform; `src` indicates the source and `dest` indicates the destination. The `cwd` variable indicates the current working directory. Note how, instead of a wildcard expression, we could also match a certain `src` pattern. For example, to only copy minified JS files, we could write:

```
"src": ["*.min.js"]
```

Take a look at the following screenshot:

```
[Benjamins-MBP:ch08 benjaminjakobus$ grunt copy
Running "copy:target" (copy) task
Created 86 directories, copied 585 files

Done, without errors.
```

Figure 8.7: The console output indicating the number of copied files and directories after running the copy task

Update the watch task:

```
"watch": {
    "target": {
        'files': ['src/styles/myphoto.css'],
        "tasks": ["uncss", "cssmin", "processhtml", "copy"]
    }
},
```

Test the changes by running grunt watch. All tasks should execute successfully. The last task that was executed should be the copy task.

Stripping CSS comments

Another common source for unnecessary bytes is comments. While needed during development, they serve no practical purpose in production. As such, we can configure our cssmin task to strip our CSS files of any comments by simply creating an options property and setting its nested keepSpecialComments property to 0:

```
"cssmin": {
    "target":{
        "options": {
            "keepSpecialComments": 0
        },
        "files": {
            "dist/src/styles/myphoto.min.css": ["src/styles
            /myphoto.min.css"]
        }
    }
},
```

Did you know?

You can minify class and identifier names using the lessons learned so far in this chapter. Recall our earlier discussion on class names and identifier names—long names may improve code readability and code maintainability. Short names, on the other hand, require fewer bytes to transfer. As such, developers who want a highly optimized site are caught between two fronts—maintainability versus size. Of course, in most cases, the few extra bytes caused by slightly more descriptive identifier names will not be a cause for major concern. However, it does become a point of consideration once your website reaches a specific volume. Therefore, meet the Grunt class and id minifier at `https://www.npmjs.com/package /grunt-class-id-minifier`. Another useful and alternative tool is Munch at `https://www.npmjs.com/package/munch`.

JavaScript file concatenation

Just as we minified and concatenated our style sheets, we shall now go ahead and minify and concatenate our JavaScript files. Go ahead and take a look at `grunt-contrib-uglify`. Visit `https://github.com/gruntjs/grunt-contrib-uglify` for more.

Install this by typing:

```
sudo npm install grunt-contrib-uglify -save-dev
```

And, as always, enable it by adding `grunt.loadNpmTasks('grunt-contrib-uglify');` to our `Gruntfile.js`. Next, create a new task:

```
"uglify": {
    "target": {
        "files": {
            "dist/src/js/myphoto.min.js": ["src/js/*.js"]
        }
    }
}
```

Running `grunt uglify` should produce the following output:

```
[Benjamins-MacBook-Pro:ch08 benjaminjakobus$ grunt uglify
Running "uglify:target" (uglify) task
>> 1 file created.

Done, without errors.
```

Figure 8.8: The console output after running the uglify task

The folder `dist/js` should now contain a file called `myphoto.min.js`. Open it and verify that the JavaScript code has been minified. As a next step, we need to be sure that our minified JavaScript file will actually be used by our production-ready `index.html`. We will use `grunt-processhtml`, which we installed in the previous section. All that we need to do is wrap our `link` tags inside a special build comment: `<!-- build:js js/myphoto.min.js ->`:

```
<!-- build:js js/myphoto.min.js -->
    <script src="js/alert.js"></script>
    <script src="js/carousel.js"></script>
    <script src="js/a11yhcm.js"></script>
<!-- /build ->
```

Next will add our `uglify` task to our `watch` task list:

```
"watch": {
    "target": {
        "files": ["src/styles/myphoto.css"],
        "tasks": ["uncss", "cssmin", "processhtml", "uglify",
        "copy"],
    }
},
```

Golden rules when working with Grunt
When developing a Grunt file (or any build file for that matter), there are a few practices that you should keep in mind:

- The `dist` folder should not contain any unprocessed source files. `src` is the "unprocessed" code, `dist` is the result of "processing" `src` to create a distributable.

- Typically, you should create a Grunt build task to run the appropriate tasks to create and populate the `dist` directory. You should also create a Grunt `serve` task to run the appropriate tasks for a development server, with the watch task being the final task that is run.

- The watch task should be watching all source files. In our case, we watched just one, in order to keep the example simple and easy to understand.

Summary

In this chapter, we touched upon the basics of website optimization, and how to use the build tool Grunt to automate the more common and mundane optimization tasks. Specifically, we summarized the most important rules that help you to write better, more efficient CSS. We then showed you how to automatically compress and concatenate files, how to deploy assets, and how to strip source files off comments. The aim of these lessons was to provide you with a grounding that would allow you to perform further optimizations, using Grunt, although these are not explicitly covered in depth within this chapter. As such, we encourage you to read the documentation of the various Grunt tasks covered within this chapter. The majority of these tasks are highly customizable and offer many additional benefits not covered here. Knowing how to optimize MyPhoto prior to deployment, we can now move on to our final chapter and learn how to integrate both AngularJS and React with MyPhoto.

9
Integrating with AngularJS and React

At this stage of our journey through mastering Bootstrap, we have built the MyPhoto web page using Bootstrap, along with various third-party libraries and plugins, and have optimized the web page. MyPhoto is now complete in terms of functionality.

In this chapter, we are not going to develop any new functionality. Instead, we will integrate MyPhoto with two of the currently most popular and powerful JavaScript frameworks—AngularJS (https://angularjs.org/) and React (https://facebook.github .io/react/).

AngularJS is a Model-View-* (MVC, MVV, and so on) JavaScript framework, while React is a JavaScript library which concentrates solely on the View part of the **Model-View-Controller (MVC)** type stack. To readers unfamiliar with the MVC, the term refers to a design pattern whereby the logic for modeling and representing the data, and the logic for creating the bridge between the two are strictly separated. This development approach is extremely powerful, and consequently a vast amount of web pages are built with frameworks or libraries such as AngularJS and React, as they provide very useful abstractions on top of JavaScript and the DOM.

At this point, we will fork MyPhoto, creating an AngularJS version and a React version. We will concentrate only on how AngularJS and React can help improve reusability and maintainability, and handle dynamic data. While AngularJS and React have other great functionalities, they are beyond the scope of this book.

In this chapter we will:

- Integrate AngularJS with MyPhoto
- Integrate React with MyPhoto

Introducing AngularJS

AngularJS is a popular and powerful JavaScript framework created by Google. AngularJS provides easily consumable abstractions on top of JavaScript to aid in the development of web applications. These abstractions include easy-to-use form validation, two-way data binding, custom HTML attributes called *directives* for dynamic data and rendering, a simple interface for **XMLHttpRequest** (**XHR**), the ability to create custom directives, single page application routing, and more.

We are not going to cover the intricacies and the vastness of AngularJS, but we will learn how to leverage AngularJS's built-in directives, how to create custom directives and services, and how to use AngularJS's XHR interface.

First, let's add AngularJS to our project.

Setting up AngularJS

The AngularJS team maintains a Bower package with the latest release. Let's install AngularJS. We are going to use version 1.4.8 of AngularJS:

1. In the terminal, from the `src` directory, run:

   ```
   bower install angular#1.4.8
   ```

2. Create a copy of `src/index.html`, called `src/index-angular.html`. Let's add the minified version of AngularJS into the `head` of `index-angular.html`:

   ```
   <script src="bower_components/angular/angular.min.js"></script>
   ```

AngularJS requires a module definition, which is basically your application container, to hook into, so that AngularJS knows which parts of the DOM to execute upon:

1. First, create a file, `src/app/myphoto.module.js`, and add the following module definition:

   ```
   angular.module('MyPhoto', [])
   ```

   The AngularJS Module Definition
   ```
   angular.module('MyName', [])
   ```
   This is the simplest of module definitions. We're creating a new AngularJS module, `MyPhoto`. The square brackets is the definition of dependencies the `MyPhoto` module requires.

This is an array of other modules, which AngularJS will then load via its **Dependency Injection (DI)** system. `MyPhoto` has no dependencies, so we leave this array empty.

2. Next, add the module definition to the `head` of the `index-angular.html`:

```
<script src="bower_components/angular/angular.min.js">
</script>
<script src="app/myphoto.module.js"></script>
```

3. Next, we need to *bootstrap*. In this instance, *bootstrap* means loading the module and hooking it to a part of the DOM, and is not to be confused with the framework that this book is based upon! To do this, we use the **ngApp** AngularJS directive. The ngApp directive will automatically bootstrap the defined module to the element it is attached to, using that element as the root element of the application. We will apply `ng-app` to the `body` element of `index-angular.html`:

```
<body ng-app="MyPhoto" data-spy="scroll" data-
target=".navbar" class="animated fadeIn">
```

As you can see, we add the `ng-app` attribute with the value of `"MyPhoto"`, the name we used when defining the module in `myphoto.module.js`. Now, `MyPhoto` has been bootstrapped with an AngularJS module and is now technically an AngularJS application, although AngularJS doesn't execute or manipulate anything.

Now, let's see how we can leverage core AngularJS features, such as directives, data binding, and JavaScript abstractions to build reusable and dynamic components for MyPhoto.

Improving the testimonials component

In `Chapter 7`, *Integrating Bootstrap with Third-Party Plugins*, we built a testimonials component to demonstrate the powers of Salvattore, Hover, and Animate.css. When building this component, we hardcoded all the content and introduced a lot of repetition:

```
<div role="tabpanel" class="tab-pane" id="services-testimonials">
    <div class="container">
        <div class="myphoto-testimonial-grid animated fadeIn"
        data-columns>
            <div class="myphoto-testimonial-column hvr-grow-shadow
            hvr-sweep-to-top">
```

```
        <h6>Debbie</h6>
        <p>Great service! Would recommend to friends!</p>
    </div>
    <div class="myphoto-testimonial-column hvr-grow-shadow
    hvr-sweep-to-top">
        <h6>Anne</h6>
        <p>Really high quality prints!</p>
    </div>
    <div class="myphoto-testimonial-column hvr-grow-shadow
    hvr-sweep-to-top">
        <h6>Oscar</h6>
        <p>Declared their greatness, exhibited greatness.</p>
    </div>
    <div class="myphoto-testimonial-column hvr-grow-shadow
    hvr-sweep-to-top">
        <h6>Joey</h6>
        <p>5 stars! Thanks for the great photos!</p>
    </div>
    <div class="myphoto-testimonial-column hvr-grow-shadow
    hvr-sweep-to-top">
        <h6>Mary</h6>
        <p>Made a stressful event much easier!
        Absolute professionals!</p>
    </div>
    <div class="myphoto-testimonial-column hvr-grow-shadow
    hvr-sweep-to-top">
        <h6>Alice</h6>
        <p>Wonderful! Exactly as I imagined they would
        turn out!</p>
    </div>
    <div class="myphoto-testimonial-column hvr-grow-shadow
    hvr-sweep-to-top">
        <h6>Jack & Jill</h6>
        <p>So happy with how the photos turned out! Thanks
        for capturing the memories of our day!</p>
    </div>
    <div class="myphoto-testimonial-column hvr-grow-shadow
    hvr-sweep-to-top">
        <h6>Nick</h6>
        <p>Perfectly captured the mood of our gig.
        Top notch.</p>
    </div>
    <div class="myphoto-testimonial-column hvr-grow-shadow
        hvr-sweep-to-top">
        <h6>Tony</h6>
        <p>Captured our Cup final win! Great stuff!</p>
    </div>
</div>
```

```
        </div>
    </div>
```

We could drastically improve the maintainability of this component by making the content dynamic and then leveraging AngularJS to recursively add individual `testimonials` to the DOM.

Let's learn how to load dynamic content using AngularJS.

Making testimonials dynamic

AngularJS provides an abstraction on top of XHR, the `$http` service, with a more usable interface than Vanilla JavaScript, using a Promise-based interface as opposed to Callbacks. A `service` is a singleton object that provides some core functionality across your application, increasing reusability. We can use `$http` to dynamically load data to use in our testimonials component.

It is good practice to use `$http` within an AngularJS service. In other words, any interaction between the application and a server should be wrapped within a `service`. Let's create a `testimonialsService`. Create a file, `src/app/services/testimonials.service.js`, with the following content:

```
angular.module('MyPhoto')
.service('testimonialsService', function($http) {
})
```

Here, we are attaching a new service, `testimonialsService`, to the `MyPhoto` module, and declaring that it has a dependency on the core AngularJS `$http` service. The `testimonialsService` will now be instantiated only when a component within `MyPhoto` depends on it, and that dependency can be declared in the same way as the `$http` service is declared here. Let's add some functionality. We want this `service` to provide a way to load data for the `testimonials` component in a JSON format. Ideally, this would come from a database backed API, but here we will just load it from the filesystem. Let's create a JSON file, `src/data/testimonials.json`, with the data for `testimonials`:

```
[
    {
        "name":"Debbie",
        "message":"Great service! Would recommend to friends!"
    },
    {
        "name":"Anne",
        "message":"Really high quality prints!"
    },
```

```
        {
            "name":"Oscar",
            "message":"Declared their greatness, exhibited greatness."
        },
        {
            "name":"Joey",
            "message":"5 stars! Thanks for the great photos!"
        },
        {
            "name":"Mary",
            "message":"Made a stressful event much easier!
            Absolute professionals!"
        },
        {
            "name":"Alice",
            "message":"Wonderful! Exactly as I imagined they would turn out!"
        },
        {
            "name":"Jack & Jill",
            "message":"So happy with how the photos turned
            out! Thanks for capturing the memories of our day!"
        },
        {
            "name":"Nick",
            "message":"Perfectly captured the mood of our gig. Top notch."
        },
        {
            "name":"Tony",
            "message":"Captured our Cup final win! Great stuff!"
        }
    ]
```

With the data in place, let's update `testimonialsService` with a function to retrieve `testimonials.json`:

```
angular.module('MyPhoto')
.service('testimonialsService', function($http) {
    function getTestimonials() {
        $http.get('./data/testimonials.json')
        .then(
            function(success) {
                return success.data
            },
            function(error) {
                return error
            }
        )
    }
```

```
    return {
        getTestimonials: getTestimonials
    }
})
```

Making a Promise with $q

AngularJS includes a service based on Promises to allow for asynchronous functions, called $q. As the `getTestimonials` function includes an asynchronous request, we need to make the function itself asynchronous. To do this, first we add a dependency on $q to `testimonialsService`. We then create a `deferred` object, which will `resolve` when the HTTP request succeeds, or `reject` when the request fails. Finally, we return a Promise, which will eventually resolve:

```
angular.module('MyPhoto')
//Declare the service and any dependencies, attaching
it to the MyPhoto module..
.service('testimonialsService', function($http, $q) {
    function getTestimonials() {
        //Create the deferred object
        var deferred = $q.defer()
        //Use $http.get to create a promise to load testimonials.json
        $http.get('/data/testimonials.json')
         //Call the then method of the promise
        .then(
            //Define what happens if the promise returns
            successfully
            function(success) {
                //Resolve the deferred and return the data
                property of the success object
                deferred.resolve(success.data)
            },
            //Define what happens if the promise returns an error
            function(error) {
                //Reject the deferred, returning the error value
                deferred.reject(error)
            }
        )
        //Return the deferred promise
        return deferred.promise
    }
    return {
        getTestimonials: getTestimonials
    }
})
```

Now, our function returns a Promise, which will resolve to either the data part of our success object, or reject and return the error object. The usage of getTesimonials would now be something like:

```
testimonialsService.getTestimonials()
.then(
    function(response) {
        console.log(response)
    },
    function(error) {
        console.error(error)
    }
)
```

What is happening here is self-explanatory. We call the getTestimonials function of testimonialsService. The getTestimonials function has a then property. We pass two functions to then: the first function takes the successful response as a parameter and defines what to do when the Promise resolves; the second function takes the rejected response and defines what to do when the Promise is rejected. Now that we have a service that will return the list of testimonials, let's create an AngularJS directive to render the component.

Creating an AngularJS directive

AngularJS provides an API for extending HTML with custom elements, attributes, comments, and classes. The AngularJS compiler will recognize a custom directive in the DOM and execute a certain specified behavior on the attached element. We are going to build the testimonial's directive using the directive interface. Let's create a new file, src/app/directives/testimonials.directive.js, with the following content:

```
angular.module('myPhoto')
.directive('testimonials', function(testimonialsService) {
    return {
        restrict: 'EA',
        replace: true,
        templateUrl: './app/templates/testimonials.html',
        controller: function($scope) {
        },
        link: function(scope, elem, attr, ctrl) {
        }
    }
})
```

Here, we are adding a new directive—`testimonials`—to the `MyPhoto` module, which has a dependency on `testimonialsService`. Directives return an object with a set of properties that are interpreted by AngularJS. We will touch on a few of them here.

First, we have `restrict: 'EA'`. This means that the directive can be used as either an element or an attribute. For instance, we can use as the directive in either of the following ways:

```
<testimonials></testimonials>
<div testimonials></div>
```

There are two other ways of using a directive—as a class, by adding `C` to the `restrict` property, and as a comment, by adding `M` to the `restrict` property.

Next, we have the `replace` property. By setting this to `true`, the DOM elements generated by the directive will directly replace the DOM element calling it. If `replace` is set to `false`, then the generated elements will be nested within the calling element.

After `replace`, we have the `templateUrl` property. The `templateUrl` is a path to a partial HTML template which will be generated and executed upon by the directive. There is a `template` property also available, to allow for inline HTML in the directive. We are going to store the `testimonials` template in `src/app/templates/testimonials.html`. As `src` will effectively be the root of our deployed application, we will use an absolute path to the application directory.

The `controller` property is next, where we pass in the `$scope` object. The scope in AngularJS represents the data model of the current application, or the current context of the application. The `$scope` model here is exclusive to this instance of the testimonials directive, and cannot be manipulated by any other part of the application. The `controller` code is the first to be executed when a directive is instantiated, so makes for the perfect place to gather necessary data or set scope variables for the directive to use.

Finally, we have the `link` function. The `link` function is the last code to be executed during the directive life cycle. The `link` function is executed immediately after the `directive` template has been added to the DOM, so is perfect for setting event listeners or emitters, or for interacting with third-party scripts. We pass in four variables into the `link` function:

- `scope`: This is a reference to the $scope of the directive
- `elem`: This is a reference to the rendered DOM element
- `attr`: This is a reference to the attributes of the element
- `ctrl`: This is a reference to the previously defined controller

The variable names are unimportant here, they can be anything, but these names are pretty standard.

This is just a skeleton of a directive. AngularJS directives have many more features and intricacies than described here, and this example is just one way of writing a directive; there are many other styles. For the purposes of this example, the form of this directive is perfect.

We want the `testimonials` directive to render the `testimonials` component. To do that, it will need a list of said testimonials. In the `controller` function, we can use `testimonialsService` to retrieve the list:

```
.directive('testimonials', function(testimonialsService) {
    return {
        restrict: 'EA',
        replace: true,
        templateUrl: './app/templates/testimonials.html',
        controller: function($scope) {
            testimonialsService.getTestimonials()
            .then(function(response) {
                $scope.testimonials = response
            }, function(error) {
                console.error(error)
            })
        },
        link: function(scope, elem, attr, ctrl) {
        }
    }
})
```

Writing the testimonials template

In the `controller` function, we call `testimonialsService.getTestimonials`. When `getTestimonials` resolves, we create a `scope` variable, `testimonials`, with the value of the `response`. If the Promise does not resolve, we output an error to the console. With this, our directive has a list of testimonials before it renders, as the `controller` is the first step of the directive life cycle. Now, let's write the `testimonials` template.

Create `src/app/templates/testimonials.html` with the following content:

```
<div class="myphoto-testimonial-grid animated fadeIn" data-columns>
    <div ng-repeat="testimonial in testimonials track by $index"
    class="myphoto-testimonial-column hvr-grow-shadow hvr-sweep-to
    -top">
        <h6>{{testimonial.name}}</h6>
        <p>{{testimonial.message}}</p>
```

```
        </div>
    </div>
```

That's it. Compare this to the hard coded version and notice the difference in the amount of HTML we wrote. So, what is going on here? Well, we took the raw HTML for the testimonial component and removed the individual testimonial elements. We then added a new attribute, ng-repeat, to the myphoto-testimonials-columndiv element. The ng-repeat attribute is actually an AngularJS directive itself. The ng-repeat attribute loops through the data passed to it, repeatedly adding the element which is an attribute of the DOM. We give ng-repeat the value of "testimonial in testimonials track by $index". Simply, we are saying repeat this element for every entry in the testimonials property of the directive's scope, giving each value the reference testimonial. We are also telling ng-repeat to track each entry by $index, which is the position of the entry in testimonials. Using track by has great performance benefits for ng-repeat. Without track by, AngularJS will only identify the entries by its own built-in unique identifier, $id. If the data used for the entries is reloaded, AngularJS will recreate each DOM element in the list again. Using track by $index allows AngularJS to just reuse the entries, as it now knows which DOM elements need to be recreated and which can be reused. One caveat with using $index for tracking is that AngularJS will expect the reloaded data to be in the same order. You can use any property of the entry with track by. For example, if each object in testimonials.json had an id property, we could use track by testimonial.id. Within the myphoto-testimonial-column div, we create a h6 and p element, just like the raw HTML testimonial markup. Instead of hard coding values, we use the reference to the entries in the testimonials array, testimonial, provided by ng-repeat. Using testimonial along with handlebar notation, we can access the properties of each entry as ng-repeat loops through testimonials. As we loop through, AngularJS will execute on the handlebar notation, replacing them with the correct values.

Testing the testimonial directive

Let's test the testimonials directive out. First, add testimonials.service.js and testimonials.directive.js to the head of index-angular.html:

```
<script src="app/services/testimonials.service.js"></script>
<script src="app/directives/testimonials.directive.js"></script>
```

Next, replace the markup for the testimonials component with the directive markup. We will use the attribute form of the testimonials directive, as an attribute of a div element:

```
<div role="tabpanel" class="tab-pane" id="services-testimonials">
    <div class="container">
        <div testimonials></div>
```

```
        </div>
    </div>
```

With that in place, AngularJS will replace this element with the template defined in `testimonials.directive`, and with the testimonials from `testimonials.json`, served by `testimonialsService.getTestimonials`. Let's check it out:

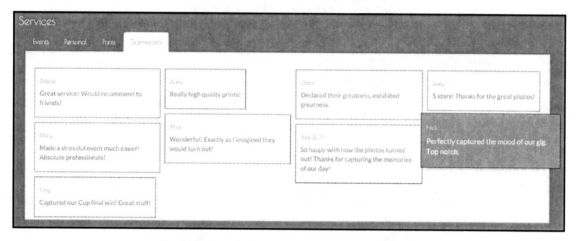

Figure 9.1: The improved testimonials section, displaying testimonials dynamically

Awesome! We now have a dynamic **Testimonials** tab, thanks to AngularJS. Something is not right here, though. Salvatorre, the dynamic grid library we introduced in Chapter 7, *Integrating Bootstrap with Third-Party Plugins* does not seem to be taking effect on this component anymore.

The reason for this is simple—by the time AngularJS has rendered the `testimonials` component, Salvatorre has already instrumented the DOM.

Importing the Salvatorre library

We need to register the `testimonials` component with Salvatorre after it has rendered. We can do this through the `link` function. First, let's add `$timeout` service as a dependency:

```
.directive('testimonials', function(testimonialsService, $timeout)
```

The `$timeout` service is the AngularJS wrapper for the `window.setTimeout` function. As you may know, AngularJS works on a digest cycle, where it uses dirty-checking techniques to see which parts of the application needs to be updated. This happens routinely, or can be forced. We can use `$timeout` to ensure that certain code is executed in a later digest cycle.

Let's update the `link` function with the following:

```
link: function(scope, elem, attr, ctrl) {
    $timeout(function() {
        salvattore.registerGrid(elem[0])
    }, 1000)
}
```

Here, we are using `$timeout` with two parameters. The latter parameter is a delay of 10 milliseconds, to ensure the code is executed in a later digest cycle; 1,000 milliseconds should be enough to ensure the `testimonial` component has completed rendering. We pass in a `function` as the first parameter, responsible for calling Salvatorre's `registerGrid` function. The `registerGrid` function forcibly instruments the passed element with Salvattore. We pass the first element in the `elem` array, which is the rendered `testimonial` component. With this in place, the **Testimonial** tab will have a dynamic grid layout.

As such, we have managed to replicate the **Testimonial** tab—which leverages Bootstrap, Salvattore, Hover, and Animate.css—through AngularJS services and directives, using dynamic content instead of hardcoded values. Time to move onto React.

Introducing React

React is a JavaScript library created by Facebook. While AngularJS positions itself as a framework, React is very clear in its position as a library. React prides itself on being responsible for the visual aspect of the application, *"Just the UI"*, as the React landing page professes. By concerning itself modularly with this single aspect, React is relatively small in size compared to AngularJS and other one-stop-shop frameworks.

React employs a modular approach to the UI, with the idea of components. Components are similar to the directives we used with AngularJS and to the idea of web components. That is, components are reusable pieces of UI functionality, adhering to the *"do one thing, do one thing well"* ideology. React really pushes the modular approach in how components are usually composed, with tight coupling between styles, HTML, and JavaScript.

Typically, all component specific code is contained within one file. The HTML, the CSS rules, and the JS logic are all included within this file. While at first glance, this approach arguably flies in the face of the approach of separation of concerns, it does totally separate the concerns of components from each other. In other words, making changes to one part of the application should have no impact on another.

React is famously fast when manipulating the DOM, using the virtual DOM approach to figuring out which parts of the UI to update, as opposed to the dirty-checking technique employed by AngularJS. The virtual DOM is essentially the idea of keeping a copy of the real DOM in memory, and updating the copy with necessary changes. The virtual DOM is then periodically compared with the *real* DOM; any differences then result in that specific piece of the DOM being re-evaluated and re-rendered.

React also promotes the usage of **JSX** with React applications. JSX is a programming language which compiles into JavaScript, thus requiring a compilation step in the development process. JSX offers a layer of object-oriented style programming on top of JavaScript, such as Java-like class systems and static typing.

Now, let's set up React.

Setting up React

There are several ways of getting setup with React. As the React team maintain a Bower package, we will use Bower as we have done throughout this book. From the terminal, let's pull down React through Bower. We are going to use 0.14.6 version of React:

```
bower install react#0.14.6
```

With that, we have a downloaded React to `src/bower_components/react`. Here you will see `react.js`, `react-dom.js`, and `react-dom-server.js`, along with their minified versions. Here `react.js` is the core React library, `react-dom.js` takes responsibility for the actual rendering of the React components in the DOM, and `react-dom-server.js` allows for server-side rendering of React components.

Create a copy of `src/index.html` to `src/index-react.html`, and add the minified versions of React and ReactDOM to the `head` of the page:

```
<script src="bower_components/react/react.min.js"></script>
<script src="bower_components/react/react-dom.min.js"></script>
```

We also need to include Babel, a JavaScript compiler which caters for JSX. Babel does not maintain a Bower package, but it is available on npm. However, Babel maintains a version of its library for browsers on a CDN. Include the following in the `head` of our page:

```
<script src="https://cdnjs.cloudflare.com/ajax/libs/babel-core/
5.8.23/browser.min.js"></script>
```

The `browser.min.js` file will transform any JSX code in HTML, within `script` tags with a `type` attribute with the value `text/babel`. Let's test it out, to make sure we have everything set up correctly. Above our `footer`, add a `div` with an `id` of `test`:

```
<div id="test"></div>
```

Next, let's write the simplest of React components. At the bottom of `index-react.js`, after the `footer` element, include the following:

```
<script type="text/babel">
    ReactDOM.render(
        <div className='container-fluid myphoto-section bg-myphoto-
        dark'>Test</div>,
        document.getElementById('test')
    );
</script>
```

Let's walk through what is happening here. First, as we said before, our `script` tag needs a `type` attribute with the value `text/babel` so that Babel knows to compile it into JavaScript before execution. Within the `script` tags, we have our first real interaction with React: ReactDOM and its `render` function. The `render` function takes two arguments here: the first is raw HTML, the second is an element selector. What is happening here is pretty self-explanatory: we want React to find the `test` element, and replace it with the HTML we passed as the first parameter. You may notice that in our HTML, we have a `className` attribute. We use `className` instead of `class`, as `class` is a reserved word in JavaScript. The `className` attribute is converted to `class` when the component is rendered in the DOM. Open `index-react.html` and check if we now have a **Test** section in our page:

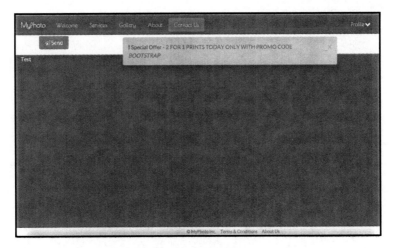

Figure 9.2: The Test section displaying as expected

We are now all set up to integrate React into `MyPhoto`. Let's do something more substantial. We are going to convert the carousel in the **Gallery** component into a React component. Before we get to that, remove the `test` component, both the `div` and the JSX we added.

Making a Gallery component in React

To understand how we can integrate React with our application, we are going to make a reusable **Gallery** component using React. The first thing we are going to do is create a new file, `src/app/components/gallery.js`, and include it in the head of `index-react.html`:

```
<script type="text/babel" src="app/components/gallery.js"></script>
```

Notice the `type` attribute, again set to `text/babel`, so `gallery.js` will be compiled to JavaScript at runtime. As you can imagine, this is a slow operation. This method is recommended to be used only for development purposes. For production, all JSX should be precompiled into JavaScript. For the purposes of this example, we will continue with the `runtime-compile` method.

Let's add some code to `gallery.js`. Take the `gallery` markup, the `div` element with the id `gallery-carousel` and its nested elements, and add it to `gallery.js` as the first argument for `ReactDOM.render`. Make sure to also change the `class` attributes to `className`. We also need to make sure that we use handlebar expressions when defining inline styles, as React parses the `style` attribute as an object, rather than a string:

```
ReactDOM.render(
    <div id="gallery-carousel" className="carousel slide"
    data-ride="carousel" data-interval="3000">
        <div className="carousel-inner" role="listbox">
            <div style={{height: 400px}} className="carousel-item
            active">
                <img data-modal-picture="#carouselModal"
                src="images/brazil.png">
                <div className="carousel-caption">
                    Brazil
                </div>
            </div>
            <div style={{height: 400px}} className="carousel-item">
                <img data-modal-picture="#carouselModal"
                src="images/datsun.png">
                <div className="carousel-caption">
                    Datsun 260Z
                </div>
            </div>
```

```
              <div style={{height: 400px}} className="carousel-item">
                  <img data-modal-picture="#carouselModal"
                  src="images/skydive.png">
                  <div className="carousel-caption">
                      Skydive
                  </div>
              </div>
          </div>
          <a className="left carousel-control" href="#gallery-
          carousel" role="button" data-slide="prev">
              <span className="icon-prev" aria-hidden="true"></span>
          </a>
          <a className="right carousel-control" href="#gallery-
          carousel" role="button" data-slide="next">
              <span className="icon-next" aria-hidden="true"></span>
          </a>
          <ol className="carousel-indicators">
          <li data-target="#gallery-carousel" data-slide-to="0"
          className="active"></li>
          <li data-target="#gallery-carousel" data-slide-to="1"></li>
          <li data-target="#gallery-carousel" data-slide-to="2"></li>
          </ol>
      </div>,
          document.getElementById('react-gallery')
  )
```

The second argument we pass is an element selector, targeting an element with an id of react-gallery. Replace the gallery-carousel element in index-react.js with the target element for the gallery.js React component:

```
<div id="react-gallery"></div>
```

Open index-react.js and we should see the **Gallery** component, but this time it is being generated by React:

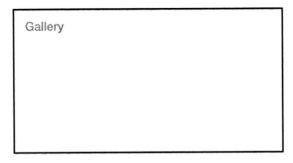

Figure 9.3: The React Gallery component

Oh, that isn't what we want. Obviously something has gone wrong here. Let's check out the browser's Developer Console to see if there are any errors reported:

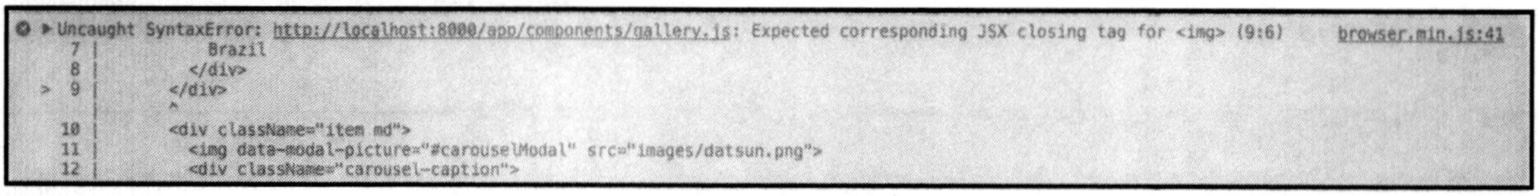

```
⊘ ▶ Uncaught SyntaxError: http://localhost:8000/app/components/gallery.js: Expected corresponding JSX closing tag for <img> (9:6)      browser.min.js:41
   7 |          Brazil
   8 |        </div>
 > 9 |      </div>
          ^
  10 |      <div className="item md">
  11 |        <img data-modal-picture="#carouselModal" src="images/datsun.png">
  12 |        <div className="carousel-caption">
```

Figure 9.4: Chrome's Developer Console displaying errors

So, Babel has thankfully given us an explicit error, it is expecting a closing tag for the `img` tags in `gallery.js`. Let's make sure all our `img` tags are closed in `gallery.js`:

```
<div style={{height: 400px}} className="carousel-item active">
    <img data-modal-picture="#carouselModal" src="images/
    brazil.png"/>
    <div className="carousel-caption">
        Brazil
    </div>
</div>
<div style={{height: 400px}} className="carousel-item">
    <img data-modal-picture="#carouselModal" src="images/datsun.png" />
    <div className="carousel-caption">
        Datsun 260Z
    </div>
</div>
<div style={{height: 400px}} className="carousel-item">
    <img data-modal-picture="#carouselModal" src="images/skydive.png"
    />
    <div className="carousel-caption">
        Skydive
    </div>
</div>
```

Let's give `index-react.js` another go and we should now have our React-powered **Gallery** tab:

Figure 9.5: The functioning React Gallery component displaying an image of the Botanical Garden in Rio de Janeiro

Great! We now have a functioning React component. But, it isn't exactly reusable in terms of a carousel. If we wanted another carousel elsewhere, we would need to create another component. Let's make the carousel reusable by passing in options to the React component.

Using carousel in React

To write a reusable component like this, we create the component as a custom React class. This class essentially returns the markup to be rendered by `ReactDOM.render`, but gives us more power to manipulate our template. Like AngularJS directive custom React classes are extensions of the DOM, allowing us to create new DOM tags. For example, we could create a `Carousel` element. Note that custom React classes always begin with an uppercase letter:

```
<Carousel></Carousel>
```

Before we do anything, let's analyze the component we have and understand which values we want to make mutable. In the root element, the `id` and `data-interval` values need to be changeable. The component also needs to allow the images and caption to be set. Ideally, this should be passed to the component as an array. Finally, the component needs to take in the value for `data-modal-picture`.

In all, the component needs to take four values. So, the markup for the component would look something like:

```
<Carousel id="<value>" interval="<value>" carousel-modal-
picture="<value>" carousel-images="<[images]"></Carousel>
```

In `gallery.js`, we can access component attributes using `this.props`. Wrapping `this.props` with curly braces allows these attribute values to be accessed within the markup of the component code. Add the following to the beginning of `gallery.js`:

```
var Carousel = React.createClass({
    render: function () {
        var props = this.props
        return (
            <div id={props.id} className="carousel slide"
            data-ride="carousel" data-interval={props.interval}>
                <div className="carousel-inner" role="listbox">
                    { props.images.map(function(item, index) {
                        var itemClass;
                        if (index === 0)
                            itemClass = "active"
                        else
                            itemClass = ""
                        return (
                            <div className={ 'carousel-item ' +
                            itemClass }>
                                <img data-modal-picture={'#' +
                                    props.carouselModalPicture}
                                    src={item.src} />
                            <div className="carousel-caption">
                                {item.caption}
                            </div>
                        </div>
                        )
                    })}
                </div>
                <a className="left carousel-control" href={'#' + props.id }
                role="button" data-slide="prev">
                    <span className="icon-prev" aria-hidden="true"></span>
                </a>
                <a className="right carousel-control" href={'#' + props.id
                }
                role="button" data-slide="next">
                    <span className="icon-next" aria-hidden="true"></span>
                </a>
                <ol className="carousel-indicators">
                    { props.images.map(function(item, index) {
                        var liClass;
```

```
            if (index === 0)
                liClass = "active"
            else
                liClass = ""
            return (
                <li data-target={'#' + props.id } data-slide-
                to={index} className={ liClass }></li>
            )
        })
    }
    </ol>
    </div>
    )
  }
})
```

We have created a new React class using `React.createClass`, which has a `render` property. The `render` property is simply a function which returns an HTML template. The template is essentially the markup for the `gallery-carousel` component, except we are accessing some dynamic properties. We have replaced all references to the carousel `id` with `this.props.id`, all references to the `id` of the modal window to open up the `carousel` modal to `this.props.carouselModalPicture`, and the `data-interval` to `this.props.interval`. We will come back to the images and the captions later. We assign this custom React class to the variable `Carousel`.

Now that we have this reusable class, we no longer need the template within the `ReactDOM.render` function. Replace the function with the following:

```
ReactDOM.render(
    <Carousel id="gallery-carousel" interval="3000"
carouselModalPicture="carouselModal"></Carousel>,
    document.getElementById('react-gallery')
)
```

We are now using the `Carousel` tag in the `render` method. We are passing three attributes to `Carousel` – `id`, `interval`, and `carouselModalPicture`. The values of these attributes will then be used in the template returned by `Carousel.render`. `ReactDOM.render` will then replace the `react-gallery` element in `index-react.js` with the carousel template, with these defined attributes. Check it out and see if we have a fully functioning carousel in the **Gallery** tab. Change some of the attribute values and see if the `carousel` component works as expected.

Now, let's put the images and image captions in as an option. In reality, these values would come from an API, or will be otherwise dynamically generated. For the sake of this example, we are going to create a variable with the array of values. To demonstrate that the values are being passed through as an attribute, we will change the captions slightly. Add the following to the beginning of gallery.js:

```
var carouselImages = [
    {
        src: "images/brazil.png",
        caption: "Lake in Brazil"
    },
    {
        src: "images/datsun.png",
        caption: "Datsun Fairlady Z"
    },
    {
        src: "images/skydive.png",
        caption: "Team Skydive"
    }
]
```

Now, we can pass carouselImages as an attribute of the Carousel tag:

```
<Carousel id="gallery-carousel" interval="3000"
carouselModalPicture="carouselModal" images={carouselImages}>
</Carousel>
```

In the carousel template, we need to loop through the data passed into the images attribute, and create a new slide for each entry, as well as a new indicator in the carousel-indicators list. We will loop through the dataset using the map function. As map creates a closure, we first need to create a reference to this.props, as this will be different in the context of the closure. At the beginning of the render function, assign this.props to props:

```
var props = this.props
```

Next, remove the slides from the carousel-inner element and add the following:

```
{ props.images.map(function(item, index) {
    var itemClass;
    if (index === 0) {
        itemClass = "active"
    } else {
        itemClass = ""
    }
    return (
```

```
                <div className={ 'item md ' + itemClass }>
                <img data-modal-picture={'#' + props.carouselModalPicture}
                src={item.src} />
                <div className="carousel-caption">
                    {item.caption}
                </div>
            </div>
        </div>
            )
    })}
```

We are looping through `props.images` using the `map` function. We want to set the first slide in the array to be the active slide, so we check its `index` and assign the `itemClass` variable accordingly. We then define the template for the slide. We pass `itemClass` into the `className` attribute to denote the initially active slide, we then use the `item.src` property as the `src` of the `img` element, and `item.caption` as the caption of the slide. Next, remove all the list items from the `carousel-indicators` list, replacing them with the following:

```
    { props.images.map(function(item, index) {
        var liClass;
        if (index === 0) {
            liClass = "active"
    } else {
        liClass = ""
    }
        return (
            <li data-target={'#' + props.id } data-slide-to
            ={index} className={ liClass }></li>
            )
        })
    }
```

Similarly, we loop through the images and assign the first slide as the active slide. That is everything our component needs to create our **Gallery** carousel. Let's check it out:

Figure 9.6: The functioning React Gallery component displaying an image of the Botanical Garden in Rio de Janeiro

As you can see from the caption, the carousel is loading from the `imagesCarousel` array. Now, we have a customizable, reusable, and easily maintainable React-powered `carousel` component that can be used anywhere across `MyPhoto`.

Summary

In this chapter, we have learned how to integrate AngularJS into our Bootstrap site. We are now able to load data dynamically, pass it into a reusable directive, and render a component which mixes AngularJS and Bootstrap, along with other third-party libraries.

We have also seen how we can leverage React to easily transform our static content into reusable, customizable, and maintainable components.

Being able to integrate frameworks and libraries such as AngularJS and React into a Bootstrap driven website is critical when building dynamic and useful user interfaces. Bootstrap complements, and is complemented by, dynamically driven content, and this chapter has hopefully given you the understanding you need to be able to use these tools to build powerful and useful websites.

Index